Women in Grenadian History

Women
in
Grenadian
History
1783–1983

Nicole Laurine Phillip

University of the West Indies Press

Jamaica • Barbados • Trinidad and Tobago

University of the West Indies Press

7A Gibraltar Hall Road   Mona

Kingston 7   Jamaica

www.uwipress.com

CATALOGUING-IN-PUBLICATION DATA

Phillip, Nicole Laurine.

Women in Grenadian society, 1783–1983 / Nicole Laurine Phillip.

p. cm.

Includes bibliographical references.

ISBN: 978-976-640-225-9

1. Women – Grenada – History. 2. Women – Grenada – Social conditions.
3. Women – Grenada – Economic conditions. 4. Women slaves – Grenada –
History. I. Title.

F2056.5.P545 2010   972.9845

Book and cover design by Robert Harris.

Set in Dante 11/15 x 24

Printed in the United States of America.

In loving memory of three very special men:

my beloved father, Osbourne Ivor O'Brien;

my uncle Garick Alban Adams; and

my lecturer and mentor Dr Fitzroy Andre Baptiste.

Their indefatigable love and guidance have made this dream a reality.

Contents

List of Tables   **viii**

Preface   **ix**

List of Abbreviations   **xi**

Note on Currency and Conversion   **xii**

Introduction   **1**

1   Historical Background   **10**

2   Women in Grenadian Slave Society, 1783–1838   **18**

3   Post-Emancipation Women, Part 1: 1838–1899   **48**

4   Post-Emancipation Women, Part 2: 1900–1950   **57**

5   Post-Emancipation Women, Part 3: 1951–1979   **80**

6   Women in the Grenada Revolution, 1979–1983   **112**

Conclusion   **145**

Postscript   **152**

Notes   **157**

Bibliography   **177**

Index   **193**

Tables

Table 2.1   Madeys Estate Plantation Accounts, 1799–1803   **24**

Table 2.2   Registered Slave Births and Deaths, Grenada, 1817–1833   **25**

Table 2.3   Population of Grenada, 1763–1830   **40**

Table 3.1   Rate of Natural Increase of Grenada's Population, 1867–1910   **52**

Table 3.2   Absolute Natural Increase of East Indian Population Grenada, 1866–1896   **54**

Table 4.1   Minimum Daily Wage Rates of Grenadian Agricultural Workers for Selected Years, 1900–1966   **58**

Table 4.2   Infant Mortality Rate (per thousand), 1928–1937   **62**

Preface

IN MY FINAL UNDERGRADUATE year at the University of the West Indies, St Augustine, Trinidad, I completed the course "Women and Gender in the English-Speaking Caribbean". This course opened my eyes and allowed me to view the history of the region and the world from a different perspective – the perspective of women. The works of Hilary Beckles, Barbara Bush, Lucille Mathurin-Mair, among others, gave me an inkling of the vastness of the silence about women in the past. They also piqued my curiosity about and interest in writing the history of my grandmothers and great-grandmothers.

The aim of this book is to provide the first full-length history of Grenadian women from the era of slavery to the People's Revolution. Works on Grenada have concentrated on general histories of the island. Accounts of women's history have been limited to a few short studies on well-known women, and on women during the revolution. In the wake of the movement towards a more gender balanced account of human history, it is necessary to examine the role of Grenadian women in my nation's history. This book is a pioneering work. It attempts to begin the process of writing women's history in the Windward Islands.

The writing of women into Grenadian history necessarily involves redefining and enlarging traditional notions of historical significance, to encompass personal and family experiences as well as public and political activities. I am venturing into unknown ground and using untapped resources; although women were in many instances absent from the official accounts, they took an active role nonetheless in the making of history. Though they were silent in the official record, they spoke eloquently on issues of political thought, economic realities and social conditions.

In writing this book, I have received invaluable support from my family and friends. I would especially like to thank my mother, Yvette Phillip; my aunt, Canice Adams; my sister, Margaret O'Brien; and my closest friends, Junia Bain, Chanelle Bain, Janine Dowden, Claudette Joseph, Daisy Hazzard, Christina Batson, Michelle Greaves-Warrick, Anthony Hood, Hugh Thomas, Dr Byron Calliste, Vannie Curwen, Besha Ottley, Bernadette Ottley, Deborah Mitchell, Dr George Mitchell, Dr Curtis Jacobs, Dr Francis Martin, Roxanne Chandler and Judith Burke (RIP). I would also like to extend a special thank you to the staff at the Public Record Office, London; the West Indian Division of the Main Library at the University of the West Indies, St Augustine; the St George's Public Library in Grenada; and the University of the West Indies Library in Grenada.

Nicole Laurine Phillip
Beausejour Gardens
St George, Grenada
2009

Abbreviations

GNP	Grenada National Party
GPP	Grenada People's Party
GULP	Grenada United Labour Party
JEWEL	Joint Endeavour for Welfare Education and Liberation
NISTEP	National In-Service Teacher Education Programme
NJM	New Jewel Movement
NWO	National Women's Organisation
PRA	People's Revolutionary Army
PRG	People's Revolutionary Government
PWA	Progressive Women's Association
YWCA	Young Women's Christian Association

Note on Currency and Conversion

IN THE PERIOD 1783 to around 1940 the currency used in Grenada was pounds, shillings and pence. For the period 1940 to the mid 1950s both the pound sterling and the West Indian dollar was used. By 1946 government accounts were kept in pounds sterling. Banks and commercial houses kept their accounts in West Indian dollars and cents: £1 was equivalent to $4.80. By 1968 the Eastern Caribbean currency or EC dollar was used.

Introduction

THE HISTORY OF HUMANKIND was traditionally and narrowly defined as "his" story. Historians were not alone in this; other social scientists also ignored women and "her" story. Historians generally held the notion that much of what women did or what was important to their lives was not a proper subject for history. The contention was that women operated in a private or personal sphere while men operated in the public world.

From the 1960s, historians and social scientists have dispelled these ideas and have insisted that personal life – including family relations and women's roles within the family – is just as crucial and as much a part of history, as any other aspect of human activity. Women's historical experiences (whether within the family or outside it) are now seen as proper subjects for the historian. Outside the "private sphere", historians have examined women's participation in social production, in political life and in social organizations.

The last two decades of the twentieth century have seen the explosion of research on women's history throughout the world and also within the Caribbean region, but the larger islands have been the main focus of historical writings on women. The smaller islands have been largely neglected. They have only been represented in a few articles and, even then, the focus is on the outstanding women in these societies.

This book is a pioneering work on the experiences of Grenadian women over two centuries of British colonialism, "Gairyism" and socialist revolution. It moves away from a narrow approach of highlighting outstanding figures and revolutionary women towards one that encompasses the experiences of women of all walks of life, over historical time and space. It presents a picture of Grenadian society through the eyes of women estate workers, domestic workers, teachers, civil servants, doctors, lawyers, revolutionaries and politicians. In this way, it seeks to capture the story of Grenadian women in all its richness and complexity.

There is a common thread running through the fabric of the work; the theme of dominance and resistance: the dominance of the colonial system in the form of slavery, resistance by running away and open rebellion; resistance to colonial authority which brings forth a people's "messiah", dominance in the form of victimization by the "messiah" and resistance again in the form of socialist revolution; dominance in the form of a socialist ethic that condoned violence, restricted speech and did little to change attitudes between men and women, resistance in the form of official letters to the Political Bureau and the Central Committee by the senior members of the National Women's Organisation (NWO), and a chance now to express discontent at aspects of the regime.

· · ·

SLAVE WOMEN WERE VALUABLE workers. By the 1780s they accounted for the majority of the plantation labour force within Grenada and other British West Indian colonies. Slave women also had the "dual burden" of production and reproduction. With a firm eye on rapid profits, many planters proved entirely willing to exploit female slaves to the limits of their physical endurance (if not beyond) with little regard to the niceties of male and female tasks.[1] The concern of planters with the reproductive capacity of the female slave peaked in the wake of the abolitionist movement in Britain. They implemented measures to improve or ameliorate the living and working conditions of the female slaves and, as such, increase the slave population internally. Grenadian planters, like their counterparts in the region, took up the challenge but in spite of their attempts, failed. With the exception of Barbados, the British sugar colonies did not show an absolute increase in slave population before 1832. It was only with the onset of emancipation and the ending of gang labour for many female ex-slaves that their fertility rate, and their health and that of their children were enhanced.

It should be noted how European gender ideology operated within the context of slave society. The slave woman was not seen as the "delicate softer sex" in need of protection by the "strong male". Slave woman were treated as if they were equal to slave men. The planters were unfailingly inspired by economic self interest which enabled them, without reservation, to discard the image of the black woman as a frail creature and convert her into the mainstay of estate manual labour.[2] In European society, "respectable women" were demarcated from lower-class "wenches". Within the West Indian context in the seventeenth century, there were white prostitutes and quasi-prostitutes that could be defined as wenches. However, by the mid to late eighteenth century, nearly all white women were elevated to a superior status of respectability. White males held power over the slave woman's body in its productive capacity as an asexual labour machine. They also controlled the slave woman's body for reproduction and pleasure. The sexual vulnerability to which black women were exposed was not faced by white women or black men. While the white males' sphere of sexual influence extended to black females, white women's sexual appetites could not be extended to the black male.

The high incidence of manumission especially of female slaves within the Grenadian slave society contributed to the extension of the free-coloured class. While sexual exploitation did exist, white men did have fond and enduring relations with black and coloured women. This could be one of the reasons for manumission, as well as a reward for faithful services. Some wealthy white men did bequeath their wealth to black or coloured "wives", as in the case of Honoré Philip. He bequeathed many estates in Grenada, Carriacou and the entire island of Petit Martinique to Jeanette Philip, a free black woman.

Enslaved Africans, like all of humankind, had a natural right to be free. The fact that this freedom, this natural right, was withheld meant that they had a natural right to reclaim that freedom. The African was torn from highly civilized West African societies where the rights of the human being and liberty were a part of the daily discourse. The African, therefore, carried that innate desire for liberty with them to the New World. Finding themselves in situations of slavery or "un-freedom", they expressed their inherent human desire for freedom through different forms of physical resistance. As such, slave resistance and rebellion ricocheted throughout the Caribbean. The slavery system impacted upon the black women in deeper and more profound ways than black men. The slave mode of production, by virtue of placing the black woman's "inner world" – her fertility, sexuality and maternity – on the market as capital assets, produced in her a "natural propensity to resist and to refuse as part of a basic self protective and survival response".[3] Within the Grenadian context, there is much evidence of female resistance. This took the form of insolence, destruction of estate property, running away and aiding in revolt. The planters were very aware of the way in which females took part in active resistance. Fred Maitland, speaking about the safety of the islands' white population in a letter to the colonial secretary in 1806, noted: "On the side of the blacks, the women though they may not fight, are able and would do services to their cause as destructive to the safety of the whites as if they carried musquets – for they would transport all the provisions and ammunition Etc."[4] By all the means available to her, the female slave sought to restore her natural right to freedom.

Emancipation was granted, but the people were not really free. Punishments of women during the apprenticeship period included hard labour on the treadmill, solitary confinement, imprisonment and being placed in the stocks. Wrongful classification of non-agricultural workers as field workers was frequent, and planters withheld indulgences commonly given under slavery. In the wake of full freedom, women retaliated. There was a movement by women away from the severely regimented work regime that characterized slavery on the sugar estates. This did not mean a restful retreat for women. They became an integral part of the household farm economy, combining production (of crops and livestock) and selling with childcare and housework.[5] This could be defined as an ex-slave family strategy or a gendered occupational strategy adopted by the former slaves. Some ex-slaves, both male and female, chose to vote with their feet and sought employment outside of their particular islands.

Like their counterparts in the region, Grenadian planters saw problems of sugar cultivation through the narrow lens of a need for a large "controlled" labour force. Sugar cultivation was on the decline in Grenada by the mid 1860s. Yet, the planters still clamoured for immigration. In the period of indenture, 1838–1885, Grenada received Maltese, Indians, Madeirans and Africans as labourers. The paucity of women, along with poor health conditions, contributed to a low rate of natural increase among the immigrant population. Despite the obvious shortage of women among the migrant groups during the period of indentureship, available evidence does not point to any significant cohabitation between Indian men and African creole women. Considering the prevalence of miscegenation throughout the history of the Caribbean, its relative absence among Indians and individuals of African ancestry up to the end of the nineteenth century is all the more revealing of racial attitudes and relations. As the missionary presence became increasingly established and Christianization of Indians took place, some of these attitudes changed gradually in the early twentieth century and miscegenation between Indians and creoles became somewhat acceptable.[6] Taking into consideration the small size of the Indian population in Grenada compared to Trinidad and British Guiana, over time it became increasingly difficult to maintain a distinct minority culture within a Grenadian society that was predominately black.

Women were paid lower wages for estate labour than men. This was so from the immediate post-emancipation period to 1980. The People's Revolutionary Government (PRG) instituted a policy of equal work for equal pay. However, it was not practised on some estates. The working and living conditions of estate women are highlighted in this book for the period 1900 to 1970. The wages they earned were examined in relation to how they supported their children in terms of food, clothing, shelter and education. The reality of their lives was poor living and working conditions, low wages, little or no education, high infant mortality and no maternity leave.

Education was the main instrument to facilitate movement off the estates, but women's meagre salaries left very little for this. In spite of the odds, some women insisted on sending their children to primary and secondary school. For those girls who did attain a secondary education, European gender ideology dictated that they be taught a partly separate curriculum from boys. When they did attain qualifications, gender ideology extended into the jobs they were allowed to perform.

Education was a means of social advancement and economic enhancement. Yet the Caribbean curriculum and the European mindset that informed it created a lack of fit with local realities. This changed drastically by the 1960s and 1970s when Caribbean women and men educated by this very system recognized its flaws and sought either by conservative or radical means to change

the political and socioeconomic status of the region. It took the form of movements towards independence, Caribbean integration, Black Power and, in the
case of Grenada, socialist revolution.

There is a complexity in the operation of European gender ideology in the
Caribbean. It was adhered to in some respects, while in others it was modified
and reformulated to operate within the Caribbean context. In the post-emancipation period, European gender ideology dictated that married women
should remain at home and take care of the children, while men should work
and provide for the home. Female exodus from plantation labour probably
had more to do with ex-slaves' family strategies than with the copying of
European ideas. Women might have left the estate labour force but they
worked on family lands and sold crops in the marketplace. In some instances,
women were seamstresses based at home who sewed for elite clients. They
also did laundry for their clients at their homes. Within the Caribbean context,
such employment by women was not seen as "work" but as an extension of
their household chores. Moreover, even when women did leave the home to
work as estate workers, domestic workers, clerks and so on, the wages they
earned were seen as supplementary to those of their husband or the man
with whom they lived. This could be a possible reason for women being paid
less than their male counterparts. Economic necessity made it impractical for
the Caribbean family structure to narrowly follow European gender ideals.
It can be ascertained that what operated within the Caribbean is what Patricia
Mohammed defined as "negotiation". What developed was a "Caribbean ideology" with respect to family forms that met the needs of its people.

Migration was one of the factors that made this "Caribbean ideology" such
a reality. The lack of stable employment that epitomized the lives of most
men in the English-speaking Caribbean had major consequences for the roles
and responsibilities undertaken by women. When men migrated they were
often likely to establish new relationships and have additional children from
these unions. Therefore, women from the original unions most often had to
assume the financial obligations for their children.[7] Such conditions, among
other factors, led to the rise of households headed by females. John Brierley
and M.G. Smith mentioned such households in Grenada in the 1950s to 1970s.
In the sampling used by Brierley, 10 per cent of the population of the parish
of St Mark was headed by females, while 35 per cent of the population of the

parish of St Patrick was headed by females.[8] The burden of subsistence was placed on these women. They developed their own family strategies to deal with their particular situation. An elaborate network of kin and neighbours provided support for the individual women and their children. Child dispersion became characteristic of Afro-Caribbean family life: a willingness on the part of women to rear children not their own, perhaps not even kin, and then give them back if the natural parents asked for them.

In the face of economic hardship, women "voted with their feet" as well. Migration to Aruba, Bonaire and Curaçao by women in search of jobs as domestic workers stretched from the 1930s to the mid 1970s. These women often left children behind in the care of grandmothers and aunts as they sought a better life. In these islands they were met with racism, the language barrier, long working hours and live-in housing arrangements. Myrtle noted that one month after arriving in Aruba, her employers packed up and left for the United States. She recounted: "They leave very little food in the house so in a few days all was finished. They did not leave any money and we had none [herself and the cook, who was her cousin]. Even if we had money we did not know where to find the shops and we don't know anybody in Aruba."[9] The children of these migrants were sometimes sent for by their mothers. Often, however, they remained home and were disciplined and parented by a combination of kin, friends and letters from their mothers. Some women stayed closer to home. Juliana Aird migrated to St Vincent in the late 1920s in search of a better life. Some women also moved to the larger Caribbean colonies like Trinidad. Movement to Trinidad by Grenadian women and men started as early as 1838 and spanned the entire period under study to the present. Nita Allen migrated to Trinidad in the aftermath of Hurricane Janet in 1955. She left her first child with her parents and siblings in Grenada. On finding a job in Trinidad, she wrote home and invited her younger sisters to migrate as well. Aymer noted that this encouragement of family and friends to migrate also took place with women moving to Aruba, Bonaire and Curaçao. Four of Nita's sisters migrated to Trinidad between 1960 and 1973. Two of her sisters also left their children in the care of parents and younger siblings.[10]

The late 1940s to mid 1970s saw the rise of women's groups in Grenada. These included the Young Women's Christian Association (YWCA), Homemakers Association, Lioness Club, Soroptomists, Grenada Women's League and the Progressive Women's Association (PWA). These groups acted as initial mobilizing units for women. Women came together, shared their experiences and enhanced their expertise. This was also the case of women's groups that developed in Trinidad in the 1920s and 1930s. The expertise gained, and the exposure to the public domain attained by these women, served as a foundation on which to build their political careers. Nadia Benjamin and Wapel Nedd both were active in women's groups and other charitable organizations. Nadia Benjamin was involved in the YWCA and the Canadian Save the Children Fund. At the YWCA, she held the posts of president, secretary and treasurer.[11]

A visible female presence in positions of authority was seen in Grenada under the Gairy regime. One can question the motives of the regime for this. Was it a genuine interest in the welfare of women or an attempt to patronize the majority of the population? The evidence from women who worked with the regime tends to swing the pendulum in the direction of the latter. Opposition to Gairy's rulership led to "excommunication" from the party. Yet Gairy could be credited with taking the initial steps to make women more "visible". Women made up the majority of the Grenadian population and as such could not be neglected; his "promotion" of women gained the support, at least initially, of the majority of the island's population. Gairy himself has been criticized for "asking or demanding" sexual favours from women as they sought employment within the government sector. Women have noted examples of Gairy's behaviour, especially at the Evening Palace in St George's. Young women were called into his office on numerous occasions for extended periods of time; and women were publicly embarrassed by him for not meeting his sexual demands or conditions.[12] That there were obvious flaws in the Gairy regime's "promotion" of women is seen in women's opposition to the regime, through their involvement with alternative political parties, for example the Grenada National Party (GNP) and New Jewel Movement (NJM). The political party that came to power through a coup d'etat was the NJM, purporting a socialist ideology.

The socialist ideology purported by the PRG sought to enhance the conditions of Grenadian women. It can be debated whether or not socialism empowered Grenadian women. Empowerment could be defined as "the acquisition of self-knowledge, self-insight into women's current status, the reasons for that status, the positive steps required to attain that goal . . . It does not mean that you have to reach the end of the goal to be empowered, since it is a process."[13] Taking this definition as a yardstick, it can be ascertained that, to an extent, Grenadian women were on the way to empowerment by the end of the revolution in 1983. Women benefited from the Maternity Leave Law, some from equal work for equal pay, free secondary education, scholarships for tertiary education and improvements in health and housing. Yet the shortcomings of the revolutionary process as it affected women cannot be ignored. There were no women in positions of power in the army. Equal work for equal pay was limited, so too was maternity leave. Lack of freedom of the press restricted women and men from criticizing aspects of the revolution. The fact that oral evidence from women who opposed aspects of the revolution could only be sourced in the post-revolution period is evidence of this. In that sense, the process of empowerment was a limited one.

This text is a product of an environment that had sidelined the important contribution of women to society. It is an effort to move towards a clearer view or vision of the past and potentially of the present. It is a conscious effort to revisit our history and reclaim our heritage. The purpose of this book is to show that Grenada was established, not only through its male inhabitants but also through the contributions of its women as well.

1 Historical Background

GRENADA IS THE MOST southerly of the Windward Islands in the Caribbean. The island is twenty-one miles in length and twelve miles in width, with a total area of 133 square miles, inclusive of the sister islands of Carriacou and Petit Martinique.

The Amerindians of the Orinoco delta in South America were the earliest inhabitants of the island. They consisted of two groups – the Taino, also known as the "Arawaks" (who spoke Arawakan) and the Kalinago, also known as the "Caribs" (who spoke Cariban). Although the Taino inhabited Grenada before the Kalinago, it was the Kalinago who controlled the island for one hundred and fifty years before the Europeans first arrived in the region.[1] The Kalinago called the island Camerhogne. In 1498, Christopher Columbus, on his third voyage to the New World, renamed the island Concepción. It was later renamed Mayo by Amerigo Vespucci. In 1511, it appears that both names – Concepción and Mayo – were used on Royal Cédulas (official proclamations) about Grenada, but Concepción was used more frequently. From 1523 onwards, these names were dropped and replaced by Granada. Under French rule (1674–1763 and 1779–1783), the island was known as La Grenade; however, as soon as the British took possession (1763–1779 and 1783–1974), it was renamed Grenada.

In 1674, Grenada officially became a French colony, but throughout the 1700s, the English and French fought between themselves for control of the Caribbean's wealth. Grenada featured prominently in this rivalry between the two nations. During this period, ownership of the island alternated between the two powers, until Grenada was ceded to Britain in the Treaty of Paris in 1763. The British controlled the island from 1763 to 1779. On the ascension of the British to power, the "Anglicization" of the island began. In addition to giving the country its final "anglicized" name (by which it would hereafter be known), the British set up an English colonial legislature based on the model of the Legislative Council and Assembly already established in the older British colonies. The state religion was changed to Anglicanism, despite the fact that most of the population was (at least nominally) Catholic.

Under British rule, Grenada became quite a profitable sugar colony. Building on the considerable progress in plantation development made by the French, the British were able to erect an economy which stood second only to Jamaica in the British Caribbean. During the War of American Independence, the French, again, took control of the island in 1779. However, the Treaty of Versailles returned Grenada to the British in 1783. The British reinforced their process of anglicization with fervour and determination in order to "repay" the French settlers for the harassment which the British had suffered during the period of French occupation. However, it was not only the white French colonists who were adversely affected by the British laws, but the "free coloureds" (free persons of mixed ancestry) as well. Many of them owned land and could be considered part of the French plantocracy. But, under the British, they suffered a steady erosion of their civil and political rights. The slaves also suffered, and (like their counterparts throughout the region) yearned for physical, social, political and economic freedom. The continued discord between the French and British in Grenada reached its climax in 1795 with the occurrence of the Fédon Rebellion.

Adopting the French revolutionary motto (Liberty, Equality and Fraternity), Julien Fédon, a free coloured planter, led the French free coloured and enslaved population in revolt against the British. By November 1795, Fédon's forces controlled all of Grenada except for the town of St George's and its immediate environs.[2] In Britain, the authorities were concerned that they were going to lose Grenada from the inside and that a second Haiti was in the making.[3] By June 1796, Fédon and his men were overpowered by the British. While his lieutenants were captured, Fédon eluded the British and was never taken.

The insurrection lasted fifteen months and resulted in a loss of property estimated at £2.5 million. Sugar works, rum distilleries and other buildings were destroyed on sixty-five estates. Cattle, horses and mules valued at approximately £65,000 were killed. Seven thousand slaves died. However, the British rallied and rebuilt their damaged property and continued plantation cultivation. Sugar was cultivated most extensively in the parish of St Andrew, followed by the parishes of St Patrick and St George.

The slave trade, which had lasted for approximately three hundred years, ended in 1807 and was followed by the amelioration policies of the British government in 1823. These policies were administered in an attempt to improve the conditions of the slaves. Because of the abolition of the slave trade, planters were now being forced to take better care of the labour force they already had. They, therefore, sought to improve the living and working conditions of slaves, particularly female slaves who they relied on to reproduce in order to replenish and increase the slave population.

The slaves received their freedom on 1 August 1834. However, they first had to serve a period of apprenticeship: six years for slaves who worked in the fields and four years for slaves who did not work in the fields. The apprenticeship system was implemented by the British government as a period of transition between emancipation and full freedom. Apprenticeship, however, ended prematurely in 1838, as many ex-slaves abandoned the estates and headed for Grenada's mountainous interior where they went to farm their own small plots of land. The freed slaves' desire for economic independence was so strong that a new class was created almost overnight – that of the small farmer.

Grenadian planters imported immigrant labourers between 1838 and 1885 to help shore up the labour force on the estates. Immigrant labourers came from Malta, Madeira, Africa and India, while Grenadian ex-slave labourers emigrated to larger Caribbean islands, like Trinidad, in search of higher wages. By 1901, the island's population was 63,438 and by 1930 it was 76,987. The population density was 578 persons per square mile. In 1930, the racial composition was as follows: 76.9 per cent black; 17.5 per cent coloured; 4.1 per cent East Indian; and 1.4 per cent white.[4] The whites and some of the landed coloureds made up the dominant class in Grenadian society.

Under the French, the Grenadian economy was centered on sugar cane and tobacco cultivation until the second decade of the eighteenth century. By 1714 the economy was diversified to include cocoa, cotton and coffee. Under the British, sugar became the chief export, but cocoa replaced sugar as the mainstay of the economy between 1857 and 1868. The nutmeg industry became prominent by the turn of the twentieth century and bananas by about 1934. Bananas, cocoa and nutmeg formed the base of the island's economy and, directly or indirectly, generated much of the income and employment in the island from 1868 to 1983.

Grenada's government had a typical "old representative government" type of constitution from the 1760s to the 1870s. This system operated with a governor at its helm, and it consisted of a Legislative Council, appointed by the governor, and an elected Assembly. The representative system was removed following the repercussions of the Morant Bay Rebellion in Jamaica in 1865.[5] Grenada became a Crown Colony in 1877. This form of government did away with the elected Assembly and consisted solely of a Legislative Council. The members of the government were therefore appointed by the governor and not by members of the public. By 1915, two journalists, William Galway Donovan and Theophilus Albert Marryshow took up the cause of the Grenadian people in a call for a more representative political system. Both journalists used their newspapers, the *West Indian* and the *Grenada People*, to mould public opinion. In 1917, the Grenada Representative Association was formed by local intelligentsia and Donovan and Marryshow were active participants. The Grenada Representative Association sent off a petition to the secretary of state to bring an end to the Crown Colony government on the grounds that it was ill-suited to Grenada. The British responded with the Wood Commission in 1921, which recommended that the Legislative Council be composed of the governor, seven officials, three nominated members and five elected members. This was not what the Grenada Representative Association had in mind, as it still did not allow for greater local autonomy, but an Order in Council outlining the new constitutional provisions was sent to Grenada in 1924.

Donovan and Marryshow failed to organize the Grenadian working class into an effective political force. Grenada, therefore, did not take part in the labour unrest of 1937 and 1938 that was plaguing the rest of the region, including St Vincent, Trinidad, St Lucia and Jamaica; the country's participation was delayed by thirteen years. The cause of the working class was subsequently taken up by Eric Matthew Gairy in February 1951, when he led the Grenadian estate and road workers in revolt against the colonial government and estate owners. He founded the Grenada Manual and Mental Workers Union and the Grenada People's Party. The union laid demands before the Grenada Agricultural Association for better working conditions and higher wages for workers. It was Grenada's first general strike in the post–World War II period and it involved agricultural and road workers throughout the island. By April 1951, most of Gairy's demands had been met. Universal adult suffrage was granted to all citizens of Grenada in September 1951. Gairy transformed the Grenada People's Party into the Grenada United Labour Party (GULP). The new party was elected into the Legislative Council in 1951.

In 1958, Grenada followed her other British Caribbean neighbours into the Federation of the West Indies, but this was dissolved in 1962. Also, in 1962, Grenada's constitution was suspended so that allegations of corrupt practices regarding the island's public expenditure under the Gairy regime could be investigated. For most of the period between 1951 and 1979, GULP was in power, although the party lost the elections in 1957 and 1962. Grenada attained Associated Statehood (a form of self-government just short of independence) in 1967. The first premier under the new constitution was H.A. Blaize, leader of the GNP. Later in 1967, Blaize's party was defeated in the general election when GULP won. Headed by Gairy, GULP led Grenada to independence on 7 February 1974.

In 1973, the NJM, a left-wing political group, was formed. This year also saw the commencement of a series of mass demonstrations against the Gairy regime for a number of reasons, including Gairy's misuse of government funds and his victimization of detractors. The People's Alliance was formed in 1976 out of this discontent against the Gairy regime, which resulted in the overthrow of the regime and the establishment of a socialist revolutionary regime on 13 March 1979. This made Grenada the first and only nation in the English-speaking Caribbean to have had a socialist revolution. The PRG, under the leadership of Maurice Bishop, ruled from 1979 to 1983. However, internal division and violence caused the regime to collapse and the island was invaded by the US military and by Caribbean forces on 25 October 1983.

WOMEN'S HISTORY

Women's history is history that investigates women as the main subject matter, though it cannot be studied in isolation from major developments in any given society or time period. The aim of writing women's history is twofold: first, to retrieve information about women's activities in past human societies and to insert this into the historical record; second, to ensure that gender as a system of organizing society and distributing power and resources is recognized and used by historians as a fundamental tool of analysis.[6]

The gender system is examined through many components, including (1) the social roles assigned to men and to women, (2) the cultural definition of masculinity and femininity, (3) the division of labour, (4) the rules regarding marriage, (5) kinship behaviour between the sexes and (6) women's position in relation to men in political and economic life.[7] Gender is used as a tool of analysis in this book, which addresses all the above-mentioned dimensions. However, while gender is a necessary tool of analysis, it is not the only one with which to investigate the history of women. Within the Grenadian context, there are other analytical categories by which to examine the story of women; for example, class, social status, colour, education and economic standing all figured prominently in how women's lives unfolded. Moreover, at this stage in Grenada's historiography, with its absence of any comprehensive historical work on women, I thought it best to write a book that is overtly women's history, rather than gender history.

METHODOLOGY

This book has employed secondary sources, including material from a number of serials and journals. However, there is a substantial reliance on primary sources as well. These include Colonial Office correspondence; Grenada estate records, 1796–1840 and 1948–1983; official reports, government documents and speeches; newspapers, 1815–1986; church records; and oral interviews. By using these various sources, I was able to capture the lived realities of Grenadian women hitherto not examined or recorded.

Estate records from the period of slavery provided information on the natural increase and decrease of the slave populations on the plantations over the period 1797 to 1834. Such information was instrumental in tracing the planters' attempts to ameliorate the conditions of female slaves as they sought to ensure the continued regeneration of their labour force from within. The records indicated the diseases from which female slaves suffered, the infant mortality rate and the level of medical care planters provided for their slaves. These records also give an account of the number of slave women who worked in the fields compared to the men, and indicate their financial value to the planters. The estate records of the 1940s and 1950s also furnished the names of women and their wages. Reports by stipendiary magistrates provided a rich source of information on the working conditions of apprentices and ex-slaves after 1834, and gave an insight into how apprenticed women felt about apprenticing their children. The voices of incorrectly classified apprenticed women and those ill-treated by the planters were brought to life through the court cases. Blue Book Reports, from the time of slavery to the 1940s, yielded statistics on race, sex, deaths, marriages and baptisms, as well as the educational and health facilities that were available on the island. Newspapers published between 1815 and 1834 gave an indication of the significant number of female runaway slaves along with their descriptions; those published between 1959 and 1983 provided speeches given by female politicians which highlighted women's support for and opposition to the Gairy regime, and recorded the existence of women's groups and their role and objectives.

The book relies heavily on oral histories, which are more personal, for the period 1900 to 1983. For women's history, it is an especially important method of collecting information, since women have generally documented their accounts in writing far less than men. Women have tended to use speech much more widely than the written word. Often, the oral mode is the only tool through which the voices of women from all walks of life and all strata of society can be captured. In order to record representative views of Grenadian women in this book, women from all economic and social backgrounds and from all parishes in Grenada as well as Carriacou and Petit Martinique were interviewed. Those interviewed included estate workers, domestic workers, housewives, teachers, nurses, civil servants, lawyers, business-women, clerks, managers, religious leaders, politicians and ambassadors. In order to record women's experiences in the early 1900s, women aged seventy-five to ninety were interviewed. Men were not excluded from the research, and were interviewed so that they could provide their perspective on the role of women in Grenadian history, particularly during the time of the People's Revolution, from 1979 to 1983. Pro-revolutionary authors had used oral sources to show female support for the PRG. By the same token, this method can now be used to record the voices of women in opposition to the revolutionary process, and to allow women who held positions of power in the PRG and in the NWO to comment retrospectively on the revolution.

2 Women in Grenadian Slave Society, 1783–1838

A MAJOR RETHINKING OF Caribbean historical discourse on slavery has placed the role of women centre stage. Slave women were a dominant part of the field labour force on British Caribbean sugar plantations from at least the end of the eighteenth century. Furthermore, there was an increased dependence upon slave women for reproduction of plantation labourers. The slave woman was both producer and reproducer. She, therefore, became valuable to planters who wished to ensure the survival of the slave system. The slave woman was also a rebel and found ingenious ways to resist captivity. Free coloured women and free black women were also important actors during the period of slavery – they were plantation owners, higglers and freedom fighters; white women also owned plantations and found employment as teachers and seamstresses.

ENSLAVED WOMEN

At the start of the slave trade in the Caribbean, female slaves were imported in smaller numbers than male slaves. This was so for Grenada in particular and the other colonies in general (British, French and Dutch colonies). Historical records show that between 1784 and 1788, a total of 8,216 male slaves and 5,346 female slaves were sold to Grenada.[1] By 1788, slave owners in Grenada estimated that for every five male slaves, there were three female slaves working on the plantations. They further noted that, in imports from Africa, the number of males in "a well assorted cargo" usually exceeded that of females by a proportion of two to one.[2] While the price difference was small, there were fewer African females imported than males. The relationship between mortality and sex in the Atlantic slave trade shows that mortality rates of females were the same as or even lower than those of males of the same age group.[3] The arrival of fewer female slaves was, therefore, not due to the fact that they were less able than their male counterparts to withstand the crossing of the Middle Passage, or due to a lack of demand for them by the planters. Rather, it had to do with the desires of those who were supplying the slaves. African traders were quite reluctant to release large numbers of women to the slave market in the New World because women figured prominently in Africa's internal slave market. Evidence from Senegambia suggests that a much higher local price was paid for female slaves than for male slaves. In this case, African slave traders would outbid their European counterparts for females that came up for sale on the African market. Women were vital for agricultural labour in West Africa and, within African polygamous societies, slave wives were valuable. Men were, therefore, more readily put up for sale to the Atlantic slave market. The shipping of more women than normal would indicate a fundamental breakdown in the economic and social viability of the African state.[4]

Throughout the British slave colonies, there was a tendency for the population to move towards a normalization of sex ratios among the slave population; that is, the colonies started off with a predominance of males under "frontier" conditions but ended up with a predominance of females upon maturity. In Barbados, as early as 1710, there was a predominance of females in the field labour force on the plantation and by 1756 the same was true for Jamaica. In the "frontier" period of Caribbean slavery, both white male servants and African male slaves were put to work in the fields. However, as the economic landscape changed, white indentured servants moved out of the fields and into managerial positions as bookkeepers and overseers. African male slaves replaced them as artisans in the sugar works, thereby creating a need for more labourers in the fields. This vacuum was filled by slave women. This is not to say that men did not work in the field, but that a much higher proportion of men than women were shifted into non-field jobs. Some scholars argue that the heavy influx of women in the field was due in part to a European perception of the "drudge" status of African women in polygynous marriages. This influx also aligned with traditional African practices in which women were the agriculturists, while men undertook the skilled, mobile and supervisory jobs for which, it was deemed, they were more "naturally" suited.[5]

In Grenada, the predominance of women labourers in the fields occurred after 1800. For example, in 1789, on the Lataste Estate in the parish of St Patrick, there was still a male majority in the field: forty-eight men and forty-three women.[6] However, by 1804, inventories for the Lower and Upper Pearls Estates in the parish of St Andrew show a significant number of women in the fields. On the Lower Pearls Estate, sixty-four of the ninety field slaves were women whereas, of the eleven domestic workers, only five were women. All the artisan and skilled jobs (such as carpenters, coopers, blacksmiths, masons, boilers, carters, mule boys and watchmen) were taken by the men. On the Upper Pearls Estate, sixty-four of the eighty-nine field slaves were women.[7] Here, too, the men were predominant in the artisan and skilled jobs. By 1811, the Lataste Estate caught up with the trend that saw more female than male workers in the fields: thirty-eight of the field slave labourers were women while twenty-four were men. Here, also, it was mostly the male slaves who were given the artisan and skilled jobs, although some female slaves held these positions as well. For instance, there were two female stock keepers – twenty-six-year-old Zabeth and sixty-year-old Adelaine; there was a hospital nurse – fifty-year-old Jenny; a washerwoman – thirty-eight-year-old Mary Catherine; a dry nurse – fifty-year-old Charlott; and a domestic – twenty-five-year-old Peggy.[8]

Slave women were expected to work just as hard as men and were punished just as severely. In the eyes of the master, the female slave was equal to the male. Slave women did land clearing, planting, hoeing, weeding, cane cutting and carried the cane to the mills. At crop time, from October to March, slaves worked from sunrise to sunset. They also did extended night work. Enough cane had to be cut before sunset to keep the mills running throughout the night. Higman estimates that the typical day worked by field slaves was twelve hours in Jamaica and ten hours in the Eastern Caribbean.[9] The field slaves performed the hardest labour and worked the longest hours. Pregnant women were not generally treated differently with respect to the severity of their work regime, nor with respect to the severity of their punishment. Being pregnant did not preclude slave women from being punished, but planters would take care to prevent injury to the unborn child by digging a hole in the ground for the women's belly to rest in as she was being flogged. The flogging of women was abolished in 1825 by the British government.[10] However, Grenadian planters bitterly protested the prohibition of this measure. They argued that

> The females compose the most numerous and effective part of the field gangs of the estate; from the indulgences already extended to them they have shown themselves to be the most turbulent description of the slaves, and would become perfectly unmanageable if they knew that this description of correction was abolished by law. It is therefore absolutely necessary (for the present) that it should be held in terrorem [as a warning] over them. If suddenly prohibited it is impossible to say what might be the consequences.[11]

Domestic workers were perhaps more vulnerable to physical abuse due to their close proximity to their masters. In their positions as domestic workers, both women and men fell prey to the whims and caprices of the master and his family. In this sense, their jobs, while considered as being a cut above field labour, had a major drawback. Although both the domestic female slave and the female field worker were subjected to sexual exploitation, this was more so for the domestic workers working in the great house. The female field slave was considered the most socially inferior of all the slaves. As such, she was seen as being available for sexual exploitation by her master and the other white men on the plantation. It can therefore be said that her exploitation took place not just in the sphere of production (through her enforced labour on the plantation), but also in the social sphere (with respect to sex).[12] bell hooks takes this argument further by charging that slave women had the odds stacked against them. In a racist, patriarchal society, black women were more subject to sexual exploitation than the black male. The black woman was an easy target since she was not protected either by law or public opinion. Racism ensured that black people would be enslaved and sexism ensured that the black woman's treatment would be harsher and more brutal than the black male's.[13]

Both domestic slaves and field slaves were offered up by owners as prostitutes to visiting friends and fellow planters. Female domestic workers were
sometimes also hired out to sailors, visiting merchants or gentlemen from
England. Often, advertisements in newspapers of the colonies offered the
services of female slaves. The real services of these women were disguised
through their description as *an excellent washerwoman* or *a seamstress* for whom
liberal wages would be expected.[14] While some advertisements were what
they seemed, others were fronts for the business of prostitution. The practice
seemed to have been recognized as being quite prevalent in Grenada as an act
was passed in 1788 to curb it. The act was known as "An Act for the Encouragement, Protection and Better Government of Slaves" or the Grenada
"Guardian Act". Clause XXII of this act made provision for the protection of
the chastity of the "wives" of slaves, as it was stated to be the custom for masters to offer female slaves to transient visitors to their estate. To prevent this,
a fine of £50 was imposed. The act also sought to prevent "married" female
slaves from being violated by their owners and managers. The act stated that
these persons (white slave owners and merchants) were not to "debauch and
have carnal knowledge" of such a slave during her "marriage", and made masters liable to a fine of £165 for non-compliance.[15]

As the end of the slave trade drew near, West Indian planters sought to
conserve the slave population they already had and to enhance it through
reproduction. The attitude of the West Indian plantocracy changed from the
premise that it was "better to buy than to breed", to one that sought to
encourage the replenishment of slaves from within the colonies. John Terry,
an overseer and manager in Grenada between 1776 and 1790, noted that he
never received instructions to "pay particular attention to pregnant woman
or their children". His employers, he said, were of the opinion that "suckling
children should die, for they [the employers] lost a great deal of the mother's
work during the infancy of the child".[16] At that time, the slave woman's role,
therefore, was to make sugar rather than to reproduce, but this changed by
1797 with the reenactment of the "Guardian Act" which ruled that mothers
of six living children be should be exempt from all field labour, and which
sought, generally, to improve the lives of female slaves. In addition, the act
ruled that a hospital was to be established in proportion to the number of
slaves on the estate, and that a hospital book was to be kept by the surgeon

with the names of slaves and the nature of their complaints; also, the planters were required to give an account of births and deaths of the slaves and the causes of death. The owner of Lataste Estate in the early 1800s expressed, by letter, his concern with the "very little increase by birth" on his estate. He claimed that the slave women were "very averse from [sic] child bearing and will frequently use their endeavours to procure abortion". He therefore advised that "fair encouragement" be rendered to them to make "their labour very easy during the time as any great exertion would be very inconvenient to them".[17] By 1810, on Lataste Estate, measures were implemented to "put a stop to the practice of picking grass for the mules and cattle by the negroes after leaving the field in the evening". This not only lessened their labour, to some degree, but "put it in their power to be in their houses" before sunset. Also, women were to be excused from work after delivery, and an addition was to be made to the allowance of flour for infants. For "further increasing the breeding of women", the annual allocation of pieces of loose linen (which could be made into baby clothes) and cotton handkerchiefs was increased.[18] These scraps of cloth would often be turned into baby clothes by the women. The owner of Lataste went on to mention that there was evidence of natural increase in the slave population in the Leeward Islands, and that this was probably due to the practice of stopping work at crop time between 9:00 p.m. and 3:00 a.m. However, such a practice was not, in his view, practical for Grenada. By 1826, Lataste was able to boast of one female slave who bore five children.[19]

In the wake of the abolition of the slave trade, the value of slaves increased. By the late eighteenth century and early nineteenth century, the monetary value of female slaves was almost on par with that of male slaves. On the Pearls Estate, in 1802, for example, the value of male and female slaves was similar. Young female slaves were valued at as much as £140, like ten-year-old Mary Louise; twelve-year-old Paul was valued at the same price as well. Even older female slaves were highly valued: Faudenie, for example, was valued at £150 at age fifty.[20]

A slave woman performed a dual role. She was not only valuable as a source of labour but as a reproducer of future labour power. The plantocracy sought to exploit and control the slave woman's reproductive capacity and sexuality in order to perpetuate their wealth which came from the production of sugar, coffee, cotton or other staple products. Amelioration came about as a result of the British government's bid to bring an end to slavery by means of a gradual process. This process had three stages: First, to end the slave trade; second, to improve the conditions of the slaves; and finally, to emancipate the slaves. The plantocracy of the British Caribbean followed the ameliorative measures out of compulsion rather than choice. Improving the conditions of female slaves was not done out of genuine concern for the slaves themselves, but out of the planters' concern about maintaining and expanding their wealth.

In spite of the measures taken by the plantocracy, in Grenada there was a natural decrease rather than increase in the slave population. As early as 1799, this process was evident from some plantation records. (See table 2.1.)

Table 2.1 Madeys Estate Plantation Accounts, 1799–1803

Year	Births	Deaths
1799	6	8
1801	5	9
1802	3	9
1803	4	7

Grenada's well-documented slave registration figures between 1817 and 1833, also give a clear indication of this trend.[21] According to these records, in the parishes of St Patrick and St Andrew in 1817, all the estates showed a decrease rather than an increase in the slave population.[22]

However, overall, the figures for Grenada showed more deaths than births among slaves, except for the years 1822, 1827, 1829 and 1833. (See table 2.2.) In comparison to the other Windward Islands, Grenada stood in the middle of the spectrum with respect to these statistics. In Dominica and St Lucia, there was evidence of deaths outweighing births from 1817 to 1825. Yet from 1826 to 1832, the opposite was true. In St Vincent and Tobago there was a steady incidence of deaths outweighing births.[23]

One of the reasons for the failure of planters to increase the numbers of their slaves through breeding was their non-conciliatory attitude towards the Guardian Act and slaves, in general. The Guardian Act was passed because

Table 2.2 Registered Slave Births and Deaths, Grenada, 1817–1833

Colony	Registration	Registered Births			Registered Deaths		
Grenada	Months	Males	Females	Total	Males	Females	Total
1817	8	212	239	451	478	424	902
1818	12	305	352	657	538	532	1,070
1819	12	339	375	714	585	584	1,169
1820	12	311	330	641	485	410	895
1821	12	352	330	682	506	422	928
1822	12	371	350	721	364	316	680
1823	12	361	358	719	398	426	824
1824	12	353	324	677	392	332	724
1825	12	337	340	677	399	360	759
1826	12	330	340	660	397	397	794
1827	12	369	335	704	360	309	669
1828	12	355	332	687	376	337	713
1829	12	377	359	736	372	358	730
1830	12	385	349	734	503	476	979
1831	12	348	336	684	500	428	928
1832	12	n.c.	n.c.	637	379	332	711
1833	12	n.c.	n.c.	808	348	307	655

Source: Higman, *Slave Populations of the British Caribbean*, 606.

the members came to a general consensus that it would be of "little" conse-
quence since "it was made by themselves against themselves" and would be
"carried into execution by themselves".[24] Planters failed to fully implement
the provisions of the Guardian Act. The specification that the guardians (the
"protectors" of slaves) were to be freeholders or men who owned at least
thirty slaves or their attorneys meant that the enforcement of the law was left
in the hands of the slave-owning class. It would therefore have been a difficult
situation for these men to fulfill such a conflicting role. For example, in an

enquiry into the operation of the Guardian Act in 1823, it was noted that planters generally refused to visit the provision grounds to see that proper food was administered. When a complaint was made by slave women on the issue of insufficient clothing, they received no redress.

Another reason for the lack of increase in the slave population resulted from the practices of the slave women themselves. Some medical practitioners in Grenada believed that female slave infertility was of their own making. Dr John Castles testified that black women were promiscuous in their younger years and took precautions to ensure that they did not have children until they were older, when they were no longer an "object of desire". Therefore, a great portion of their childbearing years went unfulfilled.

Ward and Higman have noted that slave infertility tended to be highest in the intensive sugar producing areas. In these areas, the work tended to be much more strenuous than on plantations exporting cotton, coffee, or cocoa. According to Higman, in the sugar parish of St Andrew, the death rate was 55 per 1,000 slaves in the period 1817 to 1819, as compared to 43 in the cotton producing island of Carriacou. The situation was similar in Jamaica. William Taylor, an estate manager in that colony, testified to the adverse relationship between females working on sugar plantations and fertility. He noted:

> The cane holing is . . . work that calls for very severe exertion and that I think must have a very bad effect upon the female frame. Cane hole digging and night work I considered to be partly the causes of the diminution of the population. On coffee plantations there is neither night work nor cane digging and I have always understood that they [the slaves] increase more than they do on sugar estates.[25]

The rigorous work was one of the factors contributing to female slave infertility. The other factors included poor diet, unsanitary living conditions and diseases. There was a link between malnutrition and the irregularity or absence of ovulation. Malnutrition could also considerably delay post-partum recovery which in turn impeded the ability to become pregnant again. The slave diet was one of salted meat or fish, corn, flour and ground provisions. In most of the colonies, planters gave slaves provision grounds on which to plant food to supplement what was imported. In 1799, a leading Grenadian planter, Alexander Campbell, observed that it was "the custom" in Grenada to "grant slaves a piece of land so they could work, because it had been universally considered the greatest benefit to a planter that his negroes should have a sufficient quantity of provisions".[26] On these grounds, the slaves grew mainly ground provisions like yams, eddoes, cassava, sweet potatoes; tree crops like plantain, banana and breadfruit; grains and legumes. They also reared fowls, hogs and sheep. By the 1790s, the slaves sold their excess produce at the local markets and virtually monopolized the internal market system.

It was slave women who mainly marketed the produce of the provision grounds. Slave women and free women, plantation women and urban women were all higglers, peddling and bartering provisions and dry goods between urban and rural areas. Planters gave evidence of how productive the provision grounds were. James Baillie, a Grenadian planter, claimed that some of the slaves possessed property worth £40, £50, £100 and even as much as £200 sterling. Such property, he explained, was regularly conveyed from one generation to another without any interference whatever.[27]

There were a number of problems related to the working of provision grounds and the sale of the produce. Planters seldom inspected provision grounds to monitor the state of cultivation or the fertility of the soil. The slaves had to indicate when the soil was depleted and when new grounds were needed. Provision grounds were defenceless against drought, hurricanes or theft. In the 1831 hurricane in Grenada, the provision grounds of the Lataste Estate were destroyed. The slaves, in desperation and hunger, resorted to eating unripened provisions which made them ill and forced them to rely on rations of expensive imported grain.[28] In response to abolitionist pressure in 1823, the British government curtailed the Sunday market and thereby disrupted the slaves' traditional commercial routine. It deprived them of access to the large volume of business transacted on a weekend. After 1828, higglers in the town of St George's increased the volume of produce brought into town by the rural slaves on Thursday, the new official market day, and then retailed it at inflated prices. While provision grounds might have provided slaves with a secure source of nutrition, not all slaves were able to cope with the labour demands of the plantation and the effective cultivation of provision grounds. Thus, not all the slaves had an opportunity to enhance their standard of living.

The Caribbean slave diet was high in carbohydrate and low in fat. Fresh meat was raised by some slaves but it most of it appears to have been sold to the white inhabitants. John Terry, an overseer in Grenada, testified that he had known slaves who were driven to satisfy their hunger by eating putrid carcasses. A similar condition was reported for Barbados. Slaves who reared animals might have sold some and have kept some for personal consumption, but what of those who did not own animals? They would have depended on getting their protein from the salt fish or beef or pork provided by the planter. It has been estimated by modern food standards that a herring a day contains only 19.6 grams of protein. Each slave received slightly more than one pound of preserved fish per week or 56.1 pounds per year.[29] As a result, the slaves suffered from the protein deficiency, kwashiorkor. The Caribbean slave diet was also low in calcium and deficient in vitamins A and B. These deficiencies led to other illnesses like dirt eating and edema. These dietary deficiencies were common among both male and female slaves, yet it was the women who were more adversely affected since they were the ones who required extra nutrients during pregnancy.

The high incidence of infertility on sugar intensive areas was further compounded by prolonged lactation. Prolonged lactation could be considered a kind of contraceptive measure, so by employing this practice, it can be argued that slave women probably exercised some control over their fertility. By nursing their babies for a long time, while perhaps abstaining from sexual intercourse, slave women were able to reduce the birth rate in the colonies. This practice was also an African custom that continued in the Caribbean. Within some African societies, the women would suckle their children until they were able to walk. Three years of nursing was not uncommon and, during this period, the husband devoted his attention to his other wives. One Jamaican planter, John Baillie, noted that few of the slave women weaned their children before they were two years old, in spite of his offering them two dollars (approximately eight shillings) if they would wean the child in twelve months.[30]

Slave women might have abstained from sexual intercourse in a society where the likelihood of marriage and stable family life was slim; where they would continue to face a punishing workload throughout the pregnancy and after delivery (if they delivered safely); and where there was a strong possibility that their child would die during the birth. Slave women may also have been unwilling to become pregnant because of the high maternal mortality rate. Instances of such cases are found in Grenada's historical records for the period 1817 to 1833. For example, in the parish of St George, on the Morne Rouge Estate in 1817, twenty-eight-year-old Angelique died in childbirth; and in the same year on the Morne Fendue Estate in the parish of St Patrick, thirty-five-year-old Mary Louise died from "convulsions after delivery"; on the Moliner Estate in St George in 1833, forty-year-old Aimee died in "child bed" from a "rupture of the womb".[31]

Slave women almost certainly used herbal mixtures and traditional potions from their own doctors, known as obeah men and women, to abort children. Some members of the plantocracy linked the practice of abortion by slaves to promiscuity. They claimed that, in order to maintain their attractiveness to whites and heighten their chances of improving their status, some slave women practised abortion. Slave women may have aborted as a means of resistance to the slave regime and in so doing helped to thwart planters' efforts at natural increase. For example, on 5 July 1801 on the Boccage Estate in St Patrick, Celest died of an abortion.[32] The term abortion could mean involuntary miscarriage or deliberate termination of the pregnancy. In the case of Celest, the evidence does not specify.

The slave women who did conceive, and who had a successful pregnancy and delivery were faced with a high incidence of infant mortality. Slave mothers were most likely calcium deficient as they entered their first pregnancy. Calcium, from the mother, is stored in the bones of the foetus during the last three months of intrauterine life. The amount stored can vary considerably, depending on the calcium nutrition of the mother. If the amount is low, the infant is in danger since the amount of calcium in breast milk is not enough to maintain skeletal growth without the contribution of the infant's stores.[33] The slave child would thus leave the mother's womb in a weakened state. The baby, when weaned, would then be fed mainly cornmeal or flour soups with little or no milk, in other words a diet that was high in carbohydrate and low in protein. The end result was often malnutrition.

Slave children generally suffered from worm infestations, marasmus, whooping cough and diarrhoea. Dr Castles of Grenada noted that "worm infestation was more common in the West Indies than in England".[34] He attributed this to slaves' "vegetable diet, [a] great part of which [was] used in a crude [that is, unclean] state, particularly fruits". The unsanitary conditions of estate slave huts and surroundings contributed to a number of illnesses. Plantations were usually situated on relatively flat land that was poorly drained and the stagnant water attracted disease-carrying mosquitoes and flies. Also, slaves would go "to the bush" to relieve their bowels. The result was that the water and the soil in which slave children walked were often infested with faecal matter. Such conditions led to worm infestation and gastro-intestinal diseases. The records show a long list of infant deaths from such infestations and diseases. The following examples are taken from the records of the main sugar producing areas – the parishes of St George, St Andrew and St Patrick: in St George, in 1815, on the Morne Delice Estate, Colette's child Dorothy died at four months of age from marasmus; in 1833, on the Tempe Estate, St George, Sally's child died at eighteen days old from bowel complaint and debility; in St Andrew, 1817, on the Grand Bacolet Estate, Lizette's child died at five days old of lockjaw; in 1833 on the Grand Bras Estate in St Andrew, Angelique's child, Rowley, died at twenty days old from colic; in St Patrick, on the Hermitage Estate, in 1817, Mary Ermine's infant died at two months old from measles.[35]

By 1820, Grenada had seventeen doctors. Medical services were either offered by piecework or by contract. The piecework system involved doctors visiting the estates only when they were sent for, whereas the contract system bound the doctors to visit the estates on a regular basis. There was evidence of planters paying doctors substantial sums of money to perform surgeries and provide smallpox inoculations to slaves on the Pearls, Boccage, Boulogne and Dunfermline Estates.[36] In spite of the money spent on medical treatment for the slaves, there was a natural decrease rather than an increase in the slave population in Grenada after the abolition of the slave trade.

In the final analysis, planters' primary concern was to gain as much profit from their plantation as possible. If they had sought to change the main factors that prevented the increase of their slave populations (such as a rigorous work regime for women, poor diets, unsanitary living and working conditions), then they would have had to change the entire organization of sugar cane cultivation. This would have inevitably reduced their profits, as they would have had to spend on things like better housing, proper drainage facilities and the provision of more nutritious foods. This would have meant an extensive outlay of capital and a reduction of output, but planters were unwilling to make this sacrifice.

By 1823, at the time of amelioration, planters and government officials not only sought to increase the slave population but also to cultivate proper moral and religious standards, according to European dictates, among the slaves. For this purpose, an act was passed in Grenada to remove the Sunday market from the designated day of worship. Slaves were also encouraged to be baptized. The ameliorative measures might have assisted in keeping slave families together, for example, by forcing planters to sell slave families intact (rather than splitting them up and selling slaves individually, as was usually done). While the official documents give little evidence of formal slave marriages and baptisms, it seems from the reports of the Roman Catholic Church, as recorded and reported by Father Raymond Devas, that slave unions were often long lasting. Although polygyny and other African practices persisted, the nuclear family was fairly common, especially among creole slaves in the British West Indies. In Grenada, however, it is possible that slaves lived in family units by choice rather than out of a desire to satisfy planters or church officials.

Although laws were passed, throughout the colonies, which forced slaves to practice a Christian/European lifestyle, they kept hold of their cultural and religious traditions. These persist into the present day. For example, in Grenada and the sister islands of Carriacou and Petit Martinique, obeah and big drum dancing still exist. In addition, songs with distinct African and French words have been handed down through the ages. These encapsulate stories that tell of life during slavery. For example, the song, "Pléwé Lidé", recounts the selling of a slave family:

Pléwé mwe Lidé Pléwé Maiwaz
oh hélé mwé Lidé, hélé oh Maiwaz hélé pu nu alé.
Dimâsh Pwashi bâtma-la-vol-a Vâdi ya bâtma-la-vol-a Kité, oh Maiwaz[37]

Translation:

Weep for me Lydia, weep Mary Rose,
Lament for me, Lydia, lament Mary Rose, lament for our going. Sunday next the schooner sails from Haiti, the schooner leaves oh Mary Rose

Hélé is an African word meaning to bawl out or wail. It evokes the sense of trauma felt by the husband and wife who were sold individually, without their children, to planters in Trinidad and Haiti.

During the amelioration period, Sunday school sessions were held for slave children. One such class was held by the Church of England (the Anglican Church) and another by the Catholic Church. The Wesleyan clergy also offered catechetical instruction to slave children on different estates on their weekly or fortnightly visits.[38]

FEMALE RESISTANCE TO SLAVERY

Female slave resistance was notable for its diversity of tactics. These women would employ a number of methods to weaken the system of slavery and to hasten its collapse. Sometimes their resistance was subtle – malingering on estates, feigning illness and performing self-inflicted mutilation (to purpose-fully extend their period of illness so that they would not have to work). At other times, their resistance was overt and they would commit acts of arson and theft, they would run away, poison their masters, murder members of the plantocracy, find ways to buy themselves out of slavery and participate in armed rebellion. Some women would employ "gynaecological resistance", by practising infanticide and abortion. Through these means they sought to bring a speedier end to slavery. The methods of resistance that will be dis-cussed further are resistance by running away from plantations, resistance through destruction of property and resistance through armed rebellion.

Most of the evidence of female resistance to slavery in Grenada refers to women running away from the plantations. There were numerous notices in the *St George's Chronicle and Grenada Gazette* and the *Grenada Free Press and Public Gazette* over the period 1815 to 1829 concerning female runaways. Interest-ingly, during the period 1808 to 1821, female runaways outnumbered male runaways: 62 per cent of the 703 runaways were women. Sometimes, some of the women absented themselves from the estates for long periods, never to return. For example, Mary Ursule and Sally were runaways from the Crochu Estate for twenty-three years and twenty years, respectively. Daw-phne, described as having marks on her face, was a runaway from the Grand Anse Estate in St George for fourteen years.[39] Women ran away to escape the

rigours of plantation life; even if only for a short period of time. They ran
with the full knowledge that if they were caught they would be punished.
Some ran away to see family members in other parts of the island. Others
hoped to leave the island altogether with the false hope that slavery did not
exist elsewhere or that the conditions were not as severe. From the vivid
descriptions of runaways given by the planters, one can get a sense of their
physical appearance. One such advertisement reads:

> Runaway
>
> From the subscriber about four months ago a negro woman named Mary
> Therese, about forty years of age, five feet five inches high. She has a scar on
> her left leg and one of her toes is cut off.

Another reads:

> Runaway
>
> From the subscriber on Thursday last a negro woman named Sofy about five
> feet five inches high dark complexion had on when absconded an osnaburg
> coat and white shift, speaks English and French, she has been sent out some-
> times to sell jelly pickles and preserves about the town previous to this.[41]

The advertisements also give a sense of the kinds of abilities some slave
women had (mentioning, for instance, a woman who spoke three languages:
English, French, and Spanish) and the cunning they used to aid their escape
(such as passing themselves off as free women if they had a lighter skin
colour).

The advertisements often alleged that runaways were being harboured by
friends or kin. For example, a young girl named Fancheon was allegedly harboured by friends at Grand Anse, St George's. Some runaways travelled quite
far, such as Flora who ran away from Gouyave and was seen in Richmond
Hill, St George, approximately fifteen miles away. The advertisements also
show that female slaves commonly sought to escape while in their "teens"
and earlier. For example, twelve-year-old Kitty ran away six weeks prior to
1 April 1815 and sixteen-year-old Mary, nicknamed Monkey, ran away in September 1821.[42] There was also evidence that it was not just the female slaves
on the larger island of Grenada who ran away, but also those from the sister

island of Carriacou. For example, Zabat, the slave of Mary Louise St Hillaire of Carriacou, had, by July 1815, absconded for ten months and Betsey, a twenty-two-year-old creole slave of Hope Estate, ran away in November 1823.[43]

Some women ran away with their children. Some were persistent runaways in spite of the punishment they received when they were recaptured. For example, Therese was described as an "incorrigible runaway". She received fifty lashes in 1813 and was sentenced to work in chains for six months and to be confined in the stocks, noon and night. Etienne and Susey, even after receiving thirty-nine lashes on the public parade, still resisted returning to the estate and had to be forcefully taken back. They were locked away in jail for six months.[44]

Some female slaves, however, chose to live and express their opposition to slavery through acts of vandalism, for example, by destroying crops and equipment. In 1823, John Wells, manager of Ballies Bacolet Estate in St David, noted that, on 19 February, a slave woman, Germaine, was given fifteen stripes for willfully destroying canes in the field and for general neglect of duty.[45] Other female slaves chose to participate in organized acts of rebellion, such as in Grenada's largest uprising in 1795. This was led by Julien Fédon, a free coloured planter and slave owner. Fédon and his free coloured compatriots were struggling against discrimination by the British on account of their colour and French nationality, and against restrictions on their political and social rights. The free coloured rebels were joined by the slaves who saw them as allies in the fight against the system of slavery. According to an eyewitness, John Hay, on his way to imprisonment at Fédon's camp, the headquarters of the rebels, "we were met by numbers of negroes of both sexes". He further noted that a woman, with whom one of the leaders of the revolt had a child, was taking part in plundering his property. He noted that "she was very busy packing up and sending away the few articles of glass and earthenware which had yet remained without either speaking or taking the least notice of me". On Sunday 8 March 1795, he reported that at Fédon's camp "a great number of men[,] women and children joined this day and enjoyed themselves in feasting[,] dancing and singing".[46] However, there is no evidence from authentic sources that women were actively involved in the fighting. Hay did mention that Fédon's wife and daughter were present at the massacre of the British prisoners. He described them as "unfeeling spectators" of Fédon's "horrid barbarity". There was evidence of women involved in transporting weapons, plundering provision grounds of plantations and plundering the property of planters. Women also provided food for the rebels by cultivating food crops on the small plantations owned by the leaders of the rebellion.

A number of free coloured women were supposedly involved in sending supplies to Fédon's troops. Madame Peschian and Madame Reynauds were two of the suppliers for the rebels. In fact, at the end of the rebellion, while no women were executed, a committee was established in September 1796 by the governor to "examine . . . the characters and conduct of the free coloured women[,] many of whom were lying under strong suspicion of having taken an active part with the insurgents and rebels during the insurrection". When, in May 1797, some female relations of the executed rebels attempted to re-enter Grenada from Trinidad, there was a public outcry against them. The outcry was so loud that Governor Charles Green accepted the Legislative Council's advice in refusing them permission to land.[47]

The insurrection left extensive damage in its wake. Grand Bras Estate's records noted "every building was destroyed and every negro [had] fled". Lataste Estate's damages amounted to just over £22,000.[48] Overall, slave owners' losses amounted to £2.5 million due to the destruction of plantations, loss of harvests and the death of about seven thousand slaves.

FREE BLACK AND COLOURED WOMEN

Early evidence of manumission in Grenada was documented in the 1760s and 1780s. Planters rewarded faithful slaves who assisted them in suppressing revolts, forewarned them of imminent uprisings or were useful in apprehending runaways. In 1786, a slave woman named Pauline, owned by the heirs of Honoré Philip of Carriacou, was granted her freedom for having "unearthed a very dangerous and alarming conspiracy in which a great number of valuable slaves planned to escape to the Spanish settlements".[49] Slaves also gained their freedom through self purchase or through the goodwill of their masters. For example, in Grenada, there was evidence of masters who bequeathed their slaves freedom. Louis La Grenade, the free coloured owner of the Morne Jaloux Estate in St George, bequeathed the freedom of thirteen slaves. Among them was his "favourite child Peggy", whose freedom was to be granted ten years after his death. La Grenade left instructions with his daughter that Peggy be tended to after her manumission while she was still a minor.[50]

In the move towards amelioration, manumission laws were relaxed. For example, an act in 1797 imposed a fee of one hundred pounds on all manumissions. This, however, was repealed on 27 July 1818, after which no tax or fine whatsoever was imposed by law on any manumission. While the law after 1818 appeared to be accommodating towards manumission, the minutes of the Legislative Council in 1823 expressed the dissenting views of the plantocracy. On the issue of manumission as part of amelioration measures for slaves, the president of the council, George Paterson, feared that it would be tantamount to "the ultimate ruin of the proprietors' of land".[51]

Grenada had a female to male manumission rate of at least 2:1. One possible reason for this pattern may be that masters "rewarded" those with whom they had sexual relations. The case of fifty-six-year-old Rose, a "cabresse" (that is, a coloured or mulatto person, part black and part white) slave of Springs Estate in St Andrew, leads one to speculate that this was indeed the case. It was recorded that Rose was sent to England by her former master "with a view of having the sore on her leg cured [and that] she was attended at considerable expense for that purpose by Sir William Blizard". Rose was granted her freedom.[52] Rose may have been treated so well by her owner because of her years of service to her master, or she may have been looked after so well because she was his mistress. A second possible reason for more women than men being granted manumission is that free coloured men would, at times, purchase the freedom of their spouses in order to ensure the freedom of their offspring.

The town of St George's, which in 1820 accounted for 9 per cent of the slave population, had a manumission rate of 149 persons or 47 per cent of those manumitted. The parishes of St George and St Andrew, which collectively accounted for 18 per cent of the slave population, manumitted fifty and twenty-four slaves, respectively, or 15 per cent and 7 per cent of the total manumitted. This suggests that the slaves in towns might have had more opportunities to gain employment to be able to purchase their freedom. They might also have been better informed about their right to freedom than the slaves in the rural areas. The evidence also shows that slaves of a light complexion obtained their freedom more frequently than fully black slaves. For example, between 1820 and 1826, of the 586 slaves manumitted, 41 per cent were coloured while 59 per cent were black. The numbers, alone, would seem to suggest the opposite until it is considered that coloured slaves in Grenada represented only 7 per cent of the slave population.[53] Thus, a higher proportion of coloured slaves gained their freedom than blacks.

Although freedom from slavery brought with it certain rights, it did not necessarily bring equal rights. Free blacks and coloureds were seen as having tainted blood and, thus, were discriminated against politically, socially and economically by the whites. The Grenada Election Act of 1792 restricted voting for members of the legislature to white males who were over the age of twenty-one and who owned property. In court, however, the evidence of free coloureds could be admitted, but it was rarely taken seriously. In 1769, the grand jury asserted that the custom "of taking evidence from free coloureds in cases of life and death against his majesty's white subjects is dangerous and may tend to give ideas to persons of their colour that may be of fatal consequences".[54] Socially, free coloureds were not allowed to share the same pews in church as whites or to be buried in the same section of the cemetery. These restrictions were not gender related, but were equally applied for both sexes. To an extent, economic restrictions were also applied. One example, from 1773, was when two free coloured women, Marie Francoise Tampoon and Barbe Jovanneau, applied for town lots in St George's and were rejected. The Legislative Council ruled that "lots ought not to be granted out to petitioners who were mulattoes or Negroes".[55] On the whole, however, economic restrictions were not generally as far-reaching as other restrictions, and some coloureds were able to amass considerable wealth in Grenada.

There were free coloured and free black women who owned property and estates, but they were few. Among them were Janet Paponet, who owned a nine-acre plot in St Patrick, and Piero, a free black woman of Carriacou, who owned three slaves and thirty-eight acres of land planted with cotton, worth two thousand pounds. The most remarkable, however, was a dynasty of black women, who were the heirs of estates in Carriacou, Grenada and the entire island of Petit Martinique. It all started with Jeanette Philip (a free black) who inherited her wealth from Honoré Philip (a plantation owner with whom she had nine children). The estate included a one hundred and sixty-acre property at Tyrrel Bay in Carriacou, then called Grand Anse, and the island of Petit Martinique. In a 1778 account of the Grenadines, there is a description of Petit Martinique with reference made to its owners:

> Petit Martinique lies about a mile and a half southwest from Petit St Vincent – it is the joint property of Jeanette Philip a free Negro woman, and a number of her mulatto children, left them by a French man of that name . . . [It] contains four hundred and seventy seven acres, of which four hundred and sixty-four are proper for cultivation – Both the soil and the surface of this island are better than most of the Grenadines.[56]

In a 1786 document, Jeanette Philip was recognized as heir to Honoré Philip's estates, for she had "by her labours and fidelity, assisted in making his fortune estimated at 373,723 livres".[57] Judith Philip, one of Jeanette's daughters, eventually amassed most of the family fortune. By 1793, she had gained the shares of her two brothers, Honoré and Louis, and of her sister, Suzanne. Not only did she own property at home, but also abroad as "she had access to" a leasehold house in London at 33 Great Coram Street.[58]

While some free coloureds continued to work in the field on the plantation, others took up other vocations like carpentry, shoemaking, masonry, tailoring, selling market produce and working as servants. For instance, three of Jeanette Philip's sons were carpenters (Honoré, Louis and Joachim), while Michel was a shoemaker and Nicholas Regis a mason. The free coloureds, along with the slaves, were instrumental to the operation of the internal market system within the colonies. Through the use of one example, we can get an idea of the wealth they amassed from such sales. Cumba, or Mary, a nineteen-year-old free black woman, earned the considerable sum of sixteen pounds per annum from selling goods in the market.[59]

Regarding the social and family lives of free black and coloured women, the records of the Anglican Church indicate that there was a higher rate of marriage among free coloureds in the parish of St George than in the other parishes of Grenada and on the island of Carriacou. For example, in the period 1808 to 1821, there were only nine registered marriages of free coloured persons in Carriacou, two in the united parishes of St Patrick, St Andrew and St David, one in St John and none in St Mark. Yet, in St George, there were sixty-six marriages in that same period.[60] This may be because there was a much larger free coloured population in St George. Some marriages occasionally took place between white males and free coloured females who saw these unions as a means of gaining financial security. In Grenada, there was evidence of free coloured women who married whites of high social, if not economic, standing. For example, Margaret Houston, a free coloured woman, daughter of President (of the Assembly) Andrew Houston, married James Briscoe Gaff, the governor's secretary. Margaret's sister, Jane, married James Bowler, the provost marshall. Free coloured women also married slave men. Some of these relationships might have begun while the woman was still a slave.[61]

The free coloured population in Grenada was a relatively large one. The ratio of people of colour to that of slaves in Grenada was 1:21 in 1785. In Dominica, the ratio was 1:33 in 1788; in Jamaica, it was 1:64 in 1787; and in Barbados, it was 1:74 in 1786.[62] In Grenada, by the 1800s, free coloured women outnumbered their male counterparts, possibly because they were manumitted in larger numbers.

WHITE WOMEN

The white population of Grenada was relatively small in 1777: whites were outnumbered by blacks and coloureds by a ratio of 1:27. By contrast, Dominica's ratio in 1788 was 1:12 and Barbados's, in 1783, was 1:13.[63] White women were a minority among the white population. In 1806, it was noted that "the number of white women and children was unworthy of being counted".[64] Henry Coleridge, on his visit to Grenada in 1820, expressed his shock at seeing "just forty [white] ladies on the island". Governor Shipley commented on this when he noted that, while the French inhabitants married young, British families were rare in Grenada. He also expressed concern about miscegenation and the consequent rise of the coloured or mulatto class. While the white female population dwindled, that of the free coloured and slave women increased, as shown in table 2.3.

Most of the white women were based in the parish of St George, near to the town of St George's. Few white women, like their free coloured counterparts, owned property; however, some did, mainly through inheritance.[65] A

Table 2.3 Population of Grenada, 1763–1830

Year	White				Free Coloured				Slave			
	Female	%	Male	%	Female	%	Male	%	Female	%	Male	%
1763	514	42.0	711	58.0	236	51.9	219	48.1	–	–	–	–
1771	393	23.7	1,268	76.3	216	52.1	199	47.9	–	–	–	–
1783	290	21.9	1,034	78.1	113	53.8	97	46.2	–	–	–	–
1787	276	27.7	720	72.3	–	–	–	–	14,438	58.6	10,182	41.4
1823	219	25.9	628	74.1	2,069	61.1	1,319	38.9	12,258	48.4	13,052	51.6
1824	214	25.7	617	74.3	2,085	59.8	1,401	40.2	12,101	48.4	12,871	51.6
1825	214	25.7	618	27.4	2,022	57.8	1,475	42.2	12,057	48.4	12,840	51.6
1826	222	26.6	612	73.4	2,358	60.6	1,534	39.4	11,895	48.7	12,547	51.3
1827	195	25.4	573	74.6	2,155	59.4	1,470	40.6	11,828	48.5	12,581	51.5
1828	205	26.2	577	73.8	2,236	59.7	1,507	40.3	11,777	48.4	12,565	51.6
1829	205	25.6	596	74.4	2,224	58.7	1,562	41.3	11,738	48.6	12,397	51.4
1830	193	25.4	586	74.6	2,358	58.4	1,675	41.6	11,589	48.7	12,232	51.3

Source: CO 101/28; CO 101/42; CO 101/45; CO 101/61; CO 106/17–27.

1767 law made "slaves, cattle, horses, mules, asses, coopers stills and plantation utencils [sic], real estate of inheritance and declared widows dowable of them as lands and tenements".[66] Thus in 1772, in St George parish, there were four white female landowners.[67] Accounts from Grand Bras Estates (Grenada) and Dukenfield Hall Estate (Jamaica) give an idea of the financial rewards women gained from plantation produce.[68]

White females in the colony, who did not own property, usually became teachers, and this was especially true for those who were single. The local newspapers, for example, the *St George's Chronicle and Grenada Gazette* (26 July 1834), advertised white women who offered classes in music, French and dancing to young ladies of the island. Some women opened schools with their spouses: "Mr. and Mrs. Jones most respectfully announce to the inhabitants of Grenada . . . their intention of opening on Monday the second instant in the house of Mr. Smith in Scott Street for the admission and instruction of young gentlemen and ladies." White women also offered their services as dressmakers to the gentry, as seen in the advertisement which appeared in the *Grenada Free Press and Public Gazette* (25 March 1829):

> Mrs. Cottingham having just arrived from London begs to announce to the gentry and public of Grenada that she intends carrying on her profession of dressmaking and millinery. Ladies favouring her with their orders will find them executed in a superior style.

White women took an active part in organizing social events, balls, dinners and charitable functions. In the town of St George's, for example, there was evidence of a bazaar held to sell fancy articles for charity made by "ladies of Grenada".

White women were probably as merciless as their male counterparts in their treatment of slaves, whether male or female. The famous slave and author Mary Prince described the beatings she endured at the hands of her female owner. It has been argued that they were even more brutal than their male counterparts, since it was thought necessary for an industrious wife to be severe and rigid in the punishment of her slaves.

According to the dictates of European gender ideology, the sexuality of white females of the planter class was strictly controlled. As such, they were restricted from forming liaisons with black or coloured males. There was evidence, however, of such unions during the formative years of slavery. Later, such relations might have persisted, though on a small scale. The records are silent on this matter and these relationships must have been rare.

WOMEN DURING APPRENTICESHIP

One of the most crucial provisions of the Emancipation Act of 1833 was that of "apprenticeship". All freed persons above the age of six on 1 August 1834 were to be classified as either agricultural or domestic apprentices, based on the type of labour they had performed during the twelve months before the passage of the act. Agricultural workers were to be apprenticed for six years and domestic workers for four. Planters were obliged to provide their apprentices with legally established allowances of food, clothing, lodging and medical attendance. In exchange, the apprentices were to perform forty-five hours worth of unpaid labour per week for their former owners, now their masters.

Apprenticeship did not meet the needs or expectations of either party involved. As William Green aptly put it, "Neither slave nor planters were consoled by apprenticeship. The former wanted complete freedom. The latter resenting their loss of arbitrary power feared the disintegration of a social system which had afforded them the highest rank and authority."[69] The planters adopted "an exacting rather than a conciliatory approach". For women, a number of the concessions that had been won as part of the amelioration process were obliterated. Indulgences formerly extended during slavery were removed during apprenticeship. Reports by stipendiary magistrates for a number of parishes in Grenada and the sister island of Carriacou record this. For example, in the parish of St Patrick, Stipendiary Magistrate C.L. Fraser noted, in November 1837, that "several indulgences are withheld particularly to pregnant women and nurses[;] formerly they were allowed sugar, flour, and also time in the morning to attend to their children, now many estates have discontinued this".[70] Stipendiary Magistrate John Ross of St George noted that women who had borne "a certain number of children had advantages under slavery which they do not now possess".[71] Stipendiary Magistrate Sinclair of Carriacou noted that medical assistance was withheld from the free children (that is, those under the age of six on 1 August 1834, or those born subsequently). The owner of the Clarke's Court Estate in St George only provided medical care to free black children in return for at least four days' work per year. The mothers vehemently refused to apprentice their children for the extension of this service. One stipendiary magistrate advised the women to apprentice their little ones, but the women complained that "the [Stipendiary] Magistrate wanted them to sell their children for slaves". Stipendiary Magistrate Ross further noted that the estate owner sought to "exact the repayment of the time during which women had been confined in pregnancy, and the illness consequent thereon".[72]

Punishment, for example whipping, had been restricted or reduced for females during amelioration. During apprenticeship, however, punishment was liberally meted out. The record of the amount and nature of punishment ordered for apprentices by stipendiary magistrates between 1 August 1834 and 31 July 1835 was significant: of the 10,728 females who were apprentices, 915 (approximately 9 per cent) were punished for a series of "crimes". These included refusing to work, indolence, insolence, disobeying orders and running away. For example, 639 women were punished by being given extra labour; ninety-four were given hard labour on the treadmill; and sixty-eight were given hard labour and solitary confinement.[73] The proportion of females punished was larger than that of males. Of the 10,648 males, around 7 per cent were punished. Sometimes the severity of the punishment meted out to female apprentices was not proportionate to the crime committed. For instance, Agnes, a non-praedial apprentice who was accused of running away, was initially sentenced by Stipendiary Magistrate John Ross to eight days' hard labour on the treadmill. However, after the sentence, her owner Robert Stronach decided that Agnes should get three months' imprisonment with hard labour on the treadmill, to make up for the time lost to him after her apprenticeship expired.[74]

The serious nature of some of the cases between planters and apprentices warranted the attention of the supreme court. One such case was that of Hannah and Minerve on the Clarke's Court Estate. It was claimed that both apprentices were placed in the stocks, not only as punishment, but as "treatment" for sore legs. Minerve was pregnant and lost her child while in the stocks. One of the witnesses noted that "bloody water and pieces of clotted blood came from her". Chief Justice Sanderson, after reviewing both cases, ruled that this practice was illegal as it went against statute 257 which stated that no apprentice should be confined in the stocks without the authority of a stipendiary magistrate. Moreover, he noted that for stocks to be used anywhere, this action must first be approved by the governor. Sanderson recommended that, in both cases, the jury find the defendant, Dr John Brown, executor and trustee of the estate, guilty. Unjustly, the jury returned a verdict of not guilty in both instances. These cases show not only the injustice of the times, but also how the planters' attitudes towards the black labour force had changed. With the end of the slave trade in 1807, planters had attempted to improve the living and working conditions of the slaves as a strategy to encourage natural increase in the colonies. In the wake of emancipation, however, all such exercises vanished. The manager of Clarke's Court Estate, Gilchrist, knew of Minerve's pregnancy. However, his uncaring remark before placing her in the stocks was "negroes have too much nonsense. Nothing was going to happen to her."[75]

In the spirit of amelioration, the planter looked not only to increase the number of slaves, but also to take charge of their spiritual life. Thus, the slaves were encouraged to be baptized and to attend church on Sundays. However, after emancipation, the planters' sought to "squeeze the last drops of labour" from the apprentices, punishing them if they refused to work on the sabbath. Sue and Nancy of the Clarke's Court Estate were placed in the gaol or cachot from 6:00 a.m to 6:00 p.m. for refusing to cut grass on the sabbath. Both had cut what they considered enough grass the day before, so that Sunday morning would be left free to attend the opening of the new Wesleyan chapel on Woburn Estate. Reverend Abraham Cooper asked Gilchrist, the manager, to allow the women to cut grass on Saturday so that they could attend service on Sunday. Gilchrist agreed, but on the day in question he reneged on his promise.[76]

Purposefully incorrect classifications of labourers were made frequently. In order to gain two more years' of free service from apprentices, planters often classified domestic workers as field apprentices. Two such cases were sent to the supreme court in 1837. Betsey of Montreuil Estate in St Patrick sent a letter of complaint to Stipendiary Magistrate Fraser concerning the misclassification of her status as an apprentice by her employer, Mr Leid. Stipendiary Magistrate Fraser ruled in Betsey's favour, agreeing that she was a non-praedial apprentice. When Betsey requested manumission, however, Mr Leid's defiant stance restricted the appraisers from coming to a judgement on whether she was to be classified as a praedial or non-praedial worker. The matter was then sent on to the supreme court, where Chief Justice John Sanderson ruled that Betsey was a non-praedial apprentice. She was allowed to buy off the remaining term of her apprenticeship and go free.[77] Mary Rossee and her daughter Frances were also misclassified by their master, Robert Stronach. At the supreme court, Chief Justice Sanderson ruled that both were non-praedial workers and had been wrongfully classified as praedials. Robert Stronach appealed the case but the chief justice dismissed it.[78]

Women retaliated against the system in a number of ways. Some women left plantation labour altogether from the moment they were granted full freedom from slavery. Others, under apprenticeship, ran away, bought their full freedom, withheld their children from labour, migrated or encouraged others not to work. An example of the latter can be seen in the records, whereby Susannah, a female apprentice at Clarke's Court Estate, called on her counterparts to stop working at 6:00 p.m. instead of 8:00 p.m., as the manager had stipulated. When one of the other female apprentices refused to join her, she struck the woman. Others followed her command and no canes were fed to the mill; it ran for two hours without a supply of cane.[79]

Women accounted for the majority of apprentices who purchased their freedom during apprenticeship, not only in Grenada but in the other Windward Islands as well. There was evidence of numerous female manumissions in the islands' newspapers throughout the period 1834 to 1838. Between 1 August 1834 and 1 August 1835, twenty-three of the thirty-three apprentices manumitted were women. Such women included Maxinine, who bought her freedom for £135; Jenny, who bought hers for £120; Lucretia and Gracey who bought their freedom for £105 each; and Nancy and Mary for £100 each.[80]

It was noted by the stipendiary magistrates that women who attained their discharge usually became washerwomen, higglers and house servants. It is possible that they might have been domestic workers before. Most of them moved away from plantation work and the obvious problems they faced there.

CONCLUSION

Slave women were crucial to all facets of plantation society. As producers, they generated wealth and profit for the plantocracy; as reproducers, they supplied the next generation of bonded labourers. Despite their dominant presence in the field, there was little opportunity open to them for upward mobility through skilled labour. They were not allowed to become masons or blacksmiths, for example. Being pregnant did not guarantee immunity from harsh or onerous punishment. The planters extended their control over slave women's lives by claiming their children as property. For the slave woman, her most personal possession – her body – was both an instrument of dominance and resistance. Male plantation owners, other white males on the estates and even elite black males had access to her body for personal pleasure. She expressed her resentment to the harsh work regime and being sexually abused by committing suicide, having abortions and through self-inflicted mutilation.

Manumission gained through thrift was the essence of their resistance. Slave women painstakingly and meticulously saved their earnings from provision grounds and bought their freedom. What emerged was a group of free black and free coloured women who chose an alternative route to working in the fields. Many became higglers, washerwomen and domestic workers. Other black and coloured women gained their freedom through the manumission by their owners. Slave owners may have manumitted their children or women with whom they had a relationship or as a gift for faithful service. Some of these women married plantation owners and, on their husbands' death, inherited property, including land and slaves.

There were a small number of white women in the island during the period of slavery. The majority of these women lived in the town of St George's, and a few were property owners. Property was usually inherited from their deceased husbands. Others offered their services as teachers and seamstresses to the landed gentry.

Apprenticeship, for the plantocracy, meant the continued control of the labour force. Planters made a conscious attempt to gain as much unpaid labour from the apprentices as possible within the constraints of a six-year apprenticeship period. They achieved this by misclassifying and punishing female apprentices, which in turn inspired strong resistance. Ex-slave women bluntly refused to apprentice their children. They risked punishment to gain upward mobility and true independence. In so doing, they helped to erode the autonomy of the planters.

3

Post-Emancipation Women, Part 1: 1838–1899

FEMALE EXODUS FROM THE ESTATES

IN GRENADA, AND ELSEWHERE in the Caribbean, some women, either on purchasing their freedom during slavery or immediately after emancipation in 1838, left plantation work. Often, they went to work on family lands or to raise their children. R.T. Smith aptly describes the status of women who left the estates in the immediate post-emancipation period: "The triple handicap of devalued class, race and gender status combined with the economic necessity of labour ensured that women could only exceptionally take their place in the pedestal of domestic adoration. At best, freedom meant for them not a release from back-breaking labour but rather the opportunity to labour on behalf of their own families and kin within the protected sphere of household and community."[1] This certainly was the case for some Grenadian women. In terms of agricultural labour, the men worked full time or part time on former estates while most women and children focused on domestic agriculture and selling. The lands the ex-slaves worked were usually old provision grounds or small plots of land which they owned, rented, leased or squatted on from estates adjacent to where they lived.

One of the reasons for the withdrawal of women from estate labour was that it was a part of an "ex-slave family strategy". Women and children were vulnerable to sexual and other abuses working as labourers on the estates, even after the abolition of slavery. Staying away from estate labour, therefore, would have been a way to ensure some degree of protection and security. Not working on the estates allowed women to devote more time and attention to raising their children. As one Grenadian magistrate noted, "the mother [now had] the opportunity of personally attending her child in sickness; during apprenticeship the infant was left under the care of an old person, called a nurse, while the mother was at her compulsory labour".[2] Some women withdrew from agricultural labour altogether, choosing instead to work as seamstresses, higglers, domestic servants or washerwomen. According to the 1844 Census Returns, there were 1,036 domestic servants, 661 washerwomen and 1,409 seamstresses in Grenada. However, the number of women who left the estates, compared to men, was relatively small. Between 1844 and 1891, there were 132 women to every 100 men working in agriculture. The economic reality of the post-emancipation period may have been a reason why more women than men stayed on to work on the estates. During slavery, slaves were provided with rations of food (flour, corn, salted meat or fish), clothing and shelter. With the coming of freedom the ex-slaves were now solely responsible for all these amenities. Ex-slaves, especially single women, may have found it difficult to adequately provide for themselves.

The able-bodied male agricultural labourer worked for about one shilling per day.[3] During slavery, both male and female slaves cultivated provisions and vegetables; these included yams, eddoes, sweet potatoes, cassava, corn, peas and plantains. These were often sold at the local market by women or exported. For instance, Grenada and St Vincent produced surplus provisions that were exported to Trinidad, Barbados and the French islands. This practice continued after emancipation. Stipendiary Magistrate Justyne described how provision ground cultivation in Grenada was flourishing in 1844:

> Perhaps there is not another market in the West Indies (taking into consideration the size of the island) better supplied with every kind of vegetable provision than the market in St George and the demand has considerably increased since the port had been made the depot for the vessels of the Royal Mail Steam Packet company. Quantities of provisions are weekly exported to Trinidad and Barbados and the great proportion, I may say more than 2/3, of the supply is the produce of negro cultivation on their own account.[4]

Within the period 1840 to 1876, prices of goods and wages were stable. With a wage of 10 pence per day, a worker could afford basic staples, such as four or five pounds of flour, five pounds of muscovado sugar, a pound of beef and three pounds of rice.[5] These food items were supplemented by produce from the provision grounds; they included yam, eddoes, sweet potatoes, cassava, corn, peas and plantains. Ex-slaves also supplemented their diet with meat and milk obtained from the animals they reared – fowls, pigs and goats.

As indicated in the previous chapter, during apprenticeship women refused to apprentice their "free" children to the estates for fear that they would be tied to a form of slavery. In the decade after 1838, the result was that a relatively small number of children worked on the estates. Stipendiary Magistrate Fraser, reporting from the parishes of St John and St Mark on 31 December 1845, noted: "Since emancipation, parents appear to keep their children at home in idleness or as servants to themselves, frequently employing them to carry the vegetables from their gardens to town upon the market day [Saturday]."[6] This removal of children from estate work was also a part of the ex-slave family strategy. Instead, youngsters were put to work on family lots where they could be monitored by their parents, thereby removing the risk of abuse. Parents also wanted their children to be educated, but the fees they were required to pay were often more than they could afford.

EDUCATION

During slavery, education for children (and a few adults) was limited to religious instruction and fragments of reading, writing and arithmetic. Throughout the island, by the late 1820s, the Church of England had established a Sunday school for slave children and adults every Sunday morning, and a day school was also held in the church every Monday, Wednesday and Friday for all slaves of all ages. By the 1840s, the records show a focus only on the education of children. In fact, there is no evidence that education was given to adults, whether male or female. The basics of reading, writing and arithmetic were not administered to adults by missionary groups. There was no lobbying or call for the education of working-class women, either from within their ranks or from colonial officials.

By 1865, mostly upper- and middle-class children attended the Grammar School and the Model School. The admission fee to the grammar school was four pounds, six pounds and eight pounds, per term for the three different grades of students. The model school's fee was one pence, two pence and three pence per week. In January 1876, the Sisters of St Joseph of Cluny started a fee-paying day school for young ladies (this would have included a few coloured girls from affluent families). The main objective of the school was to turn out refined, genteel young women, well trained to be founders of good Christian homes. The emphasis of the curriculum was on religious knowledge, culture, art, painting, fancy needlework, music, drama and singing. By 1880, there were 115 girls attending the school.[7] In 1891, the St George Girls High School was opened (later called the Church of England High School and now the Anglican High School). It was essentially for the daughters of middle-class Anglican families. School fees ranged from three pounds to five pounds per term.[8] The educational needs of middle- and upper-class boys were met by the Grammar School (later Grenada Boys Secondary School).

The type of education that girls were given was affected by the prevailing European gender ideology. This ideology stated that a woman's place was within the confines of the home, therefore the education that girls received was geared towards making them better wives and mothers; males, on the other hand, were groomed to be the breadwinners and so they were given an education that would prepare them for the world of work. This view of the gender roles and the impact it had on the differences in the way the sexes were educated existed throughout the region, not only in Grenada.

WOMEN AND HEALTH

In the period after emancipation, health care was provided by a few remaining estate hospitals and by the Colony Hospital in the town of St George's. These proved limited in their ability to adequately meet the needs of the populace. By 1849, the Colony Hospital was described as being "filthy in the extreme . . . There [were] neither bedsteads, bedding, furniture nor utencils, excepting two or three earthen urinals in the upper wards, also a few bottles, on two small shelves, containing medicines. The atmosphere [was] pregnant with a most revolting effluvium of filth and rottenness."[9]

Both women and men suffered from a number of illnesses, including dysentery, tuberculosis, and small pox. The illness which affected most and caused the most deaths is worthy of special mention: cholera. The pandemic hit Grenada in 1854 and by the end of its rampage, it had left 3,778 dead. Cholera was known to have been especially virulent along the banks of the St John's River, which was inhabited by a number of washerwomen. As cholera is a water-borne disease, it is not surprising that the washerwomen, who were in direct contact with contaminated water, would have been particularly vulnerable. Despite the ravages of cholera, there was a marked improvement in the rate of natural increase of the population in the post-emancipation years, as shown in table 3.1. This could be attributed to the fact that the ex-slaves had the earning capacity to purchase or lease land, to grow food for home consumption or sale. Their diets would have been richer in protein and vitamins. Because the women were better nourished, the birth rate would have improved. As well, the movement of some women of child bearing age away from strenuous plantation labour was also a major contributing factor.

Table 3.1 Rate of Natural Increase of Grenada's Population, 1867–1910

Period	Population Range	Birth Rate per 1,000	Death Rate per 1,000	Rate of Natural Increase per 1,000
1867–1870	35,993–43,807	41.5	25.2	16.3
1871–1880	38,423–43,807	44.0	27.4	16.6
1891–1900	54,062–65,523	42.7	21.1	21.6
1901–1910	64,288–75,274	38.4	21.6	16.8

Source: Brizan, *Grenada: Island of Conflict,* 241.

WOMEN DURING INDENTURESHIP

Although sugar cane production was on the decline by the mid 1860s, Grenadian planters, like their counterparts throughout the region, joined in the call for immigrant labourers to work on the estates. The problem was not that there was a shortage of labourers, but that the labourers were free and therefore were able to demand higher wages, which the planters were unwilling to pay. Indentureship allowed the planters to pay immigrant labourers less money than the ex-slave labourers for the same amount of work. During the period of indentured immigration from 1838 to1885, 164 Maltese, 3,200 Indians, 601 Madeirans (Portuguese) and 2,541 Africans (liberated Africans) were brought to Grenada.[10]

The inspector of immigrants noted that the Indians complained of not being taken care of when they were ill. He also noted that there were a number of estates with what he described as "a reputation of being unhealthy".[11] The hospital at Observatory Estate was described as being no more than a "thatched cottage consisting of two rooms, [with] no furniture, [and] poor ventilation . . . [There was] no division of the sexes . . . [and] no bedding."[12]

Men outnumbered women among Indian, Maltese and Madeiran immigrants. For example, the ship, the *Maidstone*, left India in 1857 with 268 men but only sixty-eight women, and the *Jalawa* left in 1858 with 208 men but only eighty-one women. One author, in reference to Indian immigration, noted that many estate owners were not too keen on employing women because they could not work as hard as men.[13] This statement, however, does not seem to be borne out by the evidence which indicates that Indian women were just as hard-working as their male counterparts. The reality was that fewer women than men offered themselves for indentureship. Within Indian culture, marriage and family life was a very important aspect of a woman's life. For most women, marriage took place at a very early age. This meant that the majority of the adult female populace, who were prime candidates for indentureship, was otherwise engaged with their own households. The Indian women who emigrated to Grenada were those who followed their husbands, or those who had run away from oppressive marriages or were widows. For Indian indentured women, life on the estates was quite similar to slavery. The work regime was just as rigorous and they were exposed to sexual abuse by

Table 3.2 Absolute Natural Increase of East Indian Population Grenada, 1866–1896

Year	Births	Deaths	Net Increase
1866	50	84	-34
1867	50	70	-20
1868	26	30	-04
1869	36	35	+01
1870	35	21	+14
1871	63	61	+02
1872	45	49	-04
1873	48	43	+05
1874	41	31	+10
1875	22	29	-07
1876	32	26	+06
1877	21	21	0
1878	34	46	-12
1879	39	32	+07
1880	39	34	+05
1881	40	21	+19
1882	53	21	+32
1883	52	21	+31
1884	44	26	+18
1885	46	35	+11
1886	60	15	+45
1887	24	18	+06
1888	15	08	+07
1889	38	15	+23
1890	27	16	+11
1891	34	10	+24
1892	23	11	+12
1893	21	12	+09
1894	42	24	+18
1895	29	17	+12
1896	15	09	+06

Source: Brizan, "Creole and Immigrant", 9.

the plantocracy. Like their male counterparts their movement was restricted. They needed a pass to move from one estate to the other.

The paucity of women and poor health-care facilities contributed to the low rate of natural increase among the immigrant population. Brizan noted that Indian immigrants in Grenada during the period 1857 to 1885 failed to reproduce themselves, as there were more immigrants dying than being born. For five out of the ten years over the period 1866 to 1875, the rate of natural increase was negative. After 1879, the birth rate diminished marginally, but the net increase remained positive rather than negative (see table 3.2).[14] This was likely due to the movement of Indian immigrant women away from the rigours of estate labour, towards relatively less physically taxing work on family plots which were either bought or leased.

Immigrant women, like all other women, were paid less than men. For example, men were paid one shilling per day whereas women were paid nine pence per day.[15] This disparity between wages paid to women and wages paid to men was prevalent throughout the island. It was unfair, because the work performed by women was no less strenuous than that performed by men. On sugar estates, for example, both sexes planted, weeded and harvested the canes; on cocoa estates, men picked the cocoa pods while the women collected them and carried them in baskets on their heads to the *boucan* (the shed where the cocoa was removed from the pod), which was sometimes as much as a mile away from the field. The women complained among themselves that their job was just as tiring and back-breaking as the men's, yet they made no public outcry about the disparity to their employers or the colonial authorities. They seemed to be resolved to their fate.

WOMEN VOTERS

At this time in Grenada, a person's right to vote depended on their level of income and the amount of property they owned. The recently freed ex-slaves (whether female or male), most of whom had a very small income and owned little or no property, were effectively shut out from casting their vote. By the mid 1880s, Parochial Boards were established throughout the colony. These boards were responsible for overseeing the financial affairs of each parish, and for providing and maintaining their infrastructure. Some women possessed the income and property qualifications to elect persons to these boards. According to the list of voters (1887) for the parishes of St Patrick, St Andrew, St David and St Mark, there were a few eligible female voters.[16] There were two notable women in the parish of St Patrick – Augustina Francois of Mount Craven and Marcelane Francois of La Fortune. Their given occupations were agriculturalists and their qualification to vote was that they were freeholders. In the parish of St Andrew, Cecelia Mark of Munich was a freeholder and in the parish of St David, Peggy Pierre of Windsor Forest was a freeholder. In the parish of St Mark, Jean Jno-Baptiste and Judy Andrew of Gross Point were owners of freehold property.

The records give no indication of the race of these women, or the means by which they came to own the land. However, some may have inherited property from husbands or other deceased family members; others may have saved their money from the sale of provisions, livestock and other crops and used it to purchase or lease land from neighbouring estates.

CONCLUSION

The exodus from the estates was one form of resistance employed by women after emancipation. Some women chose to work as washerwomen, seamstresses and domestic servants, rather than as agricultural labourers. Others who left the plantation opted to remain in agriculture, but to labour for themselves and sell their own produce.

Female secondary education was a privilege enjoyed by the upper and middle class, and was administered by the St Joseph's Convent and the St George Girls High School. Constraints on capital made it difficult for lower-class women to send their children to school.

Both ex-slave women and immigrant women worked on the estates for lower wages than their male counterparts. This remained a feature of Grenadian society up until 1983. It was only with the advent of the socialist revolution that this inequality was rectified.

4 Post-Emancipation Women, Part 2: 1900–1950

IN GRENADA, BETWEEN 1900 AND 1950, men were considered by society to be the primary breadwinner: they went out and worked while the women mainly stayed home and looked after the house and family. Because of their earning capacity, men were awarded greater status than women whose role as homemaker was not highly valued. Merle Collins accurately describes the tension this created between Grenadian women and men in the story she wrote which mirrors the lives of her parents in the 1940s and 1950s. One of her female characters expresses her displeasure at the lack of appreciation her husband shows for her labours within the household:

> I tell you already this is a man's world. Your Father working . . . and every day he come home and sit down and stretch out his foot and clear his throat and say how he tired and wait for me to put food on the table. At the end of the month where me salary? None. I not working you know. Is me planting the peas around the house, is me planting tomato, is me watching the cocoa he put to dry and pulling it in if rain come. But if anything sell is his you know. The man own. He might give me a dollar if he feel like it.[1]

It is likely that the sense of frustration at the injustice of the domestic situation acted as a spur for some women to encourage their daughters to pursue a secondary education so that they would have the opportunity to become economically independent from men, and not suffer the same fates as their mothers.

However, women who were employed outside the household did not travel a smooth road either, as they were at a distinct disadvantage in the labour market. Usually, they were exploited as a source of cheap labour: employers reasoned that they could be paid lower salaries, as women's earnings were deemed to be supplementary to the men's. The black working woman was considered a less valuable worker than the man.[2] Table 4.1 gives an idea of the discrepancy in the wages earned by male and female agricultural workers between 1900 and 1966.

Table 4.1 Minimum Daily Wage Rates of Grenadian Agricultural Workers for Selected Years, 1900–1966

Year	Male (daily wage rate)	Female (daily wage rate)	How Determined
1900–1935	$0.24	$0.20	By convention
1938	$0.30	$0.24	By statute
1940	$0.34	$0.28	By statute
1942	$0.50	$0.40	By statute
1945	$0.56	$0.48	By statute
1948	$0.78	$0.66	By agreement
1949	$0.78	$0.66	By statute
1950	$0.94	$0.78	By statute
1954	$1.44	$1.20	By agreement
1959	$1.80	$1.50	By agreement
1963	$2.00	$1.70	By agreement
1966	$2.20	$2.00*	By agreement

*A bonus was paid of five cents per day worked in December.

Note: Between 1900 and 1949, Grenada used two forms of currency: the pounds, shillings and pence from the colonial system, and the newly established dollars and cents. One shilling was equivalent to twenty-four cents; one pound was equivalent to four dollars and eighty cents.

Source: Department of Labour, St George's, Grenada.

Frederica Lewis's story is illustrative of what life was like for female agricultural labourers during this period of Grenada's history. She worked as an estate worker on Plaisance Estate in Florida in the parish of St John from the late 1940s to the late 1990s. As a labourer, Frederica performed a variety of tasks that required great strength. She said, "I use to bring three box of banana . . . that time ah young ah strong . . . two on me head and one below me arm."[3] This kind of intense labour was not uncommon. Although women did some relatively light work, such as collecting

Frederica Lewis, estate worker, Plaisance Estate. Courtesy Frederica Lewis.

cocoa and putting it out to dry, cutting grass, collecting nutmeg and bananas and cleaning mace, they also had gruelling workloads as seen in the example from River Antoine Estate in St Patrick:

> [The women] were required to carry ten baskets of cocoa per day, covering distances between two and three miles each way. Later on when the cocoa was transported on bull carts, if the carts broke down the women had to go home to look after their families and return at night with a torch to finish the day's work. The cocoa was carried by a system known as heading. This was a system whereby the straw from a banana tree was wrapped to form a "kota" (padding) for the labourer's head. The basket was then placed on the kota, which the labourer had on the head. The women's dresses were completely drenched after this tedious task.[4]

For her manual labour, Frederica earned twenty cents a day in the 1940s while the men who worked alongside her earned twenty-five cents per day. Interestingly, though, Frederica saw this as the natural way of things, commenting that "men must work a penny more than you, more than woman, men [must] work even . . . a five cents, a ten cents more than woman. Woman can't get same amount of money as man, men must get a penny more." Her response can be viewed as evidence of the way in which women had been indoctrinated to accept that this disparity in pay was just. Frederica recalled that estate workers had to buy food supplies from the estate: "That time ting didn't rosy as now because [of] the owner. You ha[d] to buy everything [then]. [With] the [new] owner now, ting more rosy because you [can] get two grain ah fig, you doh have to buy, you [can] get two breadfruit, you doh have to buy. The owner before . . . everything had to go on the scale and weigh [and be paid for]." Although her salary was small, and the estate management at the time was not generous in giving away free food to the workers, Frederica was able to raise her five children on it and send all of them to secondary school. Frederica paid for her children's education from her meagre salary, and this required a tremendous sacrifice on her part. Although times were still hard in the late 1940s, things were better than before. When she was growing up and going to school, Frederica says, she was not privileged to have the fine clothes children wear today. She noted, "When ah de going to school we didn't have the quality of 'drawers' [underwear] and ting. What [we had] was flour bag, taking flour bag and making whole suit, so ah go to school. Well is so me parents an dem could . . . afford."[5]

The account given by Norman Paul (a traditional healer and Orisha priest in M.G. Smith's autobiographical book *Dark Puritan*, which was set in Grenada in the 1950s) of his mother's life indicates a similar experience to Frederica's. He noted that his mother worked for twenty cents per day in the late 1890s and early 1900s. The estate used to sell bluggoes (a member of the banana family; called moco in Trinidad) to its workers. A bunch of bluggoes was sold for four or six pence depending on the size. Breadfruit and waternut were given free of charge.[6] He describes the financial hardship his mother faced:

> My Mother used to deal in a shop and I know sometimes when life was pretty hard with her, she owed the shop fourteen shillings and her wages is only eight shillings and four pence a week and when she went to the shop to get anything they would refuse giving her. It was very troublesome to maintain the nine children that was with her. Sometimes she would go to the estate to get provisions and she would hardly get. Sometimes even on Sundays we never used to drink tea because on Sundays she was unable to get sugar to make tea for us . . . She only had a small bit of garden on the estate. She plant peas and cassava sometimes corn but it . . . [didn't] . . . do very well.[7]

Thelma Francis, a seventy-six-year-old woman from the village of Morne

Jaloux in St George, on the other hand, gives a different account of her childhood. She grew up in a family where there was enough money to feed the household. Her grandfather worked as a foreman on the road for two shillings a day and her grandmother worked in the garden and sold the produce in the St George's market. She recalled:

> On a Saturday, she [her grandmother] come up [from the market] with a basket full of food and two piece of cloth at four pence a yard . . . two yards, one for me and one for Ruby [my sister] to make clothes to go to church . . . We had long time shingle house. It was kept clean and use to look nice . . . We never stay hungry . . . You could get four pence jacks that was a large bowl of jacks . . . You go and pick up mango eat; six mango, your belly full and your food on the fire.[8]

Although Thelma paints a rosy picture of her early years, the reality was that she and her sister were not sent to secondary school. This had to do with the lack of finances after the basic needs of the household had been met. There was also the general view that a woman's work involved only domestic duties, hence there was no need to send girls to school for further education.

While most women were limited by their social circumstances, some were not. By 1920, for instance, there was evidence from Carriacou of women who owned property. The ownership of land was something to which agricultural workers, female and male alike, aspired. For women, this dream was attained either through inheritance or purchase. An example of the former was M.E. Archer, who inherited three estates in Carriacou: Craigston, Prospect and Limhair. Louise Augusta-Charles, exemplified the latter. She bought two acres of land from the Craigston Estate in Carriacou and, through a system of share-cropping, employed persons to work this land on which peas, corn, peanuts and cassava were planted.[9] Both women, therefore, were not only the owners of property but also employers. They managed their own accounts and staff and were known to be hard-working and fair-minded in their relations with their employees.

HOUSING AND HEALTH

Housing conditions were grossly inadequate and health provisions were neglected by local and imperial governments. For example, on River Antoine
Estate, the quarters for labourers were built of wattle, roofed with cane straw
and had earthen floors. In the 1921 census, it was noted that "many houses
were occupied by a far greater number than they were probably capable of
accommodating with anything like a proper regard to health, comfort and
decency".[10] Poor nutrition, poor economic circumstances and crowded, unsanitary housing contributed to the prevalence of a number of debilitating diseases in Grenada in the 1900s. These diseases and illnesses included typhoid,
yaws, hookworm, tetanus, marasmus, gastro-enteritis, whooping cough and
measles. Children were particularly affected by these illnesses. Living within
their small overcrowded houses, germs that caused respiratory illnesses, such
as tuberculosis, were easily contracted and spread, while the outdoors provided ideal breeding grounds for helminths and parasites which caused
gastrointestinal illnesses, such as dysentery.[11] Infant mortality rates were
exceedingly high, as shown by the figures in table 4.2. However, it is notewor-

Table 4.2 Infant Mortality Rate (per thousand), 1928–1937

Year	Country		
	Grenada	St Lucia	St Vincent
1928	110.0	125.7	134.0
1929	109.0	150.0	149.0
1930	119.0	85.6	94.0
1931	129.0	134.1	102.0
1932	84.4	121.0	94.0
1933	94.0	92.0	73.0
1934	100.8	106.3	109.2
1935	84.0	109.0	111.2
1936	104.0	97.9	119.3
1937	115.0	101.1	117.8

Source: West India Royal Commission Report, 1938–1939 (London: HMSO, 1939), 138.

thy that Grenada was not the only island with this problem, which emanated from similar conditions of inadequate health and housing facilities.

According to the *Grenada Handbook* (1946), medical fees in 1912 were calculated according to the income of the patient. For example, persons whose income did not exceed £60 per year paid one shilling six pence for medical attention at the medical officer's house during the day and double at night; those whose wages exceeded £60, but not £120 per year, paid two shillings for medical care received at the medical officer's house in the day and double that amount at night. Patients earning less than £60 who were seen outside of the medical officer's house paid two shillings during the day and four shillings at night; those earning between £60 and £120 paid three shillings in the day and five shillings at night. With the average male labourer earning twenty-four cents a day and the female twenty cents a day, it was difficult or near impossible for individuals to afford the medical fees quoted above. Traditional medicine was, therefore, the alternative that most patients sought. In 1915, in the parish of St Patrick, Edwin Wells commented that although "numbers of cases [of yaws] existed . . . modesty and . . . false pride prevent[ed] many sufferers coming for [conventional medical] advice. The services of old grannies [were] enlisted for treatment. These old women armed with various concoctions of roots and herbs carried out experiments on the sufferers."[12] Wells's tone may be dismissive of traditional medicine, but the average labourer felt it was beneficial and saw it as a viable alternative to going to the doctor. Traditional medicine, mainly administered by women, was also more affordable, since local herbs, poultices and visits could be paid for with the produce from the recipient's garden. The provision of traditional medical services and medicines operated on a simple barter system.

Generally, estates made little or no provisions for the medical care of their labourers who they expected to cover their own health-care costs from their salary. The River Antoine Estate was one such example. Labourers who became sick were required to pay their own medical bills. They would also have to make their way to Grand Bras (an hour and thirty minutes away on foot) which was where the nearest doctor was. The worst cases were transferred to the public hospital in St George's where they received treatment free of cost. However, going to the hospital was unpopular among the labouring population, for, while the patient was in hospital, no stipend was given by the

Albertina Alexander, domestic worker, village of Morne Jaloux. Courtesy family of Albertina Alexander.

employers to maintain the family of that patient.

For women who were pregnant, they usually enlisted the services of a midwife to help them through labour. This practice of midwives helping women to give birth at home was common, especially in villages that had no doctors or nurses. Ninety-year-old Albertina Alexander of the village of Morne Jaloux, St George, spoke a little about midwives: "Mrs Debbie Marshall, she used to deliver babies . . . [as well as] . . . her sister . . . They came to the house. They were called bush midwives. They didn't have any training. You gave them a little something, whatever; because things wasn't so good. Our parents told us the ladies bring the babies in their apron. They wore a big apron."[13]

By the mid 1920s, there were some support services available to assist women during and after their pregnancy. In 1924, the Child Welfare League was formed to attend to the pre- and post-natal needs of rural women. A few months after its inauguration, it opened twelve crèches and established a weekly clinic for babies in St George's. In 1929, it was renamed the Maternity and Child Welfare League (hereafter the League). The crèches and clinics were staffed and maintained by a voluntary committee under the active patronage of Lady James, the governor's wife. The committee consisted of the wives and daughters of prominent members of the community and they were aided by a paid nurse, on loan from the medical department of the General Hospital, and girl guides. The League was supported by contributions from the public and by a grant from the government of fifty to seventy-five pounds per annum. The purpose of the crèches was to provide care for the infants whose mothers worked as labourers in the day. In order to deal with needy toddlers, a day nursery for children aged one to three was added to accommodate twelve children.

The nurse-midwife service offered by the League was established with the primary objective of getting nurses into the homes of rural women. This was deemed necessary since diarrhoea and gastro-enteritis were responsible for 95 per cent of the deaths of children under five years old. It was felt that most midwives in rural areas were untrained and this new service by district nurses would raise the standard of midwifery. This kind of assistance to welfare organizations was the trademark of many upper-class (especially white) women. For example, in 1914, Lady Haynes Sadler threw her support behind the operations of the maternity ward at the Colony Hospital and the Hospital for Consumption at Richmond Hill.

The Midwives Ordinance of 1926 indicates the kind of payment midwives could expect for their services. Government nurse-midwives' fees varied depending on the patient's background. The fee for delivery of a labourer's wife or a female labourer was ten shillings six pence and for attending her and the baby for ten days postpartum, the fee was one shilling a day. A labourer was defined as someone who worked as an agricultural worker, a menial servant, a handicraftsman, a boatman, a seaman, a porter, a washerwoman, or a seamstress, and whose annual income was not more than twenty-five pounds or whose property was valued at one hundred pounds or less. If the woman in labour was a pauper, then the government nurse-midwives were required to attend them free of charge. A pauper was defined as someone without property or income who, due to an accident or chronic illness, age or infirmity, was unable to earn a living.

RELATIONSHIPS AND PARENTHOOD

In the late 1890s and early 1900s, women got married from as young as fourteen or sixteen.[14] In relationships and marriage, there were clear distinctions made between the roles and responsibilities of men and those of women. Veronica Williams of Happy Hill noted that there were certain things that women were responsible for bringing into the marital home and certain items that men were expected to provide. She recalled, "My father gave me everything [when we got married] for the house – clothes, linens. The husband gave the ring, so he could not say you come to him empty handed."[15] In many instances, the care and the raising of children were often left solely up to the wives. This was even more pronounced in cases where the mothers were

Veronica Williams, housewife, village of Happy Hill. Courtesy Daniel Williams.

unmarried. Some men were satisfied to have produced children, as it proved their virility, but they did not necessarily accept any of the obligations and duties of parenthood. The raising of a child was generally accepted to be the woman's responsibility and there was no public censure if fathers did not acknowledge or fulfil their parental role. This is not to say that there were not many instances of fathers who, whether married or unmarried, provided emotional and financial support for their families.

Society's response to adultery was different for men and women. It was not generally frowned upon if a man was unfaithful to his wife. However, women were expected to remain faithful, and if they strayed outside of the marriage, they alone bore the brunt of society's judgement. If "outside" children came along, men expected their wives to be accepting of their indiscretion.[16] Women who were not financially independent could easily be dictated to by men in this way, and they had very little say in the matter of his adultery.

Illegitimate children born out of unions between elite men and poor women were not uncommon. Poor women usually entered into these unions with the hope that their offspring would have a better life. However, the male lover often did not support these illegitimate children, and rarely had any intention of marrying the woman who he had impregnated, as she was not of his class. In some instances, the father made special provision for the child and mother. However, if he was married, such provisions often led to conflict with his wife and her family. There was a marked difference, therefore, between the privileges enjoyed by legitimate and illegitimate children. The differences were seen in the kind of education they received, their socio-economic status and the kinds of opportunities available to them.

Single men from the elite were free to enjoy extra-marital liaisons with women from lower classes, but women from the elite who failed to marry were expected to remain spinsters and childless. It was unthinkable that they should bear illegitimate children, and their entering into liaisons with men of a lower class was particularly taboo.[17] Some unmarried women from the lower classes had relationships whereby they either lived in continuous cohabitation with their lover, or had "extra residential" relationships in which they lived separately from the lover but maintained a visiting relationship. The women in such relationships were supposed to remain faithful, and she might or might not receive monetary assistance for children born out of these unions.

EDUCATION

Although some parents were progressive in their desire to see their daughters educated to a high level, this was not a sentiment shared by all. The reality of this period, 1900 to 1950, was that most girls received only minimal education. By age fourteen or fifteen, most had left school to learn to sew or other such domestically oriented skills. Veronica Williams recalls, "We went to school with one [text]book, one slate, one exercise [book]. The book was [the] *Royal Reader*. The girls went to Happy Hill School [while the] boys went to Mr Fletcher [J.W. Fletcher Memorial in St George's]. Girls left school at fourth or fifth standard. I was sorry to leave. Our parents [told] us to go and learn to sew, become seamstresses. You had to do what they [said]."[18] Thelma Francis, echoes this view about the role of a woman (which influenced the kind of education they received): "When I was growing up I thought women had to stay home wash cook and scrub."[19] Girls usually learnt to sew from an older woman in the village. At these classes, women learnt to make their own clothes and draperies for their homes. They also learnt to do "fancy embroidery" and make children's clothing, including babies' diapers.[20] Theophilus Albert Marryshow, editor of the *West Indian* newspaper and political activist, was very aware of the limited educational opportunities for women. He wrote:

> We should like to see the lot of women of the future made much better than the existence of the present generation and in order to accomplish this, we will have to do a great deal more in their school life. In colonies like these the chances open to women for gaining a decent livelihood are few and far between. So limited are their opportunities that the respectable poor of that

sex have to engage themselves in employment which give them but a bare pittance. To condemn the fairer sex to a life of perpetual dependence can do no good.[21]

Despite this appeal, many women remained uneducated.

For those parents who had great ambitions for their daughters, they were frequently hampered by the lack of finances. Quite a number of girls from such families were barred from attaining a secondary-level education because

Lady Gloria Williams, former teacher and wife of former governor-general Sir Daniel Williams. Courtesy Lady Gloria Williams.

of monetary constraints. Lady Gloria Williams recounted her inability to sit the scholarship examination from primary to secondary school because her father could not afford the exam fees. She noted, "The principal had to send you to do the exams and your parents had to be able to afford it; for example, your books and clothes. I was never sent to do the exam because my father was not able to contribute."[22] Lady Gloria, however, was eventually able to sit the Teacher Examinations and got a job as a temporary teacher by 1953. She was eighteen years old and worked for a salary of twenty-six dollars a month. A similar constraint was placed on Dame Hilda Bynoe (first female governor of Grenada and the Commonwealth) in pursuing her studies. Although she sat and passed the Senior Cambridge School Certificate Examination in 1936, she was unable to study abroad because she did not win the one island scholarship that entitled the student to free university education abroad. With no money to fulfil her dreams to be a doctor, she became a teacher. In 1940, she won one of the Colonial Development and Welfare Fund Scholarships. These scholarships were awarded in the wake of the report made by the Moyne Commission in 1939 on the state of the Caribbean colonies including education. In 1944, she went on to pursue her goal.

The kind of education available for girls differed from the type of education available for boys, as the curricula were tailored according to sex. Enid

Charles, who was a student of St Joseph's
Convent, St George's, Grenada, in the mid
1940s, revealed that

> Subjects like Mathematics, Chemistry,
> and Biology were done at the boys'
> school . . . we just did Arithmetic. Girls
> did the Arts, like Literature and History,
> after Senior Cambridge . . . that is those
> who could do it, for they were few and
> handpicked. They did Latin Algebra,
> Geometry, French and Spanish. University
> then was still more for the boys. The odd
> girl went. Senior Cambridge was the
> highest [level of education for most girls],
> then you applied for a job in the Public
> Service and you took commercial lessons
> like typing and shorthand.[23]

*Enid Charles, former employee of W.E.
Julien. Courtesy Enid Charles.*

St Joseph's Convent was predominantly a girls' school, although there were
a few boys enrolled. Scholars at the convent paid £2 per annum. The fees were
£3 a month for boarders; four shillings for day scholars under age seven, and
eight shillings for those over age seven; and eight shillings extra for drawing
and painting and ten shillings for music.[24] By 1900, six scholarships which were
annually tenable for five years were awarded to boys from primary schools,
while four scholarships which were tenable for four years were awarded to
girls at each of the two girls' secondary schools. In this respect, Grenada's situation was more favourable for girls than some other Caribbean islands. In
St Lucia, for example, there were ten scholarships available for boys but none
for girls. However, in both islands and also in St Vincent, boys' schools
received a government grant of £250 and an additional £5 per scholar based
on results, while the two girls' schools received a government grant of £2 per
scholar per annum, which was not to exceed £100 altogether in each case. In
St Lucia's boys' schools, the subsidy was £200, while in girls' schools it was
£50 per annum.[25]

The girls from the upper middle class and the elite, whose parents could afford it, were sent away to finishing schools in Europe after they completed their secondary school education in Grenada. The purpose of the finishing school was to allow the girls to complete their Senior Cambridge Examinations as well as to provide them with exposure to European culture. Afterwards, they were not expected to work. Mollie McIntyre's life followed this trajectory for a while. She was born in Grenada in 1916 and enjoyed a privileged upbringing. She had "a governess" and attended the Church of England High School (now called Anglican High School). At the age of fifteen, she was sent to board at a finishing school in England where she completed her Senior Cambridge Examinations. She recalled that on her return to Grenada, having completed her studies in England at age nineteen, she stayed at home and "kept house". According to her, "no one [girls from the upper classes] worked in those days".[26] Alice McIntyre, born in 1924, had a similar experience after completing her education at St Joseph's Convent, St George's: "My father didn't want me to go to work or learn to drive. I was the first girl, I had to (stay home) and look after my mother."[27] Both ladies, however, eventually went out to work. The former did so with a friend of her family during World War II with the British Royal Navy, reporting the movements of the submarines in the region. The latter worked at the Grenada Cooperative Bank where her father was a major shareholder and founding member.

WOMEN AT WORK

The uneducated and semi-educated women had little choice but to take up agricultural work, domestic work or street vending. The domestic worker's duties included cooking, cleaning, washing, ironing and taking care of her employer's children. Her position was also rather unstable or precarious, because she could be easily fired if suspected of committing a crime. Nellie Payne, in her autobiographical work on Grenadian society in the 1920s, gives us an idea of the plight of domestic workers. She recalled the maid being fired on the merest suspicion of stealing a silver fork when, in fact, she and her sister were the ones who had taken it and used it as a tool to dig a grave for their doll in the re-enactment of a funeral. The upper classes treated their domestic employees with disdain. Nellie recalls that servants were provided with a separate lavatory, and she and her sister were told "NEVER to visit it as . . . it was full of germs".[28]

Some girls who were able to advance to a high level through the education system and gain qualifications, in spite of their parents' small salaries, unfortunately were often offered menial jobs. Louise Rowley is an example of this. She was able to overcome obstacles and achieve success. After the death of her father, her mother raised her and two other children on a small nurse's salary of nineteen shillings eleven pence per month. Her mother stressed the importance of achieving an education and the need to be disciplined. By the age of twelve, Louise had passed the Junior Cambridge Examination, the school leaving Certificate Examination by age fifteen and had placed third in the London Matriculation Examination at age seventeen. Louise was the first woman in Grenada to pass the London Matriculation Examination. She noted that "the news was quite the talk of the town and everybody hailed me but nobody said, 'Have a job' ". When she approached the business enterprises in search of work, she recalls: "I had the highest qualifications that were available in Grenada. I was the first woman to have all my qualifications. You know, trying to impress, I first went to the private sector and they all looked at . . . [the certificates] . . . and they were impressed . . . but I didn't have the shorthand and typing. So I decided to apply to the government."[29] In 1930, when she applied, she was given a job as a sorter in the post office. This was one of the three jobs open to women in the civil service, the others being copier and typist. Louise looks back at the experience now with a sense of amazement:

> At the time . . . I was so simple and innocent it never occurred to me I was being kept down, that I was being discriminated against. Here I was having higher qualifications than any man in the Civil Service and here I was in the post of a sorter in the Post Office. If a man had the same qualifications he could have entered at least at the clerk 3 level. It never occurred to me to revolt or to write or to complain, I was happy just to do my work and I never felt I was being oppressed. I am amazed at myself now.[30]

Through her intelligence and dedication to the job, Louise was promoted to the Treasury which, as she put it, was "the bastion of male supremacists". She was the only female there and she remembered that the day she walked in a man made the disparaging comment "change and decay all around, I see". It was difficult since they kept information from her and selected what duties she was allowed to perform. But she vowed to herself that was going to show her male colleagues that she could do the job as well as, and even better than, they could. She was finally accepted by her co-workers, but was referred to as "Mr Rowley", since, to them, "doing things good, you ceased to be a woman". Louise spoke out vehemently on the use of the category "lady clerk" at meetings of the Civil Service Association and the terminology was changed. Women were allowed to enter the service on the basis of qualifications. Louise continued to succeed in her profession and went on to become the first female permanent secretary in 1956.

Many educated women between 1900 and 1950 turned to teaching for employment. Young girls completed their primary education then went on to do a series of examinations which would qualify them to enter the teaching profession as pupil teachers. Mae Nurse recalls, "I began teaching at age twelve. I got my first pay cheque at twelve. It was five shillings a month, [or] one dollar and twenty cents . . . Teachers didn't work for [earn] . . . much money but they were contented."[31] Blanche Sylvester, who went to the teacher training college and qualified as a teacher, said that she started off earning ten shillings a month in 1931. She bemoaned this meagre salary: "What ten shilling could buy if you eh living home to get piece of food? I bought a wasicong or keds (cheap sneakers) and I boarded at Miss Felicity in town and bought four pence [worth of] food."[32] However, her salary increased over time and, by 1935, it had gone up to four pounds three shillings and four pence.

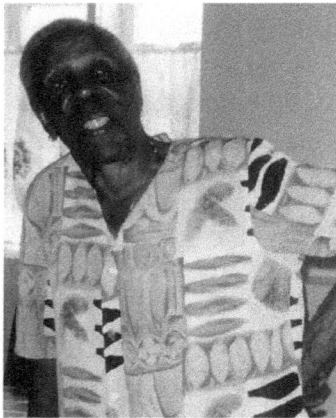

Blanche Sylvester, former teacher, village of Fontenoy. Courtesy Heather Thomas.

Within the teaching profession, especially in the denominational schools and in the wider civil service, women enjoyed a certain amount of job security. However, this security was jeopardized if the woman got married or became pregnant. Those who got married were often required to leave the job, since it was felt that they needed the time to take care of their husbands and family. Women who got pregnant, especially unwed mothers, were asked to leave permanently or take leave without pay. In the latter case, women had to return to work as quickly as possible after the delivery of the child. More often than not, they were only allowed their holiday leave. Blanche Sylvester was asked to take leave without pay for one year when she got pregnant. She said: "That was how it was done, in a decent way, not to make an alarm . . . I took leave without pay."[33]

The conditions of employment were similar in the private sector. Enid Charles noted that it was the norm to ask married women to leave the job. She was fortunate in that she and Shirley Charles were the first two married women employed at W.E. Julien and Company (hardware, furniture and appliances store as well as a shipping company) who were not asked to leave. She noted that there was no maternity leave. After she had her first child, she took vacation leave and then returned to work. She noted, "I left [my daughter with] my aunt and paid someone under my aunt's supervision to look after her. I breast fed her in the morning and at lunchtime."[34] Working women were generally discriminated against with regards to pregnancy whether they were wed or unwed. Maternity leave was unheard of. This practice continued up to 1980, when the PRG instituted the Maternity Leave Law.

By the late 1930s and mid 1940s, other jobs opened up for educated women and for those of the middle and upper classes. These included positions such as clerical officers in government offices, bank cashiers, proprietresses and head mistresses. The *Grenada Handbook* of 1946 gave many such examples: Sheila Nedd, for instance, was a typist in the Income Tax Department and Pansy Rowley was a clerk at W.E. Julien. In 1933, Muriel Glean, daughter of the owner of Mount Rodney Estate in St Patrick, was the first woman to be employed at the Grenada Cooperative Bank. Later, she was joined by Phyllis Osbourne, whose father was the founder of the St Lucia Cooperative Bank.[35] Women had also risen to more senior posts. For example, Emmeline Nunez was the headmistress of the St George's Model School. Some women, such as Rose Bell of St Andrew, Mary Hosten of St Mark, Luna Paryag of St John and Daisy Renwick of St George's, were listed as proprietresses.

By the mid 1930s there were women involved in the field of social work and at welfare organizations. The work of two such women was commended by the British Crown: Millicent Douglas and Inez Munro were awarded the

MBE (Member of the British Empire) for their exemplary service. Lottie Wells was commended in the local newspapers for her contribution to the YWCA. She went on to become the association's first Grenadian president. By 1937 Millicent Douglas was also proprietress of the Grenada Globe cinema and was instrumental in organizing the programme for Marcus Garvey's visit to Grenada.[36]

TRADE UNIONS, POLITICS AND THE JUDICIAL SYSTEM

In the period 1900 to 1930, there were no organized unions to represent employees. By 1940, however, three unions existed: the Grenada Trade Union, the St John's Labour Party/General Workers' Union and the St George's Workers' Union (also known as the Grenada Workers' Union). These unions all followed a policy of cooperation, accommodation and collaboration with the main employers of labour. The unions offered palliatives for grievances workers held rather than a radical transformation in their working conditions. For example, in 1947, the St George's Workers' Union and the St John's Labour Party demanded a daily wage rate of eighty-four cents for male workers and seventy-two cents for female workers. The Grenada Agricultural Association, an organization of estate owners geared towards protecting their own interests, rejected this and continued to pay seventy-two cents and fifty-four cents to male and female workers, respectively. On 15 January 1948, the Legislative Council appointed a Wages Committee to look into the issue of the rates of pay and working conditions. This committee recommended that a daily minimum wage of eighty-two cents be paid to men and sixty-eight cents be paid to women. The Grenada Agricultural Association was adamant that the wages it offered were suitable. It was not until 18 January 1950 that the Legislative Council put the minimum wage (recommended in 1948) into effect. It took one year and three months for the issue to be resolved, although the planters still got away with paying less than what both unions had demanded.[37]

It was anathema to take industrial action in this period of history. By the Trade Dispute, Arbitration and Inquiry Ordinance Number 5 of 1943, it was agreed by both parties (employers and unions) that there should be no strike action or lockouts. In the event of an unauthorized strike, boycott or slow down of work, the union was required to use all reasonable efforts to end such action and employers had a right to undertake disciplinary action against any employees engaged in these activities.[38] One such example took place on 15 March 1950 when 240 workers (all male) employed at the Nutmeg Curing Station in Grenville went on strike because the Grenada Cooperative Nutmeg Association refused to meet their demands for an increase in wages. When the workers finally returned to work, they found that their jobs had been given to women.[39] It is true that they paid the female replacement workers less than their male counterparts who had gone on strike, but for these women the job was a valuable source of income. It allowed them to meet the financial needs of their family. If their menfolk lost their jobs, this would reduce the family income. If she was offered the job for a smaller wage, she would take it if it meant the ability to maintain her family.

In the political arena, the ordinary man and woman were not eligible to vote for members of the Legislative Council. As in the 1800s, to be an elector in 1920s, one had to be a British subject, at least twenty-one-years-old (for men) and at least thirty-years-old (for women), have an income of thirty pounds per annum and own property valued at £150 or more. These stipulations prevented most labourers and most women from voting. Women were also excluded from becoming members of the Legislative Council as indicated in the Constitutional Order-in-Council (March 1924) which stated: "Such persons should not hold any office of employment under the crown or under municipal corporation, be a Minister of religion, a returning officer or a female person."[40] In November 1920, when the Grenada Representative Association sent a petition to the secretary of state and the king asking that the Crown Colony government be replaced by a bicameral legislature, they also requested that women be permitted to vote in both houses. This proposal, however, came at a time in the Caribbean when efforts to promote voting rights for women were sadly lacking and was, thus, unsuccessful.[41]

However, progress began to be made as female property owners between the ages of thirty and sixty were given the right to serve as jurors in 1936. These women had to own property with a minimum value of four hundred pounds or have an income (from any source) that was not less than forty pounds per annum. In 1938, there were seventy-three women listed as jurors throughout Grenada.[42] By the 1940s, women were admitted to District Boards,

which handled local affairs. There was one in each parish and they were composed of equal numbers of nominated and elected members. Mollie McIntyre
served on the board in St John, Sarah Bell and M. Emmanuel were nominated
for St George. Fay Pearce was nominated for the parish of St Mark. Agatha
Redhead was the first woman elected to the District Board in St Patrick in
1939.[43] Women also sat on the Hospital Board, notably Jane Mahy. There were
also women on the Charity Board and Public Library Committee. Sheila
Buckmire became the first female junior assistant librarian of the St George's
Public Library in 1948. However, there were still no female justices of the
peace, lawyers, judges or doctors by 1946.

MIGRATION

During this period in Grenadian history, a number of men and women from
the poorer classes chose to migrate in search of a better life and to escape
hard times. This process started with emancipation in 1838 and continues into
the present. From the late 1830s to the 1880s, Grenadians chose to migrate to
the larger British colonies of Trinidad and British Guiana; between 1885 and
1920, their preference was for Cuba, the Dominican Republic, Central America and Panama; and between 1939 and 1945, during World War II, it was
Aruba, Curaçao, the United States, Britain and Canada.[44] For every hundred
men who migrated during the decade 1911 to 1921, there were fifty-seven
female emigrants.[45] Juliana Aird, born in 1911, who migrated to St Vincent in
search of work, tells what this was like:

> I worked clearing water tanks for twenty cents a day for two months. The peo-
> ple I worked with felt sorry for me. I was poor. They gave me . . . food. I worked
> on an estate for a white man, Mr Frasier, carrying cane. The men helped me
> to put the load on my head. I . . . [earned] four pence or eight cents a day . . .
> and worked there for about two years. I saved every cent. People [were] kind
> in St Vincent; they gave me food.[46]

She recalled her determination to work and make money to help her mother.
She also had great ambitions to advance beyond the kind of work she was
doing at the time. She notes, "I was going to be somebody." She attained her

goal in the 1950s when she became the first female agent for Volkswagen in Grenada. She became a successful businesswoman and was a justice of the peace in 1972.

Between 1930 and 1950, a number of Caribbean women migrated to Aruba and Curaçao (Dutch-speaking Caribbean islands) to find employment as domestic workers. These women were usually sponsored and brought in to these countries as live-in domestic workers. Most of these emigrants travelled by schooner during World War II in the mid 1940s, often at their own peril, since there was the danger of encountering Nazi submarines in the Caribbean waters near the

Juliana Aird, first female agent for a foreign car dealer in Grenada. Courtesy Juliana Aird.

oil routes. There were flights available, but many women could not afford the airfare. On arrival in Aruba or Curaçao, they often found themselves working for families whose women treated them as second-rate citizens. The white women often remained at home to administer the household while their men went out to work. Racial tension between the female employer and the female employee was common in the household. The white woman was conscious of occupying a superior socio-economic position and the black woman resented the subordination that this entailed.[47] Some live-in domestic workers also experienced a sense of isolation. They were not Dutch speakers and were, thus, constrained by the language barrier. Edna, who left Grenada in 1943 to work as a maid in Aruba, recalls being surprised that the family that sponsored her did not live in the larger town of San Nicolas, but rather in rural Oranjestad. She was overworked, underpaid and isolated and, often went for long periods without hearing a word of spoken English. There were also strict rules in place that these migrant workers had to abide by, which had implications for their personal life. For instance, they were not allowed to live with men or become pregnant during their period of employment. They could also not be visited by their dependants unless they were on leave. Women who migrated often had to leave their children behind with a relative, usually a grandmother. Mothers tried to remain present in their children's lives, even from a distance, and endeavoured to maintain their parental role of raising and disciplining their children through their letters. They also sent food and clothes to their offspring as often as possible. Lady Williams remembers that her mother, who had migrated to Trinidad in search of work, shipped home food items, among other things, and sent clothing and money through the post office. She recalls that her mother would come to visit twice a year.

Although these working arrangements could be difficult, they had the potential to be quite lucrative because, in addition to their wages, employers provided their workers with room and board, and health insurance. Women, therefore, continued to migrate in spite of the difficulties faced. A few women migrated with their husbands, as was the case of Claire-Anna Gill. In the late 1940s, she moved with her husband to Aruba where he had accepted employment in the commissary in the army. The army provided them with a house, which Claire-Anna noted was "small with outside toilet [facilities]".[48]

For the women who remained in Grenada, life was difficult. They had the burden of maintaining the household, caring for the family as well as providing them with food and producing cash crops. Remittances, however, made it possible for the family to survive. Brizan noted that for the period April to December 1920, the post office in St George's showed that money orders from the Panama Canal zone and Cuba amounted to a substantial sum of $84,861. It was the woman's responsibility to manage the remittance money and to invest it in land or other assets.

WOMEN IN WORLD WAR II

Like their Caribbean counterparts, Grenadian men and women served in World War II. During this war, five Grenadian women – Leah Bascus, Betty Kent, Rita Kerr, Margaret Munro and Myra Woodroffe – were members of the Auxiliary Territorial Service in the army. They worked as clerks, secretaries and spies. Betty Kent distinguished herself by attaining the Overseas Service and Defence Medals.

CONCLUSION

This period in Grenadian history saw women beginning to have a greater hand in negotiating their own destinies, as they pushed beyond the gender boundaries. Women worked on estates as domestic servants; on family land, planting crops for export or sale in the market; as professionals – in nursing and teaching; and contributed to the war efforts in the army during World War II. The money they earned supplemented the family income and helped to provide food, clothing, shelter and education for their children and extended family. A number of households were headed by women and, in some cases, women were the sole breadwinner. Some Grenadian women sought their fortunes abroad. While jobs overseas could be quite lucrative, women frequently encountered racism, poor living and working conditions, and experienced feelings of isolation. Nevertheless, they persevered and this in itself can be viewed as a form of resistance as they refused to be beaten by the challenges they faced. The fact that they sought work outside the household was also a form of resistance, as women did not restrict themselves to the roles and duties that society dictated.

Women resisted against their socioeconomic restrictions. They struggled to improve their lives and the lives of their children by taking advantage of the benefits of education. Mothers hoarded their pennies to send their children to school in the hope that they would become gainfully employed in sectors other than agriculture. Girls had a hard time of it, as they were discriminated against by the education system, which favoured boys. Scholarships for girls were limited and the curriculum they were taught from was intellectually less rigorous than the boys' curriculum. In spite of that, some girls, through dint of hard work and sheer determination, achieved great educational success and went on to become professional women in the workplace.

5 Post-Emancipation Women, Part 3: 1951–1979

THE YEAR 1951 IN GRENADA is synonymous with strikes, riot and revolution. The strike action of February 1951 led to the widespread burning of estates. The radicalism that had swept through the Caribbean in the 1930s had finally and belatedly exploded at home and was presided over by Eric Matthew Gairy. While the impact of these changes affected all Grenadians, it was arguably most keenly felt by Grenadian peasants and estate workers. Agriculture was the mainstay of the Grenadian economy, therefore, agricultural workers made up the majority of the working class. For this reason, this chapter will focus on the realities of their lives and experiences.

GAIRY'S ASCENDANCY

Eric Gairy founded the Grenada Manual and Mental Workers Union in July 1950. The following year he formed the Grenada People's Party, which was later renamed the GULP. The union became the most radical trade union ever founded in Grenada. It appealed to the neglected peasants, estate and road workers, especially in the rural communities. The Grenada Manual and Mental Workers Union made a number of demands on the Grenada Agricultural Association. Some of these included an increase of 46.5 per cent on the statutory daily minimum wage; seven days' holiday with full pay to each worker who worked two hundred days in any year; fourteen days' annual sick leave on half pay; and the initiation of a better system of transport of produce from field to estate yard (for instance, the union was opposed to women carrying heavy loads when donkeys could be provided).[1] When these demands were ignored by the Grenada Agricultural Association (that is, the plantocracy) and the British colonial regime, Gairy called a strike on 19 February 1951. It was the first general strike in Grenada's history and it involved all agricultural and road workers throughout the island. The strike lasted for four weeks and resulted in the destruction of property as some workers burnt cane fields and estate houses.

On 21 February 1951, Gairy orchestrated a mass demonstration at York House, the seat of Grenada's Legislative Council, in the capital of St George's. There, he demanded an audience with the governor. Gairy used his excellent command of rhetoric to raise public support: "We shall stand together and shall die together. Don't work. Don't sleep." The Grenadian masses, female as well as male, were convinced they had found their saviour and they nick-named him "Uncle Gairy". The ruling class felt threatened.[2] They were convinced that the disturbances were not genuinely about wage disputes, but stemmed from a "communist" plot to overthrow the government and their way of life. As such, the governor refused to negotiate with Gairy and his assistant, Gascoigne Blaize. He had them arrested and sent to Carriacou. Around the island, the burning of the fields and looting intensified as workers became infuriated by the action taken by the governor. The governor realized that the only way to end the strike was to release Gairy. He demanded, however, as a pre-condition of his release, that Gairy put an end to the violence.

Universal adult suffrage was granted to all Grenadians by the British government in 1951. Gairy took that opportunity to organize his political party, the Grenada People's Party, and swept the polls in the ensuing elections. Stirred by Gairy's oratory, emboldened by his disdain for the ruling class, the masses threw their full support behind him. This was a man who, within a little over a year, had achieved what no Grenadian leader had achieved before, namely, the creation of an effective trade union organization which united town and country workers, and the transformation of trade union power into political power. More importantly, he had demonstrated to impoverished black Grenadians that domination by elite planters and merchants need not go on forever. He had shown them that the ruling class could be forced to capitulate to their demands. For example, the statutory daily minimum wage for all agricultural and road workers was reset at one dollar twenty cents for men and one dollar for women as of 1 January 1951. Workers were also to be granted seven days' annual holiday on full pay as long as they worked no less than 200 days in any one year commencing 1 January 1951. The workers were to receive back pay at the foregoing rates for every day they had worked beginning 1 August 1950, deducting what they had already received. This payment was made 27 April 1951.[3]

Wage increases continued in 1953, after another series of smaller-scale strikes. The new basic wage was now one dollar forty-four cents for men and one dollar twenty cents for women. This went up again, by 1959, to one dollar fifty-six cents for men and one dollar thirty cents for women. Emboldened by the work of the Grenada Manual and Mental Workers Union, other unions sought wage increases and gained them. For instance, the General Workers' Union successfully demanded higher salaries for clerks and shop assistants. The salaries for shop assistants (who were mainly female) in St George's increased from twenty dollars per month to thirty dollars and from eighteen dollars to thirty dollars in Grenville. Clerks in St George's were paid forty dollars per month; those in Grenville, thirty-five dollars per month; those in Sauters, thirty dollars per month; and those elsewhere were paid twenty-five dollars per month.[4]

Female support for Gairy was tremendous. Murie Francois, pioneer member of the NWO, noted: "Gairy's staunchest and most militant supporters were women. Quite a number of women were the heads of households, [and] as such Gairy's 1951 revolution would have benefited them directly. In some cases they would tell you that Gairy . . . took them out of the darkness of the cocoa estates."[5] At Gairy's campaign meetings, women outnumbered the men and they were, on the whole, more vociferous in their support of him. In the 1957 election, more women voted than men and this female admiration for Gairy continued into the 1962 election campaign, at which time the *West Indian* newspaper characterized him as an avuncular figure who was much admired, especially by the female voters. When Gairy's GULP faced its first loss with this election, a female market vendor and candidate for St George North, argued that "Uncle [had been deprived] of his rightful place" and she pledged that when she entered the Legislative Council she would fight for Uncle's right to rule Grenada again.[6]

ESTATE WORKERS AND PEASANT FARMERS

In spite of increases in salary and improvements in their living and working conditions, estate workers and peasant farmers in Grenada still struggled to make ends meet. The experiences of four women – Mary, Catherine, Rita and Delta – exemplify what life was like for a typical estate worker in 1950s and 1960s. With the salaries they received, it was a daily struggle to maintain their families and provide their children with an education. Mary Calliste from River Antoine Estate was paid one dollar and twenty cents in September 1954 for making copra. In January 1955 and 1956, she was paid the same amount for planting lacatan bananas. At this wage rate, Mary made twelve dollars per fortnight. Based on the food prices at the time, her estimated average weekly food bill would have been between two to three dollars. This would have left her with a small amount of money for other necessary expenses, such as rent, health care or tuition fees. Her counterpart, Catherine Edgar, got two cents for each rat she caught.[7] The number of rats caught determined whether she was able to feed herself and her family.

Rita Knight of Douglaston Estate in Florida, in the parish of St John, described the kind of work she did on the estate (where she worked for forty-two years) and the kind of remuneration she received from it: "I used to crack and choose nutmeg for one shilling and a penny . . . It was not an easy job. You had to be careful how you crack it. There were ladies . . . checking if it bruise and they [would] take it out [of] your pay [if it was]."[8] Rita only got as far as fourth standard in school, but she was resolved that her children would receive a secondary education. She was rewarded to see five of her nine children go to secondary school in spite of her straitened circumstances. She explains how she managed to send them to school on the small salary she received:

> I had to pay to send the girls to school. When the principal [of the school] realized [I had more than one daughter in the school], she . . . [reduced the fee] . . . I used to pay thirty dollars a term. Some of the children's fathers use to

Rita Knight, estate worker, Douglaston Estate.

help. Sister Raphael [the principal] order the books for us and we pay how we could. I had relatives abroad they use to help out.[9]

A number of women like Rita benefited from similar acts of kindness and generosity extended to them: Catholic schools were known for discounting school fees for women in reduced financial circumstances and remittances sent from family members abroad helped women to meet their family's needs.[10] The Douglaston Estate records indicate the salary Rita earned, the deductions made for food and her take home salary. It is instructive to look at snapshots of these figures. For the fortnight, 8 September to 21 September 1967, Rita worked at the boucan (the estate work house where workers cracked the nutmeg and separated the nutmeg from the mace). The daily rate was one dollar seventy-six cents. In the first week she received eight dollars and eighty cents, and in the second week three dollars and eighty-seven cents. Her total

Women sorting mace, Plaisance Estate

earnings were twelve dollars and sixty-seven cents. She was given a cash advance of two dollars and provisions worth one dollar fifty. Her total deductions amounted to three dollars fifty. Her take home pay was nine dollars and seventeen cents. From 12 January to 25 January 1968, in the first week she received fourteen dollars and twenty-six cents and nothing for the second week. Her total earnings were, therefore, fourteen dollars and twenty-six cents. She had a cash advance of one dollar fifty and thus had a take home salary of twelve dollars and seventy-six cents.[11] If Rita was paying thirty dollars a term for her children's education, then it can be seen that she truly had a difficult time making ends meet.

Delta Duprey also worked on Douglaston Estate during the same time period as Rita. She noted the nutritionally deficient diet that she fed her nine children due to an inability to afford anything better, "Breadfruit and callaloo an' a drop of hot water and call that George. They didn't have milk in those days. Breadfruit and callaloo and a bush they call zipina callaloo [was what they got]. Breadfruit and callaloo every day."[12] Delta did not attend school herself but she tried to ensure that her children did, "I was able to send all the children to school, every one. Some with shoes, some with a little paper bag on their foot. Because I didn't get [to go to school], I [made sure to] send all [of mine]."[13]

Delta Duprey, estate worker on the Douglaston Estate, with her granddaughter Cindy Duprey

It was a common practice for teenaged girls and boys to take up wage employment at the estates where their parents worked and to remain at this estate for their entire lives. In this regard, Rita Knight and Catherine Duprey followed in their mothers' footsteps. Rita learned her skills from her mother and she was the third generation in her family to work on the estate: "When I was a child going to school my father work on the estate for ten pence and my mother for six pence. My grandmother work here, my grandfather on my mother's side and father side work here. Samuel Henry, my grandfather, he was the overseer in Belair (part of Douglaston Estate)."[14] Catherine Duprey's story was similar. Her mother, Delta Duprey, worked on the estate from 1955, and Catherine followed her. Previously, she worked two days a week at the banana boxing plant (close to the estate) and went to school for three days. When she started working full time, she did domestic work, cooking and cleaning.[15] Although Catherine's daughter, Cindy, worked as a secretary at the estate from January to August 1999, her intention was to break the cycle by attaining tertiary-level education, which she did when she attended the T.A. Marryshow Community College.

As was seen in the previous periods in Grenadian history, during the 1950s and 1970s some women owned their own land. Florence Glean, for instance, inherited Panorama Estate in St Patrick and Nora Holas inherited a quarter of an acre of land in La Fortune, St Patrick.[16] Most women tended to become landowners through inheritance on the death of a husband or family member. However, there were some women who bought their own property. Celestine Mason bought two acres of land from Hope Estate in the late 1950s. There,

Nora Holas, property owner and shop owner. Courtesy Margo Holas.

Celestine Mason, property owner, village of Munich. Courtesy Dr Byron Calliste.

she planted peas and corn as well as cash crops, like cocoa and bananas. In 1968, Phyllis Pitt bought just under two acres of land from Richmond Estate, and a quarter of an acre in 1970. She used her land to plant nutmeg.[17] Monies gained from these lands, whether inherited or purchased, sometimes allowed women to be self-sufficient. Earnings from the land were used by women to financially support their families and ensure their children were educated.

EDUCATION

The curriculum for the education of girls in the 1950s had changed little since 1900. The focus remained on the domestic arts and the humanities rather than on the sciences. Interviews held with Glenda Mason-Francis, Monica Joseph, Gloria Payne-Banfield and Sister Ann Keens-Douglas revealed that science subjects were for boys and not girls. Glenda Mason-Francis, who was the principal of the Anglican High School in St George's in the 1990s, noted this about her own school days: "We [girls] didn't do much science. [We did] health science, [but] definitely no physics or chemistry. GBSS [Grenada Boys' Secondary School] had sciences like biology, chemistry, physics and, at [the] advanced level, botany and zoology."[18] According to Gloria Payne-Banfield, former cabinet secretary and contemporary of Glenda Mason-Francis, "the education facilities for girls were deficient. There were not many subjects available. We did arts and one science."[19]

The options available to women who completed secondary-level education at that time were either to get married and remain at home or find employment in the civil service. Girls were generally socialized into thinking that tertiary education was something to which they should not aspire. As Glenda Mason-Francis notes: "[Girls] left school, got a job with the [civil] service, which was a stable place, or [went] to England to do a secretarial course. Very few women were going to university; it was mainly boys . . . Women got married, had children and stayed at home."[20] However, some girls intended to go beyond society's expectations of them. Glenda Mason-Francis, for instance, went against the grain by attending the University of the West Indies and achieving her Bachelor of Arts degree. For many girls like her, the dream of acquiring a university education was very much alive but the finances to do

Gertude Protain, first female appointed to the Legislative Council. Courtesy Gertrude Protain.

so were not forthcoming. Monica Joseph, Grenada's first female judge, noted that it was difficult for a "black person to get a loan, [because] most did not have the collateral".[21] She gave typing and shorthand lessons in order to make enough money to go to England to study law. For women of the poorer classes, education was a means of social mobility. Even if they did not make it as far as university, the attainment of a secondary-level education meant being able to get a job in the civil service or in the teaching profession. It was the vehicle through which they could build a better life for themselves and their families.

Gertrude Protain, one of Grenada's first female councillors, was an advocate of higher education for girls. She led a motion in 1960 for the establishment of an annual scholarship to be awarded to girls only, but it was rejected since, generally, it was felt that certification for girls was unnecessary.[22] Up till then, only boys could compete for a sole annual scholarship to a university in the United Kingdom every two years. Her motion, if accepted, would have enabled girls to get a tertiary-level education. However, it remained that the girls had to compete with their male counterparts for scholarships.

HEALTH

Health conditions in Grenada by the 1950s and 1960s had improved since the 1930s and 1940s, and diseases like yaws and tuberculosis which were rampant in the early 1900s were on the decrease. There was an improvement in the health of children which could be attributed to efforts by the Inter Church Council to educate women, particularly rural women, on childcare and proper nutrition. Assisting the local agency was the United Nations International Children's Emergency Fund, set up in 1948 after World War II. In 1954, approximately 290,000 pounds of powdered skimmed milk was donated by the United Nations International Children's Emergency Fund for a two-year milk-feeding programme. This programme provided milk for seven thousand pre-school children and one thousand expectant and nursing mothers. The aim of the programme was to provide adequate nourishment to pregnant women, nursing mothers and young children, and it mainly targeted those in reduced financial circumstances.[23]

In addition to the Inter Church Council and the United Nations International Children's Emergency Fund, there were other groups that sought to provide food, clothing and employment for poorer women. These groups included Canadian Save the Children, the United Nations Educational Scientific and Cultural Organization and women's groups like the YWCA, the Soroptomists' Club, the Lioness Club, the Home Industries' Association, Homemakers' Association and Foresters' Social Workers League. Through these organizations poorer women got some form of relief, even though it may have been temporary, from the harsh realities of their lives. Canadian Save the Children set up a childcare project with clinics for fifteen hundred children. There, the babies were weighed, their general health was checked and they were given a monthly supply of milk. Nadia Benjamin, who was parliamentary secretary of the Ministry of Education and Social Affairs in the GULP government in 1972, gave her account of her work with Canadian Save the Children:

> There were a lot of children suffering from malnutrition. We ran clinics and provided high protein food for babies and also checked their weight. There were mothers' clubs to educate the mothers. They did not know how to prepare the skimmed milk, for example . . . We established day nurseries at Dunfermline and Sauteurs. After 4:00 p.m. we visited the homes of these families and encouraged them to come to the clinics.[24]

From July 1968 to June 1969, the Inter Church Council supplied fifty-two public schools with food and thirty-four private infant schools with milk. They also ensured a hot meal was served to approximately fifty-two hundred children in primary schools. They distributed the following commodities to poorer families between 1968 and 1969: 125,720 pounds of flour, 36,152 pounds of cornmeal, 64,980 pounds of rolled oats, 27,117 pounds of milk and 16,860 pounds of butter. The estate owners supported the project by sending weekly supplies of fruits and vegetables to all schools. The Inter Church Council also made a family feeding programme available to all disabled people who had no income; to able-bodied people who had no income due to lack of employment; and people with five or more children who had an income of less than twenty dollars per month. The Inter Church Council also held courses and lectures to try to improve family life. For example, in the parish of St Andrew, in March 1970, Sister Rose Hall, maternity tutor of the General Hospital gave a talk entitled "The First Twelve Years of Life".[25]

Although there was progress in health care, according to the Report of the Commission of Enquiry on the Colony Hospital (1959), the conditions there were still poor. The report stated that the quality of the food served was poor and often insufficient; that there was an inadequate supply of bed linen and garments in the free wards so that patients were forced to sleep in the garments they had worn all day; that there was a shortage of drugs prescribed by the doctors; and that there was inadequate clinical equipment. The report also indicated that maternity patients were sometimes required to lie on the floor in the ward due to a shortage of beds. The (mostly female) nurses were grossly overworked and, as such, found it difficult to cope with their duties. It was reported that, for the four hospitals in Grenada (the General Hospital, also known as the Colony Hospital, at St George's, the Princess Alice Hospital at Grenville, Carriacou Hospital at Hillsborough, Carriacou, and the Sanatorium at St George's), there were only eighteen qualified staff nurses.[26]

WOMEN'S GROUPS

The Home Industries' Association, the Foresters' Social Workers League, the Soroptomists' Club, the Lioness Club, the YWCA, the Homemakers' Association, the Grenada Women's League, along with the Mothers' Union and women's guilds from the various churches were some of the organizations that were around at the time and consisted exclusively of women. Their shared goal was to try to meet the needs of the poorer women, as well as those in need, in the society. In other islands, like Trinidad, for example, these women's organizations were usually led by middle- and upper-class women. This was not so for Grenada. The women who led these groups came from various social classes. There were those who were from estate-owning families and merchant families but also working-class families.

The Home Industries' Association was established in 1931 with the objective of "assist[ing] ladies in reduced circumstances to become self supporting and to encourage all forms of local industry". This association's leaders taught women how to make craft items and preserves, and how to do needlework. These products were sold at the association's retail outlet at the entrance of Sendall Tunnel in the town of St George's, and the proceeds were shared among the women.

The Foresters' Social Workers League was also established in 1931. It was not an exclusively female social work organization; however, a number of female foresters gave exceptional service especially in the establishment of a shed in St George's for serving meals to poor adults and children. The league also established a servants' depot for the training of domestic servants for service in reputable homes.

The Soroptomists' Club was founded by Louise Rowley in 1971. It raised funds for charitable institutions and helped scholarship children with books and uniforms. Mollie McIntyre, former president of the club, recalled that the club viewed "the School for the Deaf as its pet. They raised funds for the school, paid the electricity and the staff." As an offshoot of the Lions Club International, a Lionesses Club was formed in 1977 and its work was similar to that of the Soroptomists'.

The YWCA, registered in 1889, came under the dynamic leadership of Pansy Rowley, a social welfare officer, who was the first Grenadian woman to study at the London School of Economics. She changed its focus from being a bible school to one offering courses for women in domestic science, handicraft and sewing. She was instrumental in hosting the first carnival pageant and including the traditional masquerades like short-knee then called payoo and may-pole into the pag-

Pansy Rowley, leader of the YWCA and first black Grenadian women to attain a bachelor's degree, London School of Economics. Courtesy University of the West Indies Open Campus, Grenada.

Maude Hutchinson, executive member of the Homemakers Association. Courtsey Maude Hutchinson.

eant. Prior to this, the traditional masquerades were held separately. She was the founder of the School for the Deaf, the Divi Divi Dance Group and the Pygmalion Glee Club. The Pygmalion Glee Club was a cultural club that taught traditional dances and also performed plays. Pansy Rowley was awarded the MBE in 1962.

The Homemakers Association also offered similar courses to that of the YWCA. Maude Hutchinson, executive member of the Homemakers Association, noted that the group grew out of a government-sponsored ten-week programme for women to learn home economics. At the end of the programme, most of the women "missed coming [to the classes]" so she and other home economics teachers, like Agatha Pierre and Winifred Telesford, formed a non-governmental organization called the Homemakers Association. Its objective was "to meet the social, educational and spiritual needs of women, especially rural women".[27] The association would organize two-week residential conferences which would be attended by two representatives from each Homemakers group in the island. At the conferences, lectures were given on various topics and skills were taught. The representatives would then return to their smaller clubs and pass on the knowledge.

The Grenada Women's League was, for all intents and purposes, the women's arm of the GULP. Gairy, himself, noted that it was his brainchild. Like other women's organizations, it distributed food, for example at Christmas time. It organized day nurseries and held beautification schemes throughout the island. In April 1970, Gairy presented the league with twelve hundred dollars at its convention for the establishment of crèches all over the island.

Apart from the charitable organizations previously mentioned, there were other clubs and organizations that women joined to meet their recreational and cultural needs. For recreation, there were female cricket teams. Wapel Nedd, who was involved in the formation of the Woman's Cricket Association in the 1970s, noted that rural women had no recreational outlet. They watched cricket every Sunday, yet they did not play. She thought one day, "how about if they played instead of going to look".[28] This eventually led to the first Women's Cricket Competition being held in 1976, in which nine women's cricket teams competed.

For cultural organizations, there was the Bee Wee Ballet, founded in 1950 by Thelma Knight-Phillip. This group represented Grenada at the inauguration of the Parliament of the Federation of the West Indies in Trinidad and Tobago in 1958. In 1968, Mrs Knight-Phillip wrote and produced the plays *Back to Earth*, *Quest in Paradise* and

Gloria Payne-Banfield, former cabinet secretary. Courtesy Gloria Payne-Banfield.

House for Sale. For "Expo 69", held in Grenada, she wrote the script, produced and played the leading role in *Creole Language* as part of Grenada's cultural performance. In 1974, she led two cultural teams to Suriname. In 1975, she led the national cultural team to St Thomas, the United States Virgin Islands. There, she wrote and produced a script for Black History week, in which she played the leading role. Gloria Payne-Banfield (former cabinet secretary) describes her involvement in culture as "almost a crusade". She taught dancing three times a week and formed the St Paul's Academy of Dramatic Arts. In 1974, she started the Vin Vwei La Grenade Group.

For the women of the elite who may or may not have been part of a charitable organization, there were social clubs like the Richmond Hill Club, the Morne Rouge Club and the Art Club.

WOMEN IN PUBLIC OFFICE

As previously noted, women first entered public office in Grenada when they served on District Boards in the 1940s. By the 1950s, they had gained admittance into the Legislative Council. Eva Sylvester was the first woman to be elected to the Legislative Council. In the 1951 election, her husband Cyril Sylvester won his seat on a GULP ticket, but died suddenly. In a by-election,

held in 1952, Eva Sylvester ran for this position and won. She served to the
end of the term in 1954. Although Sylvester was the first woman *elected* to the
Legislative Council, Gertrude Protain was the first woman to be *appointed* to
the Legislative Council. As mentioned earlier, she championed the cause of
education for women. She also made her mark as an ambassador for Grenada
when she joined the Grenada Board of Tourism as its executive secretary. She
held this post for twenty-five years and eventually became director of the
board. In the summer of 1963, she represented Grenada at a two-week pro-
motional display in London. In 1969, she represented Grenada at the Suriname
Trade Fair and in 1978 she led the team that presented Grenada's booth that
won the first prize in the Calgary Stampede. The objective of these shows
was to present the Grenadian tourist package to an international audience,
and Gertrude Protain achieved this through her initiative, ingenuity and
strong leadership skills. She also gave radio lectures to women. These lectures
focused on women's role as mothers and on their struggle to remove the
stereotype that education is for boys only. In this capacity, Gertrude Protain
was a role model for women in her community. In recognition of her
dedicated service to tourism, she was named Member of the British Empire
by Queen Elizabeth in 1968. The citation read: "one of Grenada's finest
ambassadors".

Under the Gairy administration, at this time, the government sought to
promote the rights of women, and there was a resulting increase seen in the
number of women appointed in the government. Gairy referred to this in a
speech he presented at the twenty-third session of the United Nations in 1974,
after Grenada gained its independence:

> It is also precisely because of our faith in the sanctity of the equal rights of
> men and women that we have enshrined in our constitution the provisions
> which guarantee that the rights of Grenadian women are equated to those of
> Grenadian men . . . This philosophy is evidenced by the fact that Grenada is
> the first and only country in the British Commonwealth of Nations in which
> a woman was recommended by me as head of government and appointed
> Governor.[29]

The first female governor, who Gairy referred to in this speech, was Dame
Hilda Bynoe, appointed in June 1968. In 1974, he also appointed the first female

plenipotentiary permanent representative to the United Nations, Marie-Josephine McIntyre. In that same year Marie-Josephine McIntyre was also appointed the ambassador to the United States and the high commissioner to Canada. When she represented Grenada at the International Women's Conference in Mexico in 1975, she reiterated the sentiments expressed by Gairy, about Grenada's commitment to demonstrating the belief in the equality of women by appointing them to senior positions in the administration:

Marie-Josephine McIntyre, former ambassador to the United Nations. Courtesy Marie-Jeanne McIntyre-Symmonds.

> It has become obvious that all of humanity and not half of it must participate in the effort to solve its problems . . . Grenada is firmly committed to the equality of the sexes. This commitment is not mere rhetoric . . . My government has followed a deliberate policy of appointing women to the posts that involve them in the highest level of policy and decision making in our country. They hold positions in cabinet and in the senate.[30]

Apart from herself and Dame Hilda Bynoe, two other women were appointed to the diplomatic corp. Florence Rapier was appointed high commissioner to CARICOM and ambassador-designate to Latin America in 1978, and Jennifer Hosten replaced Marie-Josephine McIntyre as high commissioner to Canada, also in that year. Hosten was the first black woman to be crowned Miss World in 1970. Pamela Steele, former permanent secretary in the Ministry of Agriculture, Ministry of Health, and the Ministry of Communications and Works, noted that "some governments realized that they could get more out of females than men. Gairy recognized

Pamela Steele, former permanent secretary. Courtesy Pamela Steele.

Wapel Nedd, former parliamentary secretary, Ministry of Youth Development, Sports and Labour. Courtesy family of Wapel Nedd.

Nadia Benjamin, former parliamentary secretary, Ministry of Education and Social Affairs. Courtesy Nadia Benjamin.

women's work and he pushed women very early . . . others followed."³¹ Between the 1950s and the 1970s, there were three female permanent secretaries in Grenada – Florence Rapier, Mavis Fletcher and Gloria Payne-Banfield. Also in this period, Nadia Benjamin, Wapel Nedd and Cynthia Gairy took up official government posts.

Nadia Benjamin was deeply involved in women's organizations like the YWCA and charitable organizations like the Save the Children's Fund and the Inter Church Council. She described the YWCA as "a training ground for leaders". She was its president, treasurer and secretary, and she initiated the construction of a YWCA building in Grenville and established a training centre where volunteers from the community gave classes to drop-outs. Her involvement in these organizations served to open her eyes to the needs of her community and it propelled her into politics. She became parliamentary secretary in the Ministry of Education and Social Affairs in 1972. Wapel Nedd was appointed parliamentary secretary in the Ministry of Youth Development, Sports and Labour in the same year.

Mrs Cynthia Gairy was the first female to sit in the House of Representatives (1961). She was also the first female minister (1968) to be responsible for the Ministry of Social Affairs, Culture and Community Development. In a number of her speeches, she reinforced the point that agriculture was the bedrock of the economy and challenged the people to grow more local food rather than depend on foreign imports, and to manufacture local articles for sale to visitors. She encouraged self-help

Cynthia Gairy, first female minister. Courtesy Margaret Payne.

programmes in the communities and called on people to take pride in their community's welfare. Prior to her involvement in politics Cynthia had served her community by offering classes in music, sewing, embroidery, typing and shorthand.

Female support for the Gairy administration continued into the 1970s. In prayer, poetry and song, the women expressed their admiration for their leader. In the *Farmers Weekly* newsletter (3 July 1971), for example, a teacher from Beaulieu Roman Catholic School in St George wrote::

> Many years ago some old prophet had foretold that a young man would sail across the ocean blue to govern the people of this land. The natives then anxiously awaited the fulfillment of this dream for it was their desire to be lifted from the dust and smoke and be channeled into light and prosperity. In 1951 this great prophesy was fulfilled, when this very young energetic leader with an army of nine lifted the people of this land to better knowledge and understanding of their country.[32]

Gairy realized that women made up the majority of the Grenadian population. They were visible as a group and they could not be ignored. As such, he practised shrewd politics and used their votes to attain leadership. A few concessions were given to women in the process: he laid the foundation which allowed women the opportunity to move into the government service and the political arena. The PRG which followed was able to build on that foundation.

THE NATIONAL COMMISSION ON THE STATUS OF WOMEN

In light of the UN's declaration that 1975 was "International Women's Year", the Gairy administration sponsored the Caribbean Regional Seminar on Women in that same year. The seminar's objective was to discuss the specific issues, problems and concerns faced by women throughout the region. At the seminar, Cynthia Gairy expounded the view that women need not stay at home, but could make a contribution elsewhere in the community. She said that women's attendance to household duties would not necessarily be hampered by their acceptance of employment outside the home. She encouraged women to take up the challenge to be recognized as the equals of their male partners. Draft recommendations for the seminar dealt with education, employment and the establishment of a regional centre to coordinate, collect and disseminate information in order to implement the objectives.

As a spinoff from the regional seminar the Gairy administration launched a National Commission on the Status of Women later in 1975. The commission sought to improve the status of women, educate and motivate women to desire self improvement, focus public attention on the need to equalize the sexes and to encourage efforts to raise the quality of life. In accordance with these aims, twenty-six organizations were set up to study the status of women in the law, in the international arena, in education and in employment. The commission found that women were discriminated against in many aspects. It recognized that work had been done by a number of institutions to remedy the situation, but noted that the inequality of the sexes still remained. The commission found that those who tried to institute change lacked the dynamism necessary to perform such a task. It hoped to provide a cohesive body that would build on individual organizational efforts and prepare a comprehensive plan for future achievement.

The commission put forward a number of recommendations for the enhancement of women's health, education, recreation, training and employment. In the area of health, the commission recommended that services and facilities to support the dual role of women as mothers and workers should be established, that is, through the provision of day-care centres and paid maternity leave. They recommended that there should be the reorganization of the district nursing and midwifery service so that adequate post-natal care was given to mothers and their babies. In the area of recreation, the commission recommended that more recreational and cultural facilities, such as community centres and playing fields, be provided to cater to adult women and it requested that personnel from the Ministry of Culture and Youth be attached to each centre to ensure that the buildings were properly supervised and maintained. The commission also requested that facilities be provided to cater to indoor activities, such as dancing (quadrille and square dancing), card games, checkers, dominoes and bridge, for older women.

The commission further recommended that the government establish a department of career planning and placement for women and that career guidance officers be appointed to schools at both primary and secondary levels. School curricula should be broadened, they said, so as to meet the needs of those girls who had an aptitude for practical and technical subjects. It stated that classification should be based on ability and aptitude rather than on sex. The commission believed that the government should give more scholarships to encourage women to undergo such training and that they should make special efforts to retain women graduates by offering more attractive salaries and free housing. They recommended that female labourers and road workers be paid the same as their male counterparts.[33]

Although the government's staged the Caribbean Regional Seminar on Women and established the National Commission on the Status of Women, there was little or no follow through on the recommendations put forward. For example, the Gairy regime failed to implement the following: paid maternity leave, equal wages for male and female labourers and road workers, more scholarships for women. It was not until the late 1970s and early 1980s that Grenadian women attained maternity leave, equal work for equal pay and were offered a greater number of scholarships.

FEMALE OPPOSITION TO THE GAIRY REGIME

While there were quite a few female politicians in Gairy's administration, there were also female politicians in the opposing parties. Enid Charles and Gloria St Bernard were two such women. They both campaigned for the GNP. The GNP had its women's group, which campaigned for the party and raised funds for it. Like other women's groups attached to political parties, this group sought to encourage other women to join the party. The GNP women's group had its first public meeting at the Market Square in St George's for the 1967 election.

Gloria St Bernard got involved in politics as early as 1951, when she spoke on Theophilus Albert Marryshow's platform in the town of St George's. She acted as treasurer and secretary for the GNP party and ran on the GNP ticket for the parishes of St John and St Mark in the 1957 elections. She won 256 votes while GULP's Herbert McClean won 1,250 votes. St Bernard became the first female mayor of the town of St George's from 1964 to 1965. As mayor, she was responsible for the maintenance of the town. Blanche Sylvester ran for the People's Alliance for the constituency of St George North West.

It can be argued that Gairy's ideal of putting women on an equal footing with men within the Grenadian society was a farce. Nadia Benjamin and Wapel Nedd bear testimony to this. Both were sacked from the Gairy government in July 1976. According to Nadia Benjamin, "[Gairy's] policy was that you should look up to him. He was doing everything. He tried to stifle us. We were pretty vocal in expressing ourselves. He didn't like that. We were doing much more than the men. The men in the cabinet were jealous . . . He felt we were competing against him."[34] Wapel Nedd fell out with Gairy when he expressed his intention to make the women's cricket team a political entity. Both women saw themselves as being politically naïve and felt that they were used by Gairy to capture their supporters for his own interests. He resented both women's popularity. It should be noted that Gairy was unwilling to share power with any other person, not just women. What resulted was the centralization of national political power in his hands. Marie-Josephine McIntyre, on the other hand, did not see Gairy's stated desire to improve life for women as a farce. She recalls, "Gairy told me I was absolutely free to make any decisions and the government would stand by it . . . I was never asked to do anything wrong."[35] Gairy, however, lost the support of a number of women by his treatment of Benjamin and Nedd. For example, many dropped out of the Cricket Association and withdrew their financial support until it became a mere shadow of its former self.

The office of governor is a political appointment. This must be taken into consideration when analysing the role of Dame Hilda Bynoe in Grenada's history. It could be argued that her post was useless since she did little to assist the people when complaints were brought to her attention, and that her speeches held an apologetic tone

Dame Hilda Bynoe, first female governor in Grenada and in the Commonwealth. Courtesy Modern Photo Studios, Church Street, St George's Grenada.

for the Gairy regime. She did, however, call a Commission of Enquiry (Duffus Commission) in 1973 to investigate the breakdown of law and order in Grenada. The commission stated that Gairy had acted injudiciously in calling out the police aides, known as the "Mongoose Gang", which had a reputation for violence, to deal with demonstrators. While Gairy accepted the criticisms of the commission, he failed to comply with their demands to disband the gang. In her Christmas message in 1973, Bynoe tried to mediate between the opposing factions and the Gairy regime when she called for peace and unity. She called for a fresh start and pointed out that while there would always be differing views, Grenadians should concentrate on the common ground, the common purposes, and the common aspirations. She called for a spirit of tolerance and understanding and working together for the common good.

By 1974 when demonstrations increased and the crowds shouted for her removal, she resigned from her post as governor. She did see the need for a more dynamic and forceful women's organization in Grenada. In her speech to the first Biennial Conference of the Caribbean Women's Association's in April 1972, she noted that the way forward was for women to seek equal opportunity and independence rather than concentrate solely on charity and patronage, the task to which most middle-class women committed themselves.

Within the civil service and the teaching profession, there was another burning issue that angered women – the issue of maternity leave. Regarding maternity leave, the Statutory Rules and Orders Number 30 of 1967 stated that the chief personnel officer might, on the recommendation of the education officer, grant a teacher maternity leave and pay according to a formula set out, only if she was married. The unfortunate reality was that both married and unmarried women in the civil service or in the teaching profession got no maternity leave, even though the National Commission on the Status of Women had recommended that this law be adhered to. As far as a stunted career was concerned, once women married, they were discriminated against. In fact, once a woman within the service got married, she had to apply to the chief administrator to remain working in the service, for it was felt that women could not dedicate much time to work when they were married. Senior civil servant Pamela Steele, for example, noted that when she got married she was given a temporary appointment to work from month to month. Lady Scoon, another civil servant at the time, recalled that she returned to work when her son was six weeks' old. She had to take holidays to get such an extended period with her newborn. Generally married women were given two weeks' off after giving birth.

NEW POLITICAL THRUST

Discontent with the Gairy administration had been growing since the early 1960s. There was a gross misuse and misappropriation of government funds ("squandermania") as well as a fanatical and repressive hostility to all competing political organizations.

By the early 1970s, a young and progressive intelligentsia formed a new political group, the Forum, that offered the Grenadian people an alternative to the GULP and GNP. They were emboldened by the works of Walter Rodney, Frantz Fanon, Kwame Nkrumah, Martin Luther King, Malcolm X (whose mother was a Grenadian) and Fidel Castro. These young radicals, under the leadership of Maurice Bishop, passionately believed in people's rights. By 1972, the Forum had folded, but early that year Bishop was again at the head of a similar group, Movement for the Advancement of Community Effort. By

October 1972, this group evolved into a new group, known as Movement for the Assemblies of the People. Movement for the Assemblies of the People was primarily urban based, and a group known as Joint Endeavour for Welfare Education and Liberation (JEWEL) was the rural counterpart. In March 1973, JEWEL and Movement for the Assemblies of the People merged to form the New Jewel Movement.

This new political group expounded such ideas as the transformation of the Westminster-type state apparatus into one based on more popular control through assemblies of the people. It advocated the prevention of the daily rises in prices of all food, clothes and other essentials and was committed to the nationalization of banks, and the establishment of a Marketing and National Importing Board that would be responsible for imports and exports to serve the interests of the majority of the society. The aim of the Importing Board would be to provide essential imports at reduced prices and to provide an outlet for farmers' crops.

FURTHER DISCONTENT

In this context, any person, male or female, who opposed the Gairy administration, was discriminated against. They were physically abused, fired from their jobs, transferred to another department or killed. On 7 November 1970, a group of nurses staged a demonstration against the Ministry of Health and presented a letter stating their grievances. The letter voiced their concerns over poor working conditions, unhealthy facilities and the storage of medical supplies at the General Hospital. The nurses then marched through the streets of St George's with placards that read: "When patients die don't blame us. We have no tools, no drugs . . . bad administration"; "We want a hospital not an abattoir".[36] This was the first in a series of demonstrations and sit-ins at the Ministry of Health and the prime minister's office by the nurses. The nurses were strongly supported by secondary school students, other members of the public, the Council of Christian Churches and a number of trade unions, including the Grenada Union of Teachers.

The Gairy administration responded by sending out riot police, armed with tear gas, and by dismissing ten trainee nurses for taking part in the

protest action. Gairy referred to their letter as "damned rude" and referred
to them as "idlers". He then threatened those who supported the nurses. In
one radio address, Gairy threatened to exclude church leaders from the state
and to expatriate them for their support of the protest.[37] The Grenada
Women's League opposed the nurses' action and called on them to apologize.
The nurses were unrepentant and stood their ground, stating that they would
not "stoop and crawl before a man who completely ignored their concerns".[38]
It was the first time in Grenadian history that a group of women formed a
unified force and demonstrated against the government to denounce the ills
of society.

On 26 April 1974, the nurses' and midwives' graduation ceremony was held
at the Nurses Hostel in St George's. There, Gairy delivered a fiery political
address in which he stated that no one could criticize or demonstrate against
his government and expect to get away with it. He warned of immediate
dismissal if this occurred, and withheld the certificates for eight nurses who
had spoken freely, demonstrated and engaged in anti-governmental activities
function.

Persons who were opposed to the Gairy government were transferred, suspended or thrown out of jobs. At the General Hospital, for example, nurses
Yvonne Matthew, Marva John and Joan Bernard were sent to Carriacou and
Irva Brown was sent to Petit Martinique. This meant having to leave their
homes and families to move to the sister islands. Travel was by boat, at least
three hours each way. Sister Belmar was sent to Richmond Hill's Home for
the Aged. Sister Noel was sent to the classroom; Sister Holder and nurse Erma
Wilson were fired. In other government departments, June Burke, Mavis
Charles and Gloria Harris were dismissed. Joy Bowen and Pat Gilbert were
transferred. Magdalene Chateau of "Radio Grenada" was dismissed.[39]

Students were denied scholarships, despite their academic aptitude, if their
parents were not supporters of the Gairy regime. Veronica Coard (housewife
and mother of six girls) noted that there was an "unavailability of scholarships
once you were not a Gairyite". Two of her daughters, Kathleen and Helen,
were denied scholarships since it was allegedly decided that there would be
"no scholarships for the Coards".[40]

Lucy Stroude, one of the founding members of the Commercial and
Industrial Workers Union, noted that Gairy tried to persuade the workers at

French's Store in St George's to leave their union and join him. She said, "He threatened them that they would lose their jobs if they didn't. More than once the Syrian bosses downtown were so scared that they paid their workers' union dues for Gairy's union, even though they were really members of ours." Jeanette Dubois, first female president of the Grenada Union of Teachers, 1980 to 1981, noted that in 1976/1977, when the teachers called for a salary increase, they were subjected to a series of attacks. She noted:

> Gairy held a public meeting at St George's Market Square and openly invited parents and their children to intimidate the teachers. He told the people to watch them closely, spy on them, time them at work, report on them. In fact, he set up an atmosphere of psychological warfare between parents and children on one hand and the teachers on the other. This resulted in a breakdown of discipline in the schools and the verbal abuse of some teachers. This became very widespread . . . particularly in the rural areas, and some teachers who were particularly active in the union received death . . . [threats].[41]

The fear instilled by the threats led to a division in the union and there was no choice but to accept that Gairy had won.

The Gairy administration had control of the army, called the Green Beasts, and the Mongoose Gang. The latter were used to settle any unrest, demonstration or resistance from any opposing factor. Some critics have likened the Mongoose Gang to the Tonton Macoute in Haiti. Gairy boasted of his intention to recruit the most unsavoury characters to do his bidding:

> The Opposition has referred to my recruiting criminals in the reserve force . . . Does it not take steel to cut steel? I am proud of the response to my call on Grenadians regardless of their criminal record to come and join in the defence of my government and the maintenance of law and order in their colony. Indeed hundreds have come and some of the toughest and roughest rough-necks have been recruited.[42]

The NJM soon got a taste of what Gairy's army had to offer. On 4 November 1973, the NJM held a People's Congress at Seamoon in the parish of St Andrew. The congress passed a resolution accusing the Gairy regime of twenty-seven crimes against the Grenadian people. The NJM threatened that, if their demands were not met, a general strike would be called. When six members of the NJM met in Grenville to work out the details of the strike, they were met with a hail of bullets, beaten mercilessly with clubs, axe handles and pistol butts by the police and the Mongoose Gang, then thrown into prison. The following day, the six were denied bail, medical attention or visits from their families. Alimenta Bishop, Maurice Bishop's mother, recalled the day her son was beaten:

> Rupert [her husband] came and told us that Belmar [chief of police] said that not even God could help the Jewel because he would not let them out at all. Rupert brought the priest and all and they would not let him out. Next day, at Richmond Hill Prison, I saw them bring Maurice and the others in chains. Maurice was [barefoot]. When I saw their condition, [they were] bleeding, I went home and called the doctor. They were taken to the General Hospital['s] open ward. When I got there, Maurice eye "buss up", poor thing . . . Gairy['s] Green Beasts running up and down saying "they go do for them, they go kill them". Maurice had a broken jaw bone . . . It started to knit back out of place.[43]

In spite of the events, the strike was called. The strike action of 1973 spilled over into 1974. The island's economy was paralysed, as all the urban workers took strike action at the same time. There were disruptions in electricity and water supply, telephone service and at the docks. The activities of businesses and industries were also affected because workers were on strike. The three-month shut-down was marked by continuous mass protests, police violence and popular reprisals against the police. Everything came to a head on 21 January 1974, when an estimated twenty thousand persons gathered in a demonstration on the Carenage (the waterfront on St George's inner harbour). During the demonstration, over five hundred members of the Mongoose Gang approached, chanting "Jewel Behave Yourself or They Go Charge Us with Murder". The Mongoose Gang threw bottles at the crowd. Rupert Bishop, father of Maurice Bishop, was shot dead by police as he attempted to block the doorway of the building (Otway House) in which women and children had taken refuge from the violence in the street.

Those suspected of supporting the opposition were harassed by the Mongoose Gang. For example, Ethlina Thomas had her house raided on 26 September 1973 for the alleged possession of ammunition. The police claimed that they found thirty-six bullets. Mrs Thomas was arrested and taken to the station and charged. She was freed in the St David's Magistrate's Court without a single word of evidence having been pronounced against her. On Friday, 5 July 1974, Joan St Bernard, a schoolteacher at St Louis Roman Catholic Girls School, was attacked at the school by two secret police and their accomplice who was another teacher at the school. She took refuge in the staff room but was followed. She jumped out of a window and then had to be hidden in the room of a nun. It was the second attack on a female teacher. Dorris Bonaparte was also attacked and was sent on leave.[44]

Some Grenadian women took an active part in the NJM. Some sold the *New Jewel,* the newspaper of the party, which was banned. They risked being arrested. Mary Jane (pseudonym) remembers how she had to hide the newspaper from the police: "The bus [driver] would drop off the papers and slide it into the shop. We would parcel it out and send it to different areas . . . The police got wind of it and they came. I put the papers on the stool and sat on top of it with my dress covering it. They searched and never found it."[45]

The *New Jewel* newspaper, between September 1973 and May 1974, highlighted the ills of the Grenadian society at the time and encouraged the people to be vigilant and to support the NJM. The paper noted the rise in secondary school fees in September 1973 by fifteen dollars. This increase would have made it difficult for poor parents to send their children to school. The Gairy government apparently did nothing to help the situation. This was in sharp contrast to its behaviour during its rise to power in the 1950s. The paper criticized the members of the GULP for failing to meet the needs of their community. For example, Cynthia Gairy was criticized for not completing the recreation ground in St David's and not opposing the effort by Lord Bronlow, owner of La Sagesse Estate and the property surrounding it, to prevent the people of St David from using La Sagesse Beach. The governor general's wife, Lady De Gale, was ridiculed for spending two hundred dollars on dog food, while there were parents in Grenada who could not afford to spend two dollars a day to buy food for their families. Grenadian women were challenged to take an active part in the struggle:

> The Grenadian woman shattered by a history of powerlessness, wants change but shies away from actually working to create change. The new Grenadian

woman must get rid of this lethargy, this feeling of helplessness, she has seen herself as a member of the Third World Peoples working side by side with our brothers for the freedom of our people creating the kind of family life where justice and equality are meaningful elements towards the creation of a new society. The Grenadian liberation must be a conscious plan based on new values and worked out by Grenadian women for Grenadian women.[46]

This snippet from the *New Jewel* newspaper clearly illustrated how a number of Grenadian women saw themselves in the context of their nation's history. Some actually felt powerless in the face of political repression and economic hardships. Through the use of its newspaper, meetings and discussions the NJM sought to change the mindset of these women. In 1977, the NJM took the cause of women one step further with the establishment of its own women's group.

FORMATION OF NJM/NWO

The NJM established a women's caucus known as the New Jewel Movement National Women's Organisation (NJM/NWO) in 1977. Maurice Bishop believed in the sentiment expressed by Lenin that "there can be no real mass movement without the women", and echoed it when he said: "We must root out all possessive slave owner's point of view, both in the party and among the masses. This is another of our political tasks. Our relations with the sisters must be principled, must be one of raising their consciousness, making them ardent fighters against Gairyism and Imperialism."[47] Bishop asked Phyllis Coard to take up the challenge of establishing the NJM/NWO. Phyllis Coard is Jamaican and her husband, Bernard Coard, was a member of the NJM. Phyllis was asked because of her experience in the field of women's movements. She explained her previous involvement in the struggle for women's rights:

My experience of the emerging women's movement in Jamaica between 1974 [and] 1976 aroused my whole interest in the question of women's rights. There emerged in Jamaica, as part of the democratic socialist movement of Michael Manley, an increasingly vocal women's movement. I personally attended several rallies at which leading PNP [People's National Party] and a few WPJ

[Workers Party of Jamaica – Marxist/Leninist group] women members protested various social issues affecting women. There was increasing pressure for a maternity leave law, and rejoicing over minimum wage law which bene-fitted women tremendously, especially women domestic servants. Prior to that, I had grown up in a family in which equality for women was accepted as a norm. Jamaican middle-class women tend to be assertive of their right to equal-ity and almost all of them work outside the home . . . I spent almost all of nine years, 1962–1971, in Britain. There, I worked as a social worker in some of the worst slums in England. It was the terrible poverty which must have moved me, especially the suffering of the children of parents who had "given up" or been overwhelmed by their situations.[48]

A Steering Committee was established with Phyllis Coard and Rita Joseph as co-chairpersons. This committee formulated a plan of action for the NJM women's arm which would point out to women the discrimination and suf-fering they were experiencing and urge them to join the anti-Gairy struggle. Pamphlets were published to sensitize women, and members of the Steering Committee went from house to house trying to convince women to join the struggle. Patsy Romain recalled the early days of NJM/NWO:

From the different parishes we had ten sisters in all together. They went out to different areas to organise women underground. They would go out speak-ing in the homes of people they knew . . . We talked about how lower prices would be better for women and children and husbands. We had pamphlets explaining why it was necessary for a change in Grenada, what the benefits would be if there was a government that was supporting working and poor people in Grenada.[49]

Some of the early NJM/NWO groups were based in various places through-out Grenada, such as St Andrew, in the villages of Birchgrove and Paradise; St Patrick, in the villages of River Sallie and Tivoli; in the parishes of St David and St John

Women's groups like the Homemakers and the Soroptomists and those linked to the GNP and GULP had limited the participation of women to fundraising and drumming up party support in the communities. But by the 1970s, some Grenadian women were politically prepared to enter into the anti-Gairy struggle. The Black Power Movement of the late 1960s and 1970s had left its mark. Grenadian women were reading the works of Angela Davis and Eldridge Cleaver of the United States Civil Rights Movement. The NJM challenged women, through pamphlets, newsletters, talks and demonstrations, to move one step further and to fight for the right to a better life. Many women became aware of their double oppression as women and as workers and, as such, responded readily to political mobilization.[50]

On the morning of 13 March 1979, the opposition NJM led a military coup against the Gairy government. The women who supported the NJM and wanted to put an end to the Gairy regime joined volunteers to capture police stations and establish roadblocks. A twenty-six year-old woman of Byelands St Andrew noted: "We marched to our local police station, at Birchgrove, about 200 of us, mostly women, and told the police to put up the white flag. Then we took positions in different areas, cooking for the soldiers, running messages and keeping guard and listening out for any counter-revolutionary plans."[51] While many rejoiced, there were women and men who vehemently opposed the revolution; others, while supporting change, were against the NJM's method of taking power.

CONCLUSION

Gairy possessed the tenacity that others before him lacked and proved a formidable opponent to the colonial power. His rhetorical expertise, eloquent oratory and his disdain for the ruling class made him a messiah to the ordinary person. Never before had they seen one of their own stand up stolidly to the imperial dominant power. His achievements included, first, the establishment of a potent trade union that united town and country workers and, second, the transformation of trade union power into political power.

However, his political malfeasance – squandermania and commissioning acts of violence and victimization – left many Grenadians demanding radical change. Once seen as a saviour to his people, he was now viewed as a tyrant, from whom a large majority of his people yearned for liberation.

Universal adult suffrage had given men and women the right to freely choose their political representative. Women attained a milestone by being represented by their own in parliament and on the international stage. Yet, under the Gairy regime women still faced the reality of having to work for less than their male counterparts. They were denied the right to maternity leave and few scholarships were made available to them.

Socialist thought and theory, and the practical example of a working socialist state in the form of Cuba, ineluctably drew a number of young receptive persons into a radical unit seeking change. Socialist doctrine had a particular appeal to the noble and legitimate aspirations of the poor, the weak and the politically oppressed. It was to become the main tool of resistance against the Gairy regime and the instrument of change – socialist revolution.

6 Women in the Grenada Revolution, 1979–1983

On 13 March 1979, the NJM staged a military coup that marked the beginning of a new political epoch for the English-speaking Caribbean with the formation of the socialist PRG. Some Gairyite women continued to support their ousted leader, others transferred their support to the PRG, while others remained neutral. Another group, the St George's PWA, opposed the Gairy regime but did not follow the socialist line. Nevertheless, in the early years of the revolution it received some support from the PRG.

THE PROGRESSIVE WOMEN'S ASSOCIATION

The PWA was formed in early 1977. Its aims and objectives were "to raise the progressive consciousness of women . . . . To struggle to achieve material and other benefits for our women . . . . Better wages and working conditions, equal pay for working women, day nurseries training and employment opportunities, proper housing, medical sanitation, recreational and cultural facilities. To struggle against any further encroachments on democratic rights . . . and to extend rights and civil liberties."[1] Membership was open to any woman residing in Grenada who accepted the goals of the organization. The membership fee was fifty cents (in Eastern Caribbean [EC] currency) per month. For unemployed women, membership was free. According to Dessima Williams, Grenada's representative to the Organization of American States,

1979–1983, the PWA served as a small but effective urban forum for politicizing and organizing middle-class women, house-wives, teachers, professionals, students and a core of the urban working class. Its unique advantage was that, although it opposed the Gairy regime, it was allowed to operate without molestation. There was no evidence that the PWA was victimized by the Gairy regime. This was due in part to the prestige of the PWA's leadership.[2]

The PWA held a National Conference for women from the 15 to the 17 June 1979. The conference got the support of the

Dessima Williams, former Organization of American States representative. Courtesy Peggy Nesfield.

newly formed PRG. Prime Minister Maurice Bishop called for women to join with men to solve their problems and that of the society as a whole. He noted:

> The woman cannot do it by herself; the man cannot do it himself. It is by the combination of men and women together attempting to build a new process; to build a new society, to build a new civilisation, attempting to produce more; attempting to find the new value systems, to identify ideas and new ways of pushing our country forward [so that we can progress]. It is only if we achieve this unity of the man and the woman that we would be able to move forward.[3]

Phyllis Coard, member of the Central Committee of the PRG and president of the NWO, called on women "to remember that it's only our struggle that is going to win our revolution. We the women can bring women's rights and total liberation and justice for all our peoples."[4]

The conference drew up a number of resolutions that helped to define fur-ther action. It recognized the deplorable state of the health service, the impor-tance of political education for national development and the existence of discrimination against women in education, employment and the law. It resolved that

> A steering committee made up of representatives from each parish and from each women's organization be formed to find solutions to the above problems

and that women should take the lead in working towards changing the unjust societal conditions that they face.

Women take an active part in carrying forward and consolidating the revolution.

More centres providing pre- and post-natal care, immunization and parental training be created for mothers.

More educational and training opportunities be created to meet the particular needs of the society, especially those of girls and women.

There be equal economic opportunity for women in all areas of the work force, particularly in the development of agricultural production (that is, agro industries).

A programme for political education for nationals, particularly women, be adopted through the use of the media.

Antiquated and unfair laws, especially those pertaining to women, be revised and that there be a just legal code for the entire society.[5]

However, the PWA was dissolved soon after the conference. One of the reasons cited for its demise was that an autonomous organization had no place within a one-party socialist state. Since members of NJM participated in the organization and made decisions based on party discipline and solidarity, it was impossible for that organization to operate autonomously. It was predictable that independent and articulate members would sooner or later be placed in a confrontational situation with NJM members. Indeed, directly following the conference, an emotional confrontation occurred between Alice McIntyre, the chairperson of the conference, and Phyllis Coard concerning Phyllis's failure to check with the committee before inviting some of the speakers. Prior to this, there were differing views on the PWA's plans to establish a women's reading centre at Marryshow House, the University of the West Indies' centre in Grenada. Phyllis Coard allegedly saw this as a threat to the revolution. In May 1979, to counter the PWA proposal, she suggested that the NJM bureau immediately plan to start a bookshop for progressive books in order "to avoid opportunists and CIA [Central Intelligence Agency] elements bringing in revisionist Maoist and Trotskyite literature".[6]

The PRG was of the view that none of the women's groups in Grenada had, up to that time, effectively challenged the status quo. Therefore these groups could never have hoped to effect any meaningful change in the lives and status of women in the wider society. They believed that the only way women could become effective in bringing about change was when the state apparatus was made to facilitate such changes. Only a broad based well-organized revolutionary women's organization capable of mobilizing women, politicizing and unifying them into a powerful revolutionary force, could achieve this. The NJM/NWO took up this challenge, operating from within the ruling party.

EXTENSION OF NJM/NWO

Early in 1979, several women's groups in support of the revolution were formed. Claudette Pitt, executive member of the NJM/NWO, claimed that "women called in to say we want to form groups. They called and asked us to come and speak to them. We were bombarded by this."[7] According to Phyllis Coard, this was where Cuba played a role. Isabel Jamoron, representative of Cuba's Federación de Mujeres, on a visit to Grenada in May 1981 noted that what they had created in Cuba "was the establishment of a mass organisation". She noted that their communist party was small, plus there were problems of sectarianism. She further noted that was "why Fidel Castro placed so much emphasis on building the mass organisations plus building the party".[8]

The issue was discussed at the Central Committee and it was decided that the NJM\NWO should become a national group. In the words of Phyllis Coard, "It was a good idea for Grenada. We were building a government that was broad-based and we needed a broad-based women's group. It was a struggle at first to persuade NJM women to have Gairyite women join. There was such hostility, previously, between the two groups."[9] In December 1980, the first general meeting was held. A decision was reached to change the name to NWO from NJM/NWO. Phyllis Coard was elected president and Rita Joseph vice president. Other members of the executive included Claudette Pitt and Tessa Stroude. By that time, the NWO comprised fifteen hundred members operating in 47 groups in all the parishes except Carriacou. By November 1982, membership stood at sixty-five hundred women organized into 170 groups, with 11 groups in Carriacou and one in Petit Martinique.[10]

Women participating in a zonal council meeting, 1980. Courtesy Peggy Nesfield.

The hierarchical structure of the organization was as follows:

- The Congress
- The National Executive and the National Secretariat
- The National Council of Delegates
- The Parish Coordinating Teams
- The NWO Groups

The congress was the highest organ and its members met every six years. Its duties were to thoroughly assess the work of the organization during the previous six years, decide the aims, objectives and overall direction of the organization for the coming six years, discuss and adopt an in-depth programme of work for a two-year period and to elect a national executive body.[11] The national executive was the highest body of the organization when the congress was not in session. It met at least once per month and its main function was to carry out the aims and objectives that were approved by the congress and to make policy decisions for the organization on behalf of the congress when it was not in session. The national executive comprised the president, vice president and five other elected members, three delegates from

St Andrew and St George and two from each of the other parishes. The national executive appointed the national secretariat, which included the president, vice president, a financial secretary and public relations officer, and secretary. It ensured that the decisions of the national executive were carried out and oversaw the day-to-day running of the organization. The National Council of Delegates consisted of two delegates elected from each NWO group. The delegates represented their groups at the congress. The parish coordinating teams comprised the parish delegates to the National Council of Delegates and other members of each group within the parish. Each team was responsible for supervising and guiding the work of the NWO groups in its parish and ensuring that the current NWO programme of work was carried out. It also submitted monthly reports to the national executive outlining the work of all the NWO groups within the parish. It elected a chairperson, a secretary, and various committees on organization, education, finance and employment.

Theoretically, the NWO's grassroots democratic structure was based on that of the PRG. Grassroots democracy was an alternative to the Westminster model. This alternative was geared towards giving the ordinary Grenadian a say in the development of her or his community. Tessa Stroude, one of the members of the NWO's national executive, gave a detailed description of how this process actually worked. She noted:

> The [NWO] groups would identify what they wanted to do in their community. For the groups to function by themselves we [the national executive] had a system of training . . . we could not ensure that the groups functioned properly because the women were not exposed. For example, they were not sure what was the role of a chairman or a secretary or treasurer. So we did a lot of training with the leaders of the groups to ensure that they functioned. We developed a work plan at a congress meeting. We could not have all the members there but say, for example, there [were] twelve groups in St Patrick, each group would nominate three or four women and they would come with their ideas and we looked . . . at what [would] be the emphasis for the year.[12]

Phyllis Coard, NWO president, aptly expressed the objective of the organization when she noted that "the main aim was to have programmes to cover the needs of women of all types, NJM, Gairyite, GNP, old, young and all classes".[13] Tessa Stroude took the issue further when she claimed: "The objectives of the organization were to [help] women to understand what the revolution meant to them as women; to become equal in society; to become independent as a person; to understand the programmes of the revolution like the Centre for Popular Education [programme]; to develop their skills; to become involved in the militia; and to understand international issues."[14]

THE WOMEN'S DESK

The Women's Desk was established in June 1979 and acted as an intermediary between the government and the NWO. Tessa Stroude and Rita Joseph were full-time workers at the Women's Desk. Tessa Stroude explained how the Women's Desk worked in collaboration with the NWO:

> Although the Women's Desk was responsible on the government level, the NWO had workers in the field. They were the ones to identify people of need . . . . We tried not to make it partisan, so it wouldn't really be people [who were] . . . NJM supporters [who] would get the benefits, but the people who really needed it. It was said that we (NJM supporters) did all the work [while the] Gairy people [got] all the benefits, but Gairy people were the poor people and they were the ones [who] needed it.[15]

The NWO, working alongside the Women's Desk, set its work plans for 1981. These were to:

1. Ensure efficient and fair distribution of free milk [and] the effective operation of the house repair programme.
2. Ensure that health centres are repaired and epidemics are prevented through constant clean-ups of the communities.
3. Ask the Ministry of Health to organise mass health and first aid education.
4. Discuss with the Ministry of Communications and Works the areas most in need of water.
5. Maintain an active interest in [the] bringing of electricity to our rural areas.
6. Organise the full participation of all women in the Community School Day Programme (CSDP).

7.   Mobilise women to step up their work in the CPE [Centre for Popular Education] programme.

8.   Encourage NWO members to play an active part on [farmers'] boards and trade unions.[16]

Despite the efforts of the NWO to extend the organization to become a mass movement, it can be reasonably argued that it remained a tool of the PRG. Every government agency or party arm, whether socialist or capitalist, tends to propagate the views of the regime in power. If the NWO remained, to a large extent, an arm of the PRG (as it did), it fulfilled its function as part of the ruling party. It should be noted that one of the criticisms of the Gairy regime was its lack of accountability to the people. The PRG sought to rectify this by holding public meetings and explaining the programmes of the revolution to the people. The NWO groups met once a week and discussed matters of relevance to their individual communities. Once a month or once every two months, a member of the NWO executive attended these groups and explained the programmes of the revolution.

ACTIVITIES OF NWO, WOMEN'S DESK AND PRG FOR WOMEN

An examination of the activities of the NWO, the Women's Desk and the policies of the PRG as a whole would test the successes and failings of the previously mentioned work plans. The NWO was able to distribute approximately four thousand kilograms per month of free dried milk as well as cooking oil to the needy.[17] Through its efforts, cooperatives were established which provided employment to both women and men. For example, Patsy Romain, executive member of the NWO, remarked on the establishment of the Byelands Bakery Cooperative: "The government had a campaign going around to grow more food. It [was] the idle lands for idle hands programme to help ease unemployment. When we looked around Byelands there were no idle lands . . . Then the suggestion came for a bakery. The National Cooperative Development Agency did a feasibility study. The bakery has helped to employ ten sisters from NWO in Byelands and four men."[18] At Requin in St David, an agricultural cooperative was established which employed three women, one of whom was the president of the National Cooperative Development Agency, Patricia Hypolite. Patricia Hypolite noted that the cooperative planned to put four and a half acres in pumpkin, and smaller plots in tomatoes, carrots and cabbages.[19] A dried fruit project was also established in Mount Rose.

The NWO, along with the Women's Desk, took an active role in voluntary projects like road repair, building community centres, community clean-up and island-wide beautification programmes, for painting bridges and walls, clearing drains and overgrown shrubbery and house rebuilding. By December 1982, one in every nine families had received house repair materials. These families would have been selected by field officers of the NWO from among the poorest families in the island.[20] With financial aid from the Women's Desk, a schoolbooks and uniforms programme got underway. Tessa Stroude explained the difficulty in implementing the programme since there were a large number of very poor families, and most people were part-time wage earners. This presented a problem in identifying those who were most needy. In spite of this, it was one of the NWO's main social welfare programmes. The NWO was also responsible for the creation, by 1981, of six new pre-primary schools and a day nursery. Two of the former were in the island's largest parish, St Andrew, at Byelands and Conference.[21] The government provided training and salaries for the women who ran these schools.

The NWO sought to provide political education for women to make them aware of the problems facing them. Dessima Williams clearly explained this concept:

> We spent time explaining the structure of the world economy to rural women so that when they produce bananas, carry them on their heads for long distances, sell them to the National Marketing Board and are paid the small prices [for them] that they are, they do not think the government is keeping back some of the money and paying them meagre wages. We teach them that we, as one small country, do not control the price for bananas internationally.[22]

In addition, the PRG took measures to ensure that females had the opportunity to be educated to the same standard as males. These measures included:

1. A mass literacy campaign, for example the Centre for Popular Education, which began in September 1980. A high proportion of students were female.

2. First, the reduction of school fees from EC$37.00 to $12.50 per student and then free secondary education.

3. The adoption of a policy of teaching technical subjects, for example, agricultural science, carpentry, and metal work to both girls and boys.

4. A greatly increased number of scholarships to universities and further education at institutions abroad (108 scholarships in 1979 as compared to 3 in 1978), 22 per cent of which went to women.[23]

The Centre for Popular Education conducted a preliminary census in April 1980 that revealed an 8 to 10 per cent illiteracy rate. In November 1980, the Centre for Popular Education registered 2,738 illiterates, 58 per cent of whom were women.[24] More women than men volunteered as teachers in the Centre for Popular Education programme.

The national coordinator of the literacy programme was a twenty-four-year-old woman, Valerie Gordon (formerly known as Cornwall). A teacher by profession, she grasped the opportunity to serve her nation in its literacy drive. As coordinator, her duties included coordinating the work of the Centre for Popular Education in all the parishes; working on the National Technical Commission in fundraising, planning programme design, the development of methodology and pedagogy; and also co-authoring the Centre for Popular Education books. She felt that the programme was very successful in ensuring students' acquisition of skills in reading and writing, organization building at the community level and bridging the inter-generational gap within the communities. It also served as a good learning experience for the nation. Grenadians learnt about their communities and their culture and wrote their own textbooks, which was a major achievement in terms of the quality of the books. Jacqueline Creft, minister of education, declared that the "new education" was geared to equipping "all people not just a few, with the self knowledge and self confidence which would motivate them to make important decisions about and participate fully in their country's development".[25]

In an attempt to further enhance education, the PRG implemented the National In-Service Teacher Education Programme (NISTEP) and the Community School Day Programme. The programmes complemented each other. The NISTEP programme ensured that a number of female and male teachers would attain their teacher certificate while they remained in the serv-

Jacqueline Creft, former minister of education. Courtesy Peggy Nesfield.

ice. The teachers were to attend the NIS-TEP courses one day a week during the school year and for several weeks during the vacation. The day that was missed was filled in by volunteer teachers from the community, who taught a wide range of practical subjects like handicraft, agriculture, sewing, fishing, the island's cultural heritage and its oral history. Most of the teachers of Community School Day Programme were women. While they were not highly paid, the programme offered them a source of income and a sense that they were participating in something meaningful.[26]

The NWO also encouraged women to take up the challenge of doing non-traditional jobs. According to Phyllis Coard, the NWO's ideological stance embraced the dictum that "women were equal to men. They were equal in society." She noted that women were registered for carpentry, welding and woodwork courses at the Technical and Vocational Institute. A project for women in motor mechanics was established at Queen's Park in St George's. Women also registered at the True Blue Fisheries School in St George. When the National Transport Service buses came on stream in 1980, it was decided at the parish council level that all the conductors should be female.[27]

Women also assisted in the development of the youth through work in the National Youth Organization and the Pioneers. Both groups organized the nation's youth and began the process of instilling in them important qualities, such as discipline, self-confidence, creativity, commitment, leadership and patriotism. Pioneer activities included talent searches, quizzes, drama exercises and debates. All these activities came to fruition at Pioneer camp in 1981. Lorraine Felix, executive member of the National Youth Organization responsible for the pioneers, noted that the children were "encouraged to grow and be the new people and the new society, to study, work and play hard".[28]

One of the most difficult tasks of the NWO, according to Peggy Nesfield (member of the St George's NWO and chief of protocol), was the attempt to break through the patriarchal and macho attitude embedded in the fabric

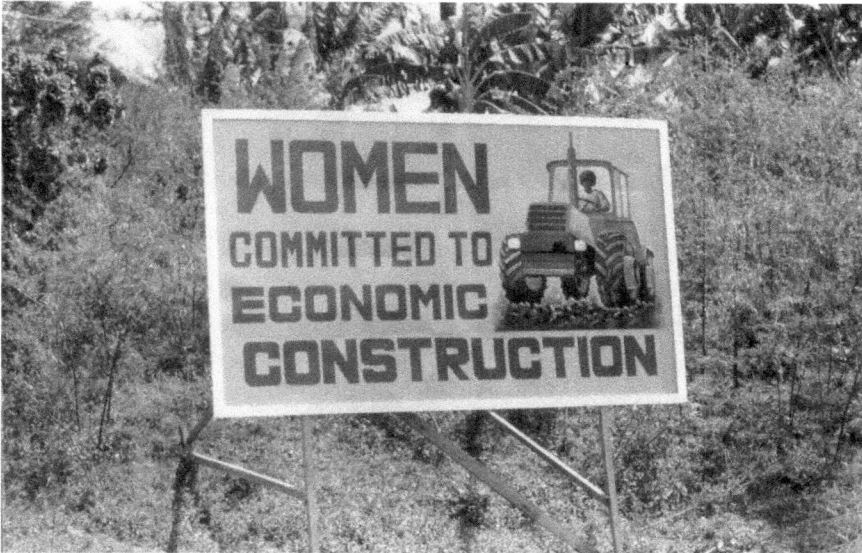

Billboard to motivate women. Courtesy Peggy Nesfield.

of Grenadian society. Within approximately four to five months of taking office, the PRG launched two significant initiatives for women: maternity leave (which was written into the law in October 1980) and equal work for equal pay).[29] Before these initiatives were drawn up, the maternity leave proposal was sent to different organizations, including other women's groups like the Lionesses, the Soroptomists, the Presbyterian Women's Guild and the Women's League. The organizations made their suggestions about what they thought should be amended. Road workers were among those who benefited from the call for equal work for equal pay. Prime Minister Maurice Bishop warned employers of the consequences they would face if they discriminated against women or asked for sexual favours in order for them to gain employment. Yet there were those, both female and male, who were against this empowering of women. Some older teachers and nurses scoffed at the idea of maternity leave. Their view was that since they had not been given that privilege, it should not be extended to the younger generation. In May 1981, one female employer was fined five hundred dollars (EC) for failing to comply with the Maternity Leave Law.[30]

Peggy Nesfield noted that this attitude extended into the personal lives of women. NWO activists, she noted, had a hard task to educate women about the role men should play in their homes. She noted that women complained of men shirking their responsibilities as fathers. Many single mothers were frustrated as they sought to keep their jobs and manage the home. The NWO and Women's Desk had to deal with the problem of incest and offered sex education for women.[31] This issue of attitude change, however, was not easily rectified and it remained a thorn in the side of the NWO throughout the revolutionary period. In fact, male chauvinism in relation to women's work in the domestic arena reared its head at the highest level of power in the PRG, namely the Central Committee, as will be discussed later (see "Shortcomings of the PRG" in this chapter).

The PRG passed the School Children's Immunization Law (or People's Law No. 41 of 1980). Under this law 12,600 children were immunized against five infectious diseases.[32] A new maternity unit was constructed between 1981 and 1982. The X-ray unit and laboratory facilities at the St George's General Hospital were refurbished. There was a reduction in the doctor to patient population ratio from 1:4,864 in 1977 to 1:2,816 in 1982. There was also a reduction in the dentist to patient population ratio from 1:53,706 in 1977 to 1:21,400 in 1982.[33] In 1981, Dr Annette Alexis became the first Grenadian female ophthalmologist to practice in Grenada.

In May 1979, the PRG passed the Trade Union Recognition Law, (or People's Law No. 9 of 1979). It made the recognition of trade unions compulsory for employers once a poll positively indicated the workers' choice of a union. The result was that the percentage of unionized workers jumped from 30 per cent to 80 per cent between May 1979 and May 1980.

Women dominated three of the largest trade unions at the membership level. Prior to this, trade unions were male dominated entities. The Grenada Manual and Mental Workers Union, which spearheaded radical changes for workers, did have a number of female organizers at the village level, including Germaine Pope. However, there were no females on the executive of any of the unions until the mid 1970s. By 1975, there were females representing categories of workers in trade unions. For example, the Grenada Civil Service Association (now the Public Workers Union) had females representing the nurses and clerical workers. According to the records, J. Japal represented the nurses in 1975.[34] Jeanette Dubois (1981–1983) headed the Grenada Union of

Teachers, one of the largest unions. Its membership comprised over 60 per cent women. Jeanette Dubois's leadership role in the trade union movement began in the late 1970s when she held the posts of secretary then vice president of the St John's Branch. Her responsibilities as president of the union included presiding over executive meetings, representing the union at regional and international conferences and meetings and collective bargaining and settling disputes. During her period in office, the health plan and credit union was started. The union fully supported the PRG's NISTEP programme. Her contribution to the union brought about the revival of the branches in the rural areas, for example St Andrew, St Patrick and St David. By 1983, she was president of the Trade Union Council.[35]

In the areas of decision and policy making, women were positively affected. Between 1979 and 1982, there was one female minister and two deputy ministers. Jacqueline Creft was minister of education, youth and social affairs; Phyllis Coard was deputy minister of women's affairs and president of the NWO and a member of the Central Committee; Claudette Pitt was deputy minister for community development; Dessima Williams was Grenada's representative to the Organization of American States. There was one female cabinet secretary and four female permanent secretaries: Marcella David was cabinet secretary; Dorcas Braveboy was permanent secretary in the Ministry of Health, Lew Bourne in the Ministry of Housing, Gloria Payne-Banfield in the Ministry of Planning and Florence Rapier in the Ministry of Legal Affairs. In programme planning, women held key roles in education, telecommunications, health and agriculture. For example, Valerie Gordon was the national coordinator for the Centre for Popular Education, Sharon Fletcher was the national coordinator for Community School and Day Programme, Candia Alleyne was coordinator of the Food and Nutrition Council, Yvonne James was health planner in the Ministry of Health, Jane Belfon was director of tourism, Pamela Buxo was secretary for tourism,

Valerie Gordon, former coordinator of the Centre for Popular Education programme. Courtesy Valerie Gordon.

Joan Ross was programme director for Television Free Grenada, Regina Taylor was general secretary of the Agency for Rural Transformation, Angela Cape was deputy manager of the National and Marketing Importing Board and Bridget Horsford was manager of the Agro-Industries Plant. Monica Joseph became Grenada's first female judge in 1982. She also acted as a diplomat, negotiating with James Mitchell's administration in St Vincent on the issue of escaped prisoners.[36]

The PRG and the NWO also encouraged women to join the militia and the army. Women joined the militia in different capacities. Some learned to fight, while others joined as cooks, first aid attendants and news runners (to take information in times of crises from one part of the island to the other, without being caught.) Albertina Alexander, then seventy-three-years-old, beamed with pride when she remembered her stint in the militia. She recalled, "There were three of us in the kitchen (army camp Fort Frederick). We cooked three separate set[s] of food. We checked the men and the plates. The men use to say, 'Ah want mammy Tina food'. When it was ready one of us would call out 'Come an' get it' and you would see them running coming down."[37]

By 1981, women constituted 35 per cent of the militia corps. The majority of casualties from the bomb blast – probably intended to eliminate the leadership of the PRG – on 19 June 1980 were women.[38] Far from intimidating women, the bomb blast catapulted women into a new consciousness and a new militancy. Slightly more than 50 per cent of all new militia volunteers after the tragedy were women. Of the ninety recruits in the Grand Roy militia, thirty-four were women. Prior to this, there were twenty-seven persons in that militia group with only five women.[39] An eighteen-year-old woman recovering from injuries after the bomb blast epitomizes the defiance of women in the face of the threat. She noted: "that still can't stop me from going to rallies, for as long as I have strength I going".[40]

Women avidly expressed their support for the militia and the revolution in poetry, songs and interviews in the local newspapers. The revolution saw a burst of cultural expression from the Grenadian people and women were by no means excluded. Merle Collins and Christine David, both writers, made their mark on the world stage during this era. For the first time in Grenada's history, a female, Lady Cinty, won the National Calypso monarch contest in

Grenada Union of Teachers' May Day Rally, 1981. Courtesy Peggy Nesfield.

1983. An example of this explosion of women onto the creative scene is seen in the popularity of the poem of a young teacher from the parish of St David, Helena Joseph. She made her poem famous through frequent public readings around the nation. She wrote:

> I Militia say
> I conscious Militia say
> You can't leave us to suffer
> Is the heavy roller for you Mr Exploiter
> Ah pick up me AK oppressor
> To fight you counter
> To free the worker
> To build Grenada
> I Militia will never surrender.[41]

In the face of regional and international pressure, spearheaded by the United States, women pledged their support and willingness to defend their revolution. United States president Ronald Reagan had repeatedly commented that the new Grenada airport was being used as a military base. Susan Lake (pseudonym) of St George noted: "We must always be on the alert, we must defend our revolution, the free milk, free health care, free education, the road projects and so on."[42] Aletta May (pseudonym) of the Prime Minister's Ministry called on the people to "stand firm. We should encourage other comrades to be alert and be vigilant. Comrades should be prepared to defend the revolution, to look out for all counter-revolutionaries and be on [their] guard. I am prepared to defend the revolution."[43] Claire Steeples (pseudonym) gave her experience of being in the People's Revolutionary Army (PRA) and being a student. She noted that she was not discriminated against because of her sex: "They (commanders) put us (herself and her sister) in front during training sessions, to do as much as the guys did."[44] She noted that a number of soldiers entered the army with literacy problems and so she got involved in education within the army. Courses were offered for those doing the School Leaving Certificate and O-level subjects. Even though she taught and worked in the armed forces, her education was not neglected. She proudly stated that she received the first scholarship of the revolution. The army funded her A-level education at the Institute for Further Education. She was responsible for counter-intelligence in the army. She gathered information on what was happening in the country and on possible threats to the revolution. She noted that her daily routine was to "change from [my] school to army uniform, [then teach], [do] sentry duties and [participate in military] training as well".[45]

As a women's group, the NWO was always questioned about its stance on feminism. The organization took the orthodox Marxist line and stated that "the NWO is not a feminist organization. We have taken the egalitarian approach. Women make up at least 50 per cent of our people; they therefore make up half of Grenada's potential for development."[46] They therefore saw men as partners in the struggle, working alongside them to overcome the forces – poverty, illiteracy, dependency, underdevelopment and neo-colonialism – that kept their society oppressed. They sought to show that advancement could be attained through women's active participation and leadership in the revolution as a whole.

WOMEN'S VIEWS ON THE REVOLUTION

Women derived substantial benefits from the work of the NWO, the Women's Desk and the PRG as whole. Phyllis Coard commented on what she saw as the most important benefits of the revolution to Grenadian women:

> I would like to emphasize that the main benefit which the revolution, in general, and the NWO brought to women was a psychological one. It was the giving to women of respect from their society which led to a tremendous rise in self-respect among women . . . . The leaders of the revolution, especially Comrade (Cde) Bishop, spoke frequently of values, about the respect to be accorded to women, then they backed it up with actions – the maternity leave law, the CPE [Centre for Popular Education], the primary health care, the distribution of free milk and the insistence by Cde Austin that members of the People's Revolutionary Army support their children. In how many Caribbean countries would you find hundreds of women with no more than primary education confidently leading group meetings, as well as organizing cultural activities, fund-raising, field trips and many other activities? . . . . This is why I said that the tremendous rise in self-respect, self-confidence and leadership skills [was] the main success of the NWO; though, of course, they were equally the successes of the revolution itself with regard to women.[47]

Rita Joseph, Claudette Pitt, Tessa Stroude and other women of the NWO executive shared Phyllis Coard's view. But what was the view of the ordinary women? How did they feel about the NWO and the work of the revolution, as it affected them? A seventy-two-year-old great grandmother from Birchgrove had this to say: "I am with the revolution and the government one thousand and nine per cent. After the revolution we formed our women's group here in Birchgrove. Progress gave me new energy. I wanted to fight on for my grandchildren because I saw in it some future. Woman is real real out now . . . we feeling more confident. We heart open now."[48] Eighteen-year-old Lorraine Felix of Vincennes in the parish of St David had this to say: "I joined the militia, the NWO and the NYO [National Youth Organization] . . . In the NYO we tried to tackle the problems of truancy, identifying children who didn't go to school, visiting their homes, finding out [their] problems and speaking to the parents about education."[49] Twenty-two-year-old Catherine

Mapp of L'Esterre Village in Carriacou reported: "Above almost everything, the revolution has been a revolution for women. Women definitely see it as a change in their direction, something which they could benefit from directly. Free secondary education, free milk distribution, electricity at last in our village and the maternity leave law. These are the things which affect their daily life and make a real difference to them."[50] It should be noted, however, that the last two sources quoted here were essentially governmental and would inevitably reflect pro-PRG views. Anti-PRG views were not recorded in Grenada during the period of the revolution.

There were shortcomings of the NWO, and the PRG was hardly above criticism in its relations with women. There were Grenadian women who vehemently opposed the revolution as a whole and others who opposed aspects of the process. The NWO itself noted its own shortcomings in its work plan for 1983 to 1989, which included political education, organizational and leadership training, community news boards and the NWO newsletter. It noted that there were few members at the executive level who were able to effectively deal with political education and leadership training. There was a lack of sufficient supervision at the national level and a lack of transport to take women to meetings, especially on the west coast, and in St Patrick and St Mark.[51] The organization also faced the problem of women not attending meetings since they had no one to take care of their children. There were programmes to develop day-care facilities. However, there seemed to be no consideration for providing childcare during meetings. Women were expected to come to meetings without their children. While the NWO was involved in vital areas of work, there were other important areas like sports, legal reform and research into women's problems that they did not address.

The NWO has been criticized for encouraging women to enter the field of male-dominated jobs while failing to re-evaluate the female-dominated fields. The NWO, it has been argued, should have given similar encouragement to boys and men to enter such fields, for example home economics, early childhood education and secretarial studies. The organization has also been criticized for not measuring up to its claim to be a mass organization. It has been pointed out that it did not involve middle-class women's organizations. It made no attempt to ally with the existing women's groups or encourage their participation whether or not they had been supportive of the revolution. The older organizations went dormant during the PRG, losing their younger members and craft and nutrition teachers to the NWO. The only exception was the Airport Development Committee that was organized and led by women.[52] In answer to this criticism, Phyllis Coard noted:

> I am not certain whether a women's organization could have been built [to include] all classes of women, without the upper middle-class women dominating the groups, simply because of their higher educational level and much greater self-confidence. Given that the revolution was a revolution of and for the working people, the NWO had to be an organization in which the majority – working-class, peasant and lower middle-class women – led and benefited the most. However, what I think the failure was, was not even to be aware that this would be a problem, and would cause serious hurt feelings and a sense of being excluded among the upper middle-class women who were, after all, part of the society too. Had I been aware of the problem at more than a superficial level, I would then have taken some form of action to reach out to them. As it was, I let my total preoccupation with building an organization that could develop working-class women blind me to the fact that another section of women of the upper middle-class largely felt marginalized. As president of the NWO from 1979 to 1983, I have to take responsibility for that.[53]

The NWO has been charged with being too aggressive in its rhetoric and proposing radical ideas (that marriage was an outdated institution, for instance). Furthermore, certain crucial laws affecting women were not dealt with. For example, the maximum punishment for rape remained a minimal three-year sentence, and restrictive laws against illegitimate children remained in place up to 1983.[54] The organization was further criticized for not confronting the issue of the abuse of power and violence within the revolution. The NWO supported the involvement of women and youth in the armed forces.[55] The revolution, as whole, has been criticized by women both inside and outside of Grenada for the extension of violence (that is, the spread of violence) in the society, the breaking up of families and the reduction of regular church-going during the period. One woman, Mary Jane (pseudonym), noted that the community clean-up was held on Sundays. Some of the older folks preferred to go to church on that day; however, they were "reported" to the revolution by their own children. Older persons, who did not under-

stand the revolutionary process or were opposed to it were seen as being sub-
versive. She also complained of children handling guns such as AK 47s from
an early age. She noted seeing boys between eight and ten-years-old, who
were blindfolded, putting guns together in the Grenville car park in St
Andrew.[56] Mary Jane also claimed that, prior to the revolution, pregnancy outside of marriage was seen as shameful. During the revolution, however, young
girls were encouraged to have children, especially those who joined the militia
and army. They were reportedly told they would produce the flowers of the
revolution.[57] She had risked imprisonment in the mid 1970s to sell the *New
Jewel* newspaper, yet by 1983 she had reservations. She noted, "I was turned
off when, on the first anniversary of the revolution, Daniel Ortega gave
Maurice Bishop a gun from the freedom-loving people of Nicaragua to the
freedom-loving people of Grenada. Guns meant death and destruction. I just
stopped."[58]

Lucy Lace (pseudonym) complained of a lack of freedom of speech: "You
could not say anything with a semblance of disagreement; you had to be careful what you said."[59] One woman noted that she did not get involved in the
revolution because "it was a coup and it was not as popular as they tried to
make it [out to be]".[60] Another believed that the revolution was in league with
the Russians. She claimed that "a Russian" viewed the St George's harbour
from her home. She claimed that the plan was for "the Russians to take over
the area overlooking the harbour". She believed that the proposed International Airport was really "a jumping-off point for the Russians to take over
South America".[61] This aligned with the theory advocated by some writers
that Grenada was to be used by the Soviet Union as a launching pad for
moving into South America.

As far as the other programmes of the revolution were concerned, there
were problems with NISTEP and the Community School Day Programme.
Often, there were not enough volunteer members of the community willing
to take classes when the teachers went off to their training programme. It
was noted that at the Methodist school in St Andrew, there were often only
three teachers left to handle the children.[62]

SHORTCOMINGS OF THE PRG

While the PRG did take the placement of women in areas of decision-making further than the previous regime, it has still been criticized for not taking the process far enough. For example, there were no female majors, lieutenants or colonels in the army. Bernard Coard (deputy prime minister of the PRG and member of the Central Committee) explained why this was the case in Grenada. He noted that the under-representation of women in positions of power in the military was a global phenomenon, since the army has "always been conceived of traditionally as a male preserve".[63] However, in relation to Grenada, he recalled that there was one woman in the armed wing of the NJM or National Liberation Army. This army existed from 1973. He noted: "She received exactly the same military training as the men. She was on par with them, militarily, in terms of skill and training. However, when the revolution came, she branched out into other areas of work, non-military areas of work. Had she stayed in the military, she would have been one of the top commanders."[64] He further noted that the men who filled the positions as commanders in the PRA were members of the National Liberation Army. They had proved themselves through the years and, as such, gained senior positions in the army. He was of the opinion that, over time, some women would have risen to the top, but by 1983 none of them had.

The women who did hold decision-making posts in the PRG had the serious problem of balancing their work with their home life. In May 1982, Phyllis Coard, as chairperson of the Women's Committee of the NJM, noted the complaints of her colleagues and wrote a letter to the Political Bureau. She identified the following as the main problems.

> The special problems of women with children are rarely if ever considered when fixing hours of study classes and committee or PCB (Parish Coordinating Bodies) meetings. When some women members raised the problems of having no one to leave their babies with at 5:00 a.m. or no one to get the children breakfast or ready for school, the attitude of many heads of PCB's, committees and study groups has frequently been that "you just have to solve that problem". As a result, some women members have been deemed "indisciplined' [for] missing meetings, others have taken serious risks with their children like

leaving babies in the care of young children of ten or twelve years. Some have faced criticisms [from] the masses for "neglecting" their children.

The maternity leave law must be respected by the party. The experience over the past two years shows us that even some senior party comrades expect that women members will continue political work almost until she gives birth and will take on work again shortly afterwards. Furthermore, women with babies or young children should always be consulted before being directed to go abroad for the party, to ensure that arrangements can be made to look after [their] children.

The party should seek actively to change the attitude of party men to the questions of babysitting, child care, housework and should ensure that all fathers support their children equally, both financially and psychologically. The party should make male party members understand that it [is] their duty to spend equal time looking after their children whether or not they live in the same house as the mother. Party men are *pressing* sisters to have babies for them yet afterwards they take little or no responsibility for them. All party members,' men and women, must share housework and baby care equally in order that both should have an equal opportunity to develop as party cadres. Otherwise women party cadres will always be held back in their development . . . relative to what they are capable of.[65]

At a meeting on 22 September 1982, the Political Bureau admitted that there was a lack of day-care centres and pre-primary schools, men had shown a lack of concern and support for the women and the women had developed an attitude of laziness and ill discipline.[66] By July 1983, the matter reached the Central Committee, yet little was done to address the women's plight and the chauvinist attitude of the men remained. According to the Central Committee, the work of the Women's Committee was weak, due to "deep, petty bourgeoisie trends" in some of the members, though concrete attempts were being made to solve the problems faced by women through the provision of day-care centres, kindergartens, pre-primary facilities, and skills training. The Central Committee further noted, following standard Marxist rhetoric, that it "would not encourage weakness, or breed cynicism or put the party in the position of a privileged clique or encourage disunity between men and women in the party's rank and file".[67]

It has been alleged that one of the flaws of the revolution was that men within the PRG and NJM used their positions of power to extract sexual favours from women. Byron Campbell, Chairman of the National Transport Service, claimed that some women were penalized for not submitting. He presented evidence of at least one woman who was accepted to study in Bulgaria, but who was refused permission to go because she failed to perform sexual favours demanded of her by a member of the PRG. He noted: "We accuse the Gairy regime, but we have to be honest with ourselves. This happened to some extent during the revolution. It may not have been widespread, but there were incidences of it happening."[68]

In general, Marxist ideology does not deal with the relations between men and women. Sheila Rowbotham noted that "Marx's thought could be applied by women to reveal and illuminate aspects of their oppression, but in his work, women's relations to men and women's capacity to shape society and culture are extrinsic. Although Marx was formally committed to the legal emancipation of women and to their right to work, his intellectual passion was not directed towards the relations between men and women but towards class."[69]

Frederick Engels, in his seminal Marxist work *The Origins of the Family, Private Property and the State*, did not shed much light on the issue either. While he saw women's subordination as being linked to certain social processes along with biological differences, he did not address the relations between men and women. He stated that women's emancipation could only take place when their participation in social production had increased and domestic work claimed only an insignificant amount of their time. He did not say whether they could obtain this with the support of men. Within the Grenadian context, the Central Committee followed orthodox Marxist doctrine which did not provide them with a cue to follow regarding the relations between men and women. In spite of the attempts of the Political Bureau and the Central Committee to "sweep the problem under the carpet", the problem was a very real one and the issue remained a thorn in the side of the regime until its collapse. Two of the women in positions of power explained how they coped. Tessa Stroude noted:

> Every day of the week there was something to do (NWO meeting[s], militia, selling of party papers, community work and party meetings). You hardly had

enough time to yourself. We were doing it because we were committed to a cause and we were doing what was best for a cause and we were doing what was best for the country. You found ways and means to continue family life but it was difficult.[70]

She recalled taking the children with her to do party work:

I used to take the children with me. As NWO organizer I used to do spot checks. I would go up to the country and I took the children in the back of the car with me . . . . As party members, we had (herself and her husband, Lieutenant Chris Stroude) to sell the party paper on Saturdays. We would make it a family thing; we would sell the paper together and take the children with us for the walk. On Sunday morning, [it was] compulsory for us . . . to go to a community and do community work. We took the children. The children enjoyed it. They had fun, they could play and it was good for them, too, to understand the concept of community. In the evening (Sunday) we took the children to the beach.[71]

Another such couple called in baby sitters: "They did the work of mother and father for us."[72] The mother recalled the "serious debates" held in the party on the issue and noted that the men treated it "chauvinistically".

COLLAPSE OF THE REVOLUTION

Some of the women within the PRG and NJM agreed to the proposal for joint leadership that led to the demise of the revolution. These discussions were held in mid September 1983. The proposal for joint leadership was the culmination of a one-year discussion on methods to enhance the "application of a Leninist standard of discipline, consistency, and seriousness" within the party and the government. The members of the Central Committee who proposed joint leadership were of the opinion that little or nothing had been done towards the "consolidation of a Leninist vanguard". Joint leadership was an attempt to marry the strengths of Bishop and Coard. Bishop would concentrate on work among the masses (focus on propaganda, production, organs of democracy), militia mobilization and regional and international work, while Coard would concentrate on party organizational development, strategy and tactics.[73] The Central Committee was divided on the issue: while the majority agreed, George Louison, Unison Whiteman and Fitzroy Bain disagreed. Bishop felt it was a vote of "no confidence" against him. Phyllis Coard, as the only female on the Central Committee, agreed with the idea "not only for a short term but on the long term basis". In retrospect, she noted:

> I had mixed feelings. On one hand it was necessary with the amount of work the revolution had undertaken. Maurice became exhausted; he had too much on his plate. It was done based on their strengths. Bernard was not on the Central Committee at the time. It was embarrassing for me. I did not wish to be seen as pushing my husband. It was a difficult situation for me. I represented the women in the party. I had to take the position of what the other women would have wanted, not a personal position. They wanted joint leadership. They were totally frustrated. Women spoke of . . . resigning from the party. Therefore I voted for joint leadership on the sixteenth of September.[74]

While the Central Committee had agreed to joint leadership, the issue was taken before the General Meeting of the NJM on 25 September 1983 for a final decision. Here, some party women voiced their opinion on the issue. It can be seen from their responses that the failure to resolve their problems was intricately tied to what was viewed as the weakness of the party as a whole. It was disappointing to them that, by 25 September 1983, Bishop was still hesitant to implement joint leadership – the sole strategy, in their view to deal with the problems of the party and to push the revolution forward. Edlyn Lambert expressed her shock and disappointment at Bishop's attitude to the decision of the Central Committee and to "democratic centralism and free, frank and honest criticism". She reminded Bishop that, in May 1983, he had called on every party member to walk the extra mile. She then asked, "How can we walk the extra mile if you don't set the pace for us?" She asked him to think of the many lives that would be lost if the party did not come out of the crisis so that the revolution could move forward. Claudette Pitt reminded Bishop that, in a weekend party seminar, he had said democratic centralism was a norm of party life. She expressed her shock to hear his position and his unwillingness, in practice, to accept the Central Committee's decision on joint leadership, and reminded him that in the years before the Revolution he had always singled out the excellent hard work, energy and foresight of Coard.

Faye Thompson, former NJM member.
Courtesy Faye Thompson.

Loraine Lewis noted that the main weakness of the NJM was the failure of its members to be firm. Faye Thompson believed that Bishop's behaviour was unexpected and rude. Maureen St Bernard commented that Bishop's problem was that he did not mingle with the rank and file of the party and, so, could not understand the changes that were taking place within the party. Murie Francois called on Bishop to accept the criticism.[75]

Bishop agreed to joint leadership after this meeting of 25 September 1983. On his return from a trip to Eastern Europe, he reconsidered. He allegedly spread a rumour that Phyllis and Bernard Coard were trying to kill him, and was placed under house arrest. There is a continuing argument about whether or not Bishop actually spread the rumour. It has been argued that Bishop did spread the rumour in order to discredit Bernard and Phyllis Coard in the eyes of the Grenadian public and, thereby, neutralize the perceived threat that Bernard Coard posed to his leadership. It has also been argued that the Coards used the rumour as a pretext to have Bishop arrested and, thus, make it easier for them to seize the leadership of the government. While negotiations were still being held between Bishop and the Central Committee, the Grenadian public took matters into their own hands and staged demonstrations in St George's and Grenville. They had gotten wind of the conflict brewing in the government. They had heard snippets of information about joint leadership, the rumour about Bernard Coard and his wife threatening to kill Bishop and Bishop's house arrest. The demonstrators demanded that the government give a statement on the precise nature of the disagreement. The public eventually stormed Bishop's house (Mount Wheldale) and took Bishop to Fort Rupert. One woman from the parish of St Andrew described her involvement in the demonstrations. She noted that she made placards in the back of her shop. On 18 October, the demonstrators blocked the runway of Pearls Airport "with barrels and stones". She noted that as early as 2:00 a.m. on the Wednesday morning (19 October 1983), people left Grenville and commandeered every vehicle they could find to take them to St George's to free their "Comrade Leader" (Bishop).[76]

Phyllis Coard was convinced that Bishop had spread the rumour and it made her realize how strongly opposed he was to joint leadership. She noted that she and her husband felt threatened on 19 October. The angry crowd had called out to them on freeing Bishop from his house which was in close proximity to that of the Coards: "We coming back for you all." She sent her children to Mount Mortiz and she and Bernard went to Fort Frederick. She said that they felt that the best thing to do was to leave the island until everything had simmered down.[77]

Claudette Pitt, in retrospect, noted that maybe joint leadership was the wrong approach in solving the issues in the party. However, she claimed that those who instilled the fear of losing power in Maurice Bishop were the ones responsible for his death. She argued:

> Maurice did not have the qualities to be leader. Decisions had to be made and you could not please everybody. Maurice tried to do that. Bernard was the party organizer, most of the projects of the revolution were created and started by him . . . . Any problem anyone had, [they] went to Bernard. If you went to Maurice, he would say go to Bernard. Dynamism and charisma are not the only qualities for leadership. This goes back to cultism. There were some who created confusion in his (Maurice's) mind. I blame those who did so for his death.[78]

While she was vehemently against the killing of Maurice Bishop, Claudette Pitt tried to explain the reasons why it happened and the possible psyche of his killers (members of the PRA) She explained: "They were so mad, disappointed and confused. They had no life. Their whole life was dedicated to the revolution. They felt totally disappointed by October nineteenth. Maurice had betrayed them."[79] Faye Thompson further described the mood of some party members on hearing of Bishop's failure to comply with joint leadership. She noted:

> That was the utmost betrayal as a party member, that was what incensed people . . . . Coming out of the September twenty-fifth meeting, everyone [who] was present was on such a high, because you thought that you had

thrashed it out. People had spoken frankly . . . and now for the first time we [were] on the same wavelength, we [were] on the same page, reading the same book and we could move forward.[80]

She felt that Fort Rupert, being a military base, should not have been allowed to be overrun by civilians. Yet, she noted, there was absolutely no justification for the killings. She gave an idea of what the mood was like in the fort on that fateful day and, from her recollections, it seemed as though the battle lines had been drawn. She recalled:

It was after the release of Maurice [that] we took the decision to put the guns in the tunnel (safe spot on Fort Rupert). We spent most of the morning doing that, up until the point when the masses arrived. That was when the soldiers in charge of the fort were arrested and cached. It shows you, then, that the party lines were drawn. As party members, there were nineteen of us. We were [told]: "Wait there and we will deal with you [later]." From there (the room into which they were ordered), we saw people moving with guns that had been retrieved from the tunnel. Vincent Noel was down on the bottom landing saying "All those with militia training come forward and arm [yourselves] because we have some hooligans to deal with on Fort Frederick" (the fort where Coard, Austin and other members of PRG had congregated).[81]

Nancy Lou (pseudonym) was with Maurice Bishop and Jacqueline Creft in their last hour and witnessed the carnage at Fort Rupert. She recalled:

I was making cups of coffee. Matron Grant, Senator, Norris Bain's wife, Merle Hodge, Chris Stroude, Porgie Cherubim, Avis and Jackie were in the room. Jackie said, "I don't like this, I am scared I know these guys go do something stupid." Avis said, "I never see so much people in one place." Then there was a loud explosion. Something pushed me against a wall, physically lifted me. When I looked, Avis was totally dismantled [had been blown to pieces]. There [was] fatty [tissue] floating in blood and body fluid. Where I was, heavy gunfire was hitting the wall. If I got up to run I would get hit. I decided to stay right there. Matron Grant was praying, saying "Stop the hands of the slaughterers Jesus." Maurice said, "See where the firing is coming from." I lost it. I said to myself if I had to die, let me die with no pain. I was about to stand up [but] Senator threw himself at me and locked my neck. Porgie said, "I would try to see if there is anything I could do. Langaigne, hold your fire, there are many

injured people in here." "Drop your fu—
—g guns and come out with your hands
in the air." "There is no one with guns in
here." The threat was repeated. Maurice
said, "Let the women and children go." I
was covered in blood. I could not lift my
right hand [because] a bullet had hit me. I
felt like sticks were poking me in my side.
Jackie Creft held on to my pants, what
was left of my jeans. Gemma Belmar was
still breathing [but] there was a bullet
straight through her head. Vincent Noel
was lying in the veranda. He said, "Help
me, help me." I proceeded to go down the

*Avis Ferguson, died at Fort Rupert, 19
October 1983. Courtesy Peggy Nesfield.*

steps. Jackie held on to my sleeve. Someone said, "Look at Jackie Creft. Don't
let the mother so and so get away." I got to the hospital gate.[82]

Maurice Bishop, Jacqueline Creft, Unison Whiteman and five others (trade
union leaders and supporters of the revolution) were marched to the parade
square at the upper level of the fort and executed. On 25 October 1983, forces
from the United States and the Caribbean invaded Grenada to try to restore
order and return the island to a democratic system of government.

How did the Grenadian people fare in the wake of this? The testimony of
three women gives some idea of their
plight. The first was Lady Esmai Scoon, the
wife of the then governor general. She gave
her story of a night of horror at Government House. Lady Scoon noted:

The PRA were shooting at the building
(Government House). It was coming
from Richmond Hill. We were lying on
the dining room floor. There were US
soldiers on the compound of Government House. PRA armoured cars were
coming through the gate from St Paul's
side during the night. About 8:00 p.m., a

*Lady Esmai Scoon, wife of former gover-
nor general Sir Paul Scoon. Courtesy Sir
Paul Scoon.*

helicopter flew over and blew [them] up. That was frightening, I wept bitterly. At 8:00 a.m. next morning sixty marines walked with us to Queens Park. We passed the back way Mount Royal to River Road, down the steps. There were shots coming from down the steps. I felt I would get one of the bullets. When we got to River Road the people said, "Sir Paul, we behind you. God bless you."[83]

Mary Louise (pseudonym), a former NWO executive member, gave the second testimony. She recalled of her 19 October 1983 experience:

I had lost everything. All I had was my clothes on my back . . . At Point Salines, we used the bathroom at night. It was open and you had to climb up to it. To bathe, a pipe ran overhead with a hose. Four of us had to bathe together. The soldier said "WET" and he opened the water then he closed it and said "SOAP" then "RINSE" . . . . [The parents of one of the detainees] found out where we were and sent us three panties and a toothbrush. We shared the panties and this one toothbrush . . . . Phyllis and the men were kept in small box-like cells and every morning at about 4:00 a.m. the soldiers would beat the cells with pieces of wood and iron.[84]

Claire Steeples (pseudonym) (member of the PRA) the third informant, shared her experiences of defending her country in the wake of foreign invasion. She recalled:

At home, I dressed in my uniform and took my gold chain and my school ring, the only two pieces of jewellery I had, and gave them to my mother and [told her] if anything happens to me, [she should] take care of my boys (she has twin boys) and give each of them these. When I remember this, I get very emotional because I was willing my children to my parents.[85]

She recalled the disappointment they felt that Cuba had not joined the battle on their side. At one point in the battle, she was the only female:

Being in St George's cemetery according to military training our formation was poor and disorganized. We could easily get killed. I was lying on a Syrian grave and I felt a oneness with that grave. On the Park Bridge there was absolutely no cover, we saw F16s and we thought that they were MIGs. We were disappointed. We expected help from Cuba. We would fight for some time and they would come and assist us. The other female soldiers were freaking out and crying and when I looked around after a while, I was the only female, the rest had gone home.[86]

She recalled the brutishness of military training and the effect it had on the psyche: "As a soldier one [learns] who the enemy is and they become not a person who has ideas and thoughts and [who] could reason, but a mere ant that could be crushed. During the invasion, I wanted so much to kill a Yankee soldier, to slit his throat and feel the knife cutting into his flesh. It is amazing what war can do to you."[87] She was inter-rogated by US soldiers and then set free.

In the aftermath of the US invasion of 25 October 1983, twenty persons, including Phyllis Coard, were accused of the murder of Maurice Bishop, his cabinet ministers and others. A trial later ensued in which, among others, seven female witnesses, including the wife of Norris Bain and the mother of Gemma Belmar, gave evidence about when they last saw their loved ones. Anne Bain recalled: "Norris was flat on the floor in front of me. I was clutching his belt and praying . . . . As we were leaving, I looked back and saw Norris for the last time. He was in a line of people coming from the room with their hands up."[88] Sylvia Belmar, mother of Gemma Bel-mar, recalled going from the fort to the hospital where she saw her daughter taken by a few schoolmates. She noted that Gemma was bleeding from a wound to her head, and her school uniform and sneakers were soaked in blood. Gemma never spoke again; she died.[89]

Gemma Belmar, died at Fort Rupert, 19 October 1983. Courtesy Peggy Nesfield.

Seventeen of those accused were convicted, including Phyllis Coard, and were sentenced to be hanged. However, in 1992, a mercy committee met to decide on their fate and they were granted life imprisonment. Between 1992 and 2007 they have filed several motions with the High Court, the Court of Appeal and the Privy Council. In 2001, Phyllis Coard was released for medical reasons. Three of the seventeen were convicted of manslaughter. They served their time and were released in March 2007. The fate of the other thirteen would be determined by a re-sentencing, carded for June 2007.[90]

CONCLUSION

The 13 March socialist revolution took the English-speaking Caribbean by surprise. It was the first time a former British colony was aligned to socialist bloc nations. Women took their place alongside their men-folk and heeded the clarion call for resistance in the form of socialist revolution. What developed was a form of jingoistic nationalism among many Grenadians, men and women alike.

Armed with the ideological arsenal of Marxism, the NJM/NWO (later, the NWO) took the lead in forging women's way forward. There were immutable differences between this group and other existing groups, like the PWA, which remained unresolved. As such, the seeds of discontent were sown, and later resulted in the PWA's outright opposition to the revolutionary process.

Under the leadership of the NWO, Grenadian women succeeded at securing equal work for equal pay, maternity leave, scholarships for tertiary education and free secondary education. Women proved themselves resourceful, industrious and productive through the establishment of cooperatives, for example, in agriculture. The PRG must also be commended for building on the lead taken by Gairy in extending the role of women in positions of power between the period 1979 and 1983.

The revolutionary process led to the empowerment of Grenadian women. However, there were limitations. While job security was ensured with the Maternity Leave Law of 1980, female revolutionary leaders had a difficult time convincing their male counterparts that leave should be extended to them. A number of women rose to positions of power, yet the positions secured tended to be inherently linked to their traditional role of mother and caregiver. Empowerment should also have been extended to their ability to fearlessly express views that were contrary to that of the revolution. However, such vocal resistance had to wait until the process ended.

Conclusion

IN THE PAST, THE STORY of women had been ignored, but today, we see the value of illuminating women's contributions to society. History is often forged by the anvil of riot, strike and revolution, and women have taken part in the formation of its chapters. The world is finally recognizing the rhythm of female voices, and this acclamation serves to reinforce the female sense of identity and possibility.

In the heyday of slavery, the British Caribbean plantocracy valued slave women as work units more than as breeding units. However, in the wake of the abolitionist movement within Britain and with the impending demise of the slave trade, planters sought to implement ameliorative measures that would enhance population growth. In spite of their concerted efforts to encourage reproduction, the slave population of all the sugar colonies, except Barbados, declined until emancipation in 1834. In Grenada, a combination of factors – poor diet, unhealthy surroundings, diseases, a severe work regime and the non-conciliatory attitude of the planters – led to a decline in the population, except in the years 1822, 1827 and 1833. While on the one hand the planters sought to introduce measures to encourage female slaves to reproduce, on the other hand they thwarted their own efforts. For example, it was not until 1825 that the whip was removed from the fields in Grenada. The Legislative Council objected and described women as "troublesome". There were noticeable flaws in Grenada's Guardian Act: the guardians themselves were members of the plantocracy and the upper class and, thus, not objective. Complaints made by slaves were merely ignored.

The planters' efforts did eventually bear fruit; however, it only materialized in 1834 at emancipation. Judging from the efforts of planters in Jamaica and Barbados, there was a long interval between the introduction of ameliorative measures and the gaining of results. Barbados implemented ameliorative measures in about 1750, yet an increase in birth rates only occurred in 1817; Jamaica implemented measures in 1780, but only saw results in 1838; and Grenada saw changes in 1834, forty-six years after implementing ameliorative measures. With the exception of Barbados, the planters' efforts might have had little impact on birth rates. However, emancipation itself did have an impact. The end of gang labour for many female slaves enhanced their fertility rate, their health and their children's health.

The family life of the enslaved was fraught with challenges, such as female sexual exploitation and transient males. Yet evidence from the Roman Catholic Church suggests that the slaves found ways to overcome these obstacles and formed nuclear families. While the dominant class sought to strip them of their dignity, slave women endured and maintained their cultural identity. Big drum dancing, for example, has survived to the present day. The women were and still are the main dancers of the big drum dance. They were also the ones who ensured that the dance was passed along from one generation to the next.

By 1820, Grenada had one of the highest manumission rates in the region, with an average of 2.1 out of every 1,000 slaves being freed each year. For purposes of comparison, St Kitts had a manumission rate of 2.4 slaves per year; Dominica, 2.2; St Lucia, 1.6; and St Vincent, 1.0.[1] In Grenada, like all her British colonial counterparts, free female blacks and coloureds outnumbered males. The high incidence of female manumission has been attributed to male plantation owners rewarding female slaves for sexual or social favours. In Grenada, as elsewhere in the region, once freed, discriminating laws made the lives of former slaves uncomfortable. Also, the threat that they could be sent back into slavery was very real. However, economically, some were able to break through the barriers. Most outstanding were the Philip women who owned land in the tri-island state of Grenada, Carriacou and Petit Martinique.

White females formed a minuscule part of Grenada's society during the period of slavery. Despite the paucity of their numbers, they held a certain amount of power as members of the ruling elite: they owned land, although mainly through inheritance; they owned slaves and punished them. They organized social events and provided education for members of their class. They did not deviate from their prescribed role in plantation society.

The system of slavery was just as degrading and repressive for slave women as it was for men. The slave woman was seen by her owner as a prime worker and a breeder. Slave women held the dichotomous position of person and property, rebel and conservative. On the auction block, in the field and in the masters' home, the female was subjected to the use of chains, collars and whips, and suffered sexual molestation. These were just a few of the innumerable acts of violence perpetrated against her, stemming from notions of dominance and hierarchy and for the purpose of economic gain. As property, she was expected to remain in awe and thralldom of her master, and unquestionably accept this treatment. As a person, however, she had an inherent right to resist. Like her male counterparts, she rebelled against the plantocracy and sought to forge her own future. The withdrawal, by the planters, of "customary" privileges and "indulgences" to mothers, and the precarious position of free children during apprenticeship, strengthened ex-slave women's resolve to leave the plantations after full freedom was granted.

It cannot be questioned that there was an exodus from the estates after full freedom in 1838. There is no conclusive figure for Grenada of the number of women who left plantation labour during apprenticeship and immediately afterward. However, the figures for those who remained were significantly high. Those who left the plantations did so because of the exacting nature of the work and the oppressive attitude of the plantocracy. They also left as part of an ex-slave family strategy. The withdrawal of women from the drudgery of gang labour on the estates enhanced their fertility, their health, and the health of their children. A gendered occupational strategy was adopted by the ex-slaves, whereby the men sought employment as estate labourers or artisans while the women and children were involved in domestic production and selling.[2]

Migration was a form of resistance employed by the ex-slave populace. Between 1839 and 1845, 2,239 ex-slaves migrated from Grenada compared to 959 from St Vincent and 82 from St Lucia.[3] Unfortunately, the data on those who migrated does not indicate what proportion were men and what proportion were women. In this instance, as well, a gendered strategy was adopted. Men migrated in larger numbers than women. For example, in Carriacou men often migrated around the harvest seasons of the year to larger neighbouring islands in search of work, while the women remained at home, cultivated small plots and nurtured the children. By the 1940s, women moved to the islands of Aruba, Bonaire and Curaçao in search of jobs. They faced harsh working conditions and racism. In spite of these trials, they persevered in order to send remittances home to support their children and their extended families.

From the money earned, the ex-slaves sought to make improvements to their homes and build new ones, yet their surroundings were still unsanitary. Health officials did little or nothing to educate the newly freed class on the merits of healthy living conditions. At the end of slavery, little or no work had been done to establish infrastructure in the colony in the form of proper roads, drains, water supply and so on. Due largely to this, the cholera pandemic claimed many lives in Grenada, as it did all over the world.

Life, for the female peasant or estate worker, in the first five decades of the twentieth century was characterized by difficulties. Meagre wages, substandard living and working conditions, a primary education system that was based mainly on imparting religious instruction and only a rudimentary knowledge of the three Rs was the order of the day. In addition to that, women had to deal with grossly inadequate health care, a high infant mortality rate and no maternity leave. Education was a tool of resistance employed by women. A number of mothers made it a point to send their children to secondary schools. They defied European gender ideology and its archaic stance that higher learning should only be for boys. In spite of the differences in the curriculum between boys' and girls' schools, a small minority of women still attained their goal of tertiary education, becoming qualified in the fields of medicine and law.

The attainment of higher wages in the period 1950 to 1979 was a major achievement for both female and male agricultural workers, shop assistants and clerks due to Eric Gairy championing their cause with the colonial masters and plantation owners. They shared in the struggle and reaped the benefits. They had found a saviour. At regional, international and local forums, the Gairy regime projected an image of support for the "promotion, encouragement, and enhancement of women". Under Gairy's government, Grenada had the first female governor in the British Commonwealth, women served as ambassadors and permanent secretaries, and there was a female minister and two parliamentary secretaries.

By the late 1960s and early 1970s, however, a number of women of all classes joined with their male folk in launching a trenchant attack on the Gairy regime. In their opinion, his messianic glory had dwindled in the face of numerous misdemeanours. These included the squandering of government funds, the lack of paid maternity leave, the disparity in wages between men and women, "sexploitation" of women, few education scholarships for women, and the use of punitive measures for anyone who opposed the Gairy regime. A number of women, therefore, threw their support behind the NJM and marshalled Grenada towards socialist revolution.

Were Grenadian women empowered in the period 1979 to 1983? Did the revolutionary process transform their lives? Under the Gairy regime, some women were placed in positions of power within the government. The PRG took the process further. However, how much further the process was taken can be questioned. Grenada was on par with Barbados in this period in terms of the number of women in the highest echelons of government;[4] however, Grenada was ahead of Dominica and Montserrat, for instance.[5] In the number of permanent secretaries in government ministries, Grenada ranked highly in the region. Yet, in spite of its socialist revolution, positions of power held by women in Grenada were of the "kitchen cabinet" type. Grenadian women were placed at the head of ministries like education and women's affairs. While the Grenadian revolution may have numerically increased the number of women in positions of power, it did not revolutionize the type of positions they held. The female government minister was limited to her traditional role as social worker and teacher.

Although the PRG passed legislation for equal pay for equal work, the evidence from estates such as Douglaston and Westerhall showed that, up until 1983, men were still paid more than women. The PRG issued the Maternity Leave Law in 1980. Oral evidence has established that rank and file Grenadian women benefited from this. However, Phyllis Coard, an executive member of the PRG, noted that women in the party were expected to work immediately after delivering their babies. When confronted with the contradictions, the Central Committee took a doctrinaire stance that did not deal with the issue at hand.

The shortcomings of the policies of the PRG and the work of the NWO and the Women's Desk beg the question whether Marxist ideology, in its strictest sense, superimposed onto a Grenadian context had worked. Could Marxist ideas of a classless society work in Grenada or any other Caribbean territory? Marxist ideology did not prioritize the struggle for the equality of women. Grenadian women who demanded equality were not going to get it in this relatively short period of time (1979 to 1983). Grenadian women would have had to experience a revolution within a revolution to address their needs. The argument rages on as to whether or not socialism rather than capitalism was instrumental in enhancing the conditions of women. According to Sheila Rowbotham:

> Marx was primarily concerned with the social consequences of class antago-
> nism not conflict between men and women. By the time he wrote *Capital* he
> concentrated on exploitation and alienation of the worker who sells his or her
> capacity to labour to the owner of capital who gives only part back in the form
> of wages. Though this covers the situation of the working-class women as a
> wage earner, it does not explore the position of women working in the family,
> the sexual relations between men and women, our relationships to our bodies.
> In *Capital* Marx takes for granted the necessity of women's labour in maintain-
> ing and reproducing wage earners but he does not examine this in any detail
> or discuss its implications for women's consciousness.[6]

The failure of Marxism to deal with this issue manifested itself, in the Grenadian context, in strained relations between men and women in the PRG and the NJM. The problems included the responsibility for childcare and household chores devolving largely on women when both sexes had to attend meetings or functions. Also, women within the party were not expected to take maternity leave. The concern of the revolutionary leadership to end women's confinement to traditional roles too often seemed limited to making their labour available to the regime. Women became as free as men to work outside the home while men remained free from work within it.[7] Grenadian women were not alone in this problem of interpersonal relationships between men and women in the revolutionary process. Commenting on the early socialist movement in England, a working-class female shop worker retorted: "Even my Sunday leisure was gone[.] I soon found out a lot of Socialist talk about freedom was only talk and these Socialist young men expected Sunday dinners and huge teas with home made cakes, potted meats and pies exactly like their reactionary fellows."[8]

Commenting on the Indian experience, Rowbotham noted that the communist's imbued women with a vision of a future society based on equality and well-being. Their ideas of universal equality, however, failed to address actual gender differences, which had social and cultural consequences for women. The Communist Party tended to blame women for infidelities and assumed childcare was the woman's responsibility.[9] This was clearly manifested in the line taken by the Grenadian Central Committee in response to complaints by women. They referred to the women as exhibiting "deep petty bourgeois trends". They were defined as being "lazy and ill disciplined".[10]

The Revolution of 1979 attained victories for women in the areas of education, health, housing and representation in government. Yet there were shortcomings, such as limited equal work for equal pay, problems of implementation of maternity leave for NJM members, and the absence of females in positions of power in the army. It can be ascertained that the transformation was not complete.

Two centuries have passed. Grenadian women have been caught in a maelstrom of incessant struggle against varying forces of domination. They formed a cohesive phalanx bent on resistance. Their resistance took many forms: subtle nuances, feigned acceptance, synchronized strikes and artifice, and insurgency. In these centuries past, they were tried and challenged by systems quiescent with paternal despotism, yet they stood resolute, dauntless, in their quest to make their voices heard and to be counted as making a worthwhile contribution to their society.

Postscript

IN THE AFTERMATH OF the 1979 Revolution, the Ministry of Women's Affairs was replaced by a smaller Women's Affairs Department. In 2000, the name changed from Women's Affairs to Gender and Family Affairs. Presently, there is a division of Gender and Family Affairs under the Ministry of Social Development. The division is currently working on a gender policy, which is at the draft stage.

The Maternity Leave Act passed under the PRG was amended in 1989. The amended act stipulates that the employer must pay 40 per cent of the woman's earnings for two months' maternity leave and that the National Insurance Scheme must pay 60 per cent. In 1998, the National Insurance Scheme increased its payment by 5 per cent. The criteria for an employee to qualify for paid leave from an employer remained the same as for the period 1979 to 1983. The National Insurance Scheme's criteria for qualification state, among other things, that (1) the claimant must have been registered for thirty weeks with the scheme, (2) the claimant must have paid contributions into the scheme for twenty weeks, and (3) the claimant must be between the ages of sixteen and sixty. In 1994, the National Insurance Scheme introduced a maternity grant, which is paid to the husband of a woman who did not qualify for a benefit.

In the post-1983 period, there was at least one female minister appointed by each subsequent government. Under the New National Party (1984–1988), there were two female ministers: Pauline Andrews and Grace Duncan. Under the National Democratic Congress government (1990–1995), there was one, Joan Purcell. Also in this period there was the first female president of the senate, Margaret Neckles. Winnifred Strachan served as the first female leader of the opposition (GULP) between 1990 and 1995. Under the New National Party (1995–2007), there were six female ministers of government. In 2007, the ministers were as follows: Brenda Hood, responsible for the Ministry of Tourism, Civil Aviation and Culture; Ann David-Antoine, responsible for Health and the Environment; Clarice Modeste-Curwen, responsible for the Ministry of Communications, Works and Public Utilities; Claris Charles, responsible for the Ministry of Education and Labour; Yolande Bain-Horsford, responsible for the Ministry of Social Development; and Emmaline Pierre, responsible for the Ministry of Youth Development. Also, in 2007, there were seven female permanent secretaries in the Ministry of Tourism, the Ministry of Sports, the Ministry of Health, the Ministry of Agriculture, the Prime Minister's Ministry and the Department of Personnel and Management Services. On 8 July 2008, the National Democratic Congress won the general election. Under the present National Democratic Congress administration, there are three female ministers of government: Glenis Roberts – minister of tourism; Franka Bernadine – minister of education; and Ann Peters – minister of health. Joan Purcell is president of the senate. The seven female permanent secretaries under the previous administration have remained.

The PRA was disbanded with the collapse of the revolution in 1983. The Royal Grenada Police Force – which consisted of fire, immigration, coast-guard and regular police branches, as well as a special branch and drug squad and prosecution branches – was revamped and now includes a para-military branch. The Royal Grenada Police Force, however, still remains a male dominated entity. The highest rank attained by a female – Magdeline Duncan (1990–1995) – within the Royal Grenada Police Force was that of superintendent of police. In 2007, there were three females holding the post of inspector of police. They have now been promoted to assistant superintendent of police. These three positions of inspector of police were filled by other female officers. One more such position was added. Thus there were four female inspectors of police in 2009.

Women have conquered some of the traditionally male dominated jobs like the legal profession. Between 1989 and 2007, women held the prestigious positions of crown counsel, director of public prosecution, registrar and deputy registrar.

The opportunity for free education offered by the PRG helped to make secondary and tertiary education attainable by the Grenadian populace, especially women. Over the last twenty-five years, statistics in education have revealed more females attending secondary schools than males. Girls have been bestowed the Marryshow Award for excellent performance in the Caribbean Secondary Education Certificate Examinations sixteen times in twenty-four years. Three of these young ladies, Akima Paul, Ferdisha Snagg and Kaywana Raeburn, have won the Caribbean Secondary Education Certificate Caribbean Award.

Women's groups like the YWCA and the Mother's Unions of the various churches continued their work in the post-Revolution years. However, the close ties between women's groups and political parties have diminished. Today, the main women's group in Grenada is the Grenada National Organization of Women, which is a non-governmental organization that was formed on 23 April 1995. The organization's mission is to create a social and culture change in the power relations between women and men. They aim to do this through sensitization campaigns that promote equal participation in the household, the community, the workplace and in everyday life. The organization acts as an umbrella for all women's groups in Grenada. It provides resources and support, such as leadership training, technical expertise, and facilitates celebrations of international events, like International Women's Day.

The Grenada National Organization of Women has been involved in the promotion of gender equality in the workforce. It has assisted the United States Agency for International Development, the T.A. Marryshow Community College and the New Life Organization in running skills training programmes. It has helped to prepare women and men to enter the construction, marine and tourism industries in the period after Hurricane Ivan (7 September 2004). The organization was also involved in setting up the Home Career Programme. This programme enabled twenty-six women, from the parishes of St Patrick and St Mark, to graduate from a course on caring for the elderly. In January 2007, the Grenada National Organization of Women conducted a Gender Sexuality and HIV Workshop with secondary school students, as well as a workshop for educators of Health and Family Life Education in October 2006.

Grenadian women have proven their resilience through the trials and triumphs of two centuries and beyond. They were far from being apathetic observers of history, but were, in fact, active participants in directing its course. They challenged plantation authority by running away, through disobedience and sabotage. They endorsed the ascension of a people's messiah who openly defied the authority of the British government. Through riots and uprisings, they sanctioned the socialist revolution and played an integral part in its existence. They have used, and continue to use, education as a means of advancement. The sacrifices of our "foremothers" have given us a sanguine view of the future. We should commemorate and celebrate their achievements.

Notes

INTRODUCTION

1.   Elizabeth Fox-Genovese, "Strategies and Forms of Resistance: Focus on Slave Women in the United States", in *In Resistance: Studies in African Caribbean and Afro-American History*, ed. Gary Okihiro (Amherst: University of Massachusetts Press, 1986), 149.

2.   Lucille Mathurin-Mair, "Women Field Labourers in Jamaica During Slavery", in *Slavery Freedom and Gender: The Dynamics of Caribbean Society*, ed. Brian Moore, B.W. Higman, Carl Campbell and Patrick Bryan (Kingston: University of the West Indies Press, 2001), 188.

3.   Hilary Beckles, *Centering Women: Gender Relations in Caribbean Slave Society* (Kingston: Ian Randle, 1999), xxii.

4.   Letter from Fred Maitland to Honourable John Harvey Esquire, 1806, CO 101/43.

5.   Bridget Brereton, "Caribbean Women in the Post-Emancipation Century, 1838–1938: Agenda for Research" (paper presented at the UNESCO conference Slavery and the Shaping of Caribbean Society, University of the West Indies, St Augustine, Trinidad, December, 1988), 4.

6.   Edward Cox, "Indian Migration to Grenada and St Vincent, 1857–1885" (paper presented at International Conference on Asian Diasporas in the Americas, University of the West Indies, St Augustine, Trinidad, August 2000), 21–22.

7.   Consuelo Lopez-Springfield, ed., *Daughters of Caliban: Caribbean Women in the Twentieth Century* (Indianapolis: Indiana University Press, 1997), 47.

8.   John Brierley, "Small Farming in Grenada, West Indies. An Investigation of its Nature and Structure" (PhD thesis, Department of Geography, University of Manitoba, Winnepeg, 1974), 74.

9.   Paula Aymer, *Uprooted Women: Migrant Domestics in the Caribbean* (Westport: Praeger, 1997), 126.

10.   Nita Allen, interview with author, 21 June 1999.

11.   Nadia Benjamin, interview with author, 24 March,1999.

12.   Canice Adams, interview with author, 24 January 2001.

13.   Bernard Coard, interview with author, 17 August 2000.

CHAPTER 1

1.   The Taino inhabited the Windward Islands around AD 400; the Kalinago arrived around AD 900.

2.   Throughout, St George's refers to the town while St George refers to the parish.

3.   The slave rebellion that occurred in Haiti in 1791 resulted in the control of the island by the slaves, under the leadership of Toussaint L'Ouverture, by 1795.

4.   "Most of the resident white population in Grenada during the heyday of sugarcane cultivation left the island in the latter part of the nineteenth century." A.W. Singham, *The Hero and the Crowd in a Colonial Polity* (New Haven: Yale University Press, 1968), 74.

5.   The Morant Bay Rebellion in Jamaica brought an end to the representative system of government in the region. All the British West Indian colonies, with the exception of Barbados, subsequently adopted Crown Colony government.

6.   Bridget Brereton, "Caribbean Women in the Post-Emancipation Century, 1838–1938: Agenda for Research" (paper presented at the UNESCO conference Slavery and the Shaping of Caribbean Society, University of the West Indies, St Augustine, Trinidad, 8–10 December 1988), 1.

7.   Patricia Mohammed, "Writing Gender into History: The Negotiation of Gender Relations Among Indian Men and Women in Post Indenture Trinidadian Society 1917–1947", in *Engendering History: Caribbean Women in Historical Perspective*, ed. Verene Shepherd, Bridget Brereton and Barbara Bailey (London: James Currey, 1995), 21.

CHAPTER 2

1.   List of Slaves in Grenada since Its Restoration to the English, 1784–1788, Public Record Office (PRO), Colonial Office (CO) 101/28.

2.   Answers to Questions Submitted to the Agents for West Indian Affairs, 28 May 1788, PRO, CO 101/29.

3. Herbert Klein, "African Women in the Atlantic Slave Trade", in *Women and Slavery in Africa*, ed. C. Robertson and M. Klein (Madison: University of Wisconsin Press, 1983), 35.

4. Klein, "African Women", 36.

5. Barbara Bush, *Slave Women in Caribbean Society 1650–1838* (Kingston: Heinemann, 1990), 33.

6. List of Negroes on the Estate on the Island of Grenada Belonging to George Cornwall taken in March 1789, Lataste Plantation Accounts and Correspondences, 1785–1835, AF 57/8B, Moccas Manuscripts (Mss) (Herefordshire Record Office, Hereford).

7. An abstract of the strength of Lower Pearls Estate; An abstract of the strength of Upper Pearls Estate, Pearls Estates Annual Accounts 1804, Chancery Masters Exhibits (C) 110/105 A, No. 5.

8. General List of Slaves on Lataste Estate, June 1811, AF 57/8B/2.

9. Barry Higman, *Slave Populations of the British Caribbean, 1807–1834* (Baltimore: Johns Hopkins University Press, 1984), 187.

10. The use of the whip was abolished in islands under Crown Colony government, for example, in Trinidad. In colonies administered under the representative system, like Grenada, the act for the prohibition of the flogging of women was to be considered by the island's Assembly for implementation.

11. President Paterson to Earl Bathurst, Grenada, 23 November 1825, CO 101/65, No.80, f. 116.

12. Hilary Beckles, *Natural Rebels: A Social History of Enslaved Black Women in Barbados* (London: Zed Books, 1989), 42.

13. bell hooks, *Ain't I a Woman: Black Women and Feminism* (London: Pluto Press, 1982), 42–43.

14. Advertisements, *St George's Chronicle and Grenada Gazette*, 21 and 24 June 1815.

15. The Guardian Act of 1788, or An Act for the Encouragement, Protection and Better Government of Slaves, Clause IX, XX and XXII, 23 December 1788, CO 73/9.

16. CO 104/1 Sessional Papers, vol. 82, 1791.

17. Lataste Estate Records, 1810, AF 57/8A.

18. Ibid.

19. Some of the planters in the Leeward Islands recognized that an intensive and rigorous work regime was one of the main deterrents to attaining natural increase. As such, they sought to rectify the problem by reducing the working hours. Ibid.

20. An Account of Forfeited Estates (Duquesne, Bonair, Gross Point, Plaisance, Potterie), 10 September 1805, CO 101/42; List of Negroes in the Upper Pearls Estate, January 1802, C 110/107; An Inventory and Appraisement of Bellevue Estate, 1806, CO 101/43.

21. Slave registration was part of the amelioration process. It provided a record of slave births and deaths and a list of the causes of death. The record was signed by a physician.

22. Natural decrease on the estates in the parish of St Patrick, 1817: Hermitage Estate, five births and eleven deaths; Mount Rich Estate, five births and sixteen deaths; Morne Fendue Estate – two births and seven deaths. In the parish of St Andrew, 1817: Grand Bacolet Estate, four births and seven deaths; Lower Pearls Estate, six births and ten deaths.

23. Higman, *Slave Populations*, 606–7.

24. Evidence of Henry Dalrymple, House of Commons Accounts and Papers, vol. 30, no. 699 (1790).

25. Richard Sheridan, *Doctors and Slaves: A Medical and Demographic History of Slavery in the British West Indies, 1680–1834* (Cambridge: Cambridge University Press, 1985), 242.

26. House of Commons Sessional Papers (HCSP) 71:103; Woodville Marshall, "Provision Ground and Plantation Labour in Four Windward Islands. Competition for Resources during Slavery", in *Cultivation and Culture: Labour and the Shaping of Slave Life in the Americas*, ed. Philip Morgan and Ira Berlin (London: University of Virginia Press 1993), 205.

27. HCSP 71:187.

28. Mitchell to Baumer, Lataste Estate Papers, 3 and 25 September 1831.

29. Sheridan, *Doctors and Slaves*, 163.

30. Higman, *Slave Populations*, 354.

31. PRO 71437, Reference T 71/264, T 71/327, T 71/266.

32. Journal and Ledger, Boccage Estate, 1801, C 110/105.

33. Kenneth Kiple, *The Caribbean Slave: A Biological History* (New York: Cambridge University Press, 1984), 124.

34. Sheridan, *Doctors and Slaves*, 201.

35. PRO 71437, Reference T 71/264, T 71/266, T 71/326; PRO 71474, Reference T 71/326.

36. Lataste Plantation accounts and correspondences 1814, AF 57/8B, Moccas Mss. Journal. Ledger for Boccage, Boulogne, 1796–1823, C 110/105.

37. Lorna McDaniel, *The Big Drum Ritual of Carriacou: Praise Songs in Rememory of Flight* (Gainesville: University Press of Florida, 1988), 34–35.

38. Paterson to Bathurst, 6 November 1823, CO101/63; Blue Books 1828: Return of the Number of Schools, CO 106/22.

39. A list of slaves to Crochu estate in the parish of St. Andrew, the lawful possession of John Stokes Esq., 1833, T 71/322; Slave Registry for the town of St George's and the list of slaves for the estates of the parish of St George, 1833, T 71/265.

40. Advertisement, *St George's Chronicle and Grenada Gazette*, 7 January 1815.

41. Advertisement, *St George's Chronicle*, 25 March 1815.

42. Advertisement, *St George's Chronicle*, 1 April 1815; 26 September 1821.

43. Advertisement, *St George's Chronicle*, 5 July 1815; 26 November 1823.

44. Abstract of the proceedings of the several slave courts which have been held in the island of Grenada for the trial of slaves since May 1812 until 1818, CO 101/58.

45. Ballies Bacolet Plantation Returns, 1823.

46. John Hay, *A Narrative of the Insurrection in the Island of Grenada* (London: J. Ridgeway, 1823), 32–33.

47. Post at Madame Ache's, 9 April 1795, CO 101/34, f. 62; Green to Portland, 27 May 1797, CO 101/35.

48. Hankey to Proprietors of Grand Bras Estates, 1 July 1795, Acc.775 953/18; Estimation of the losses and damages sustained on Lataste Estate, 20 December 1788, AF 57/8B.

49. An Act to manumit and free a certain negro woman named Pauline, 20 December 1786, CO 103/8.

50. Edward Cox, *Free Coloreds in the Slave Societies of St Kitts and Grenada, 1763–1833* (Knoxville: University of Tennessee Press, 1984), 34.

51. George Paterson, Amelioration Measures for Slaves, Grenada, 23 November 1825, CO 101/65.

52. A List of Slaves belonging to Edward Julius De Poullain, proprietor of Springs Estate in the Parish of St Andrew, 1833, PRO 71474, Reference T 71/326.

53. Cox, *Free Coloreds*, 47.

54. Ibid., 93.

55. Ibid., 60.

56. S.V. Morse, "Description of the Grenadines", 1778, CO 101/16; CO 101/18, part 3.

57. Lease and Release, 1787, Land Registry, St George, Grenada.

58. Lorna McDaniel, "The Philips: A Free Mulatto Family of Grenada", *Journal of Caribbean History* 24, no. 2 (1990): 179.

59. Cox, *Free Coloreds*, 67.

60. Ibid., 120.

61. Ibid., 25.

62. Eric Williams, *From Columbus to Castro: The History of the Caribbean, 1492–1969* (London: Andre Deutsch, 1970), 190.

63. Ibid., 104–5.

64. Maitland to Harvey, 13 April 1806, CO101/43.

65. *St George's Chronicle and Grenada Gazette*, 28 February 1835, CO 105/1. From the list of the claims sent out by the office by assistant commissioners of compensation, there was evidence of women who owned slaves on plantations. For example, one of the claims shows that three women, Catherine Anderson, Anne Grant and Henrietta Grant, became slave owners in the wake of the death of Charles Grant. They were responsible for 187 slaves on River Antoine Estate in St Patrick. Judith Philip (free coloured) is also listed as being responsible for 68 slaves on Susanna Estate, 67 on Petit Anse Estate and Grand Anse Estate. The evidence does not differentiate between white, free coloured or free black women.

66. George Smith, *The Laws of Grenada from the Year 1763 to the Year 1805* (London: n.p., 1808), 21–26.

67. State of the Parish of St George, St John, St Mark, St Patrick, St David in the island of Grenada taken April 1772, CO 101/5, f. 147: These records show that one was the widow and heir of Paiserete, who owned 130 acres of land consisting of indigo trees, pastureland and provision grounds; 120 acres of woodland and bush wood and sixty slaves. The other three women owned 56 acres and twenty-eight slaves between them. In the parish of St John, there was one female plantation owner, the widow of Le Vexier, who owned 70 acres containing coffee, 20 acres of cocoa, 60 acres of woodland and thirty-six slaves. In St Patrick, there were three female plantation owners, two of whom were widows. In the parish of St David, there were two white widows, who owned 171 acres and eighty-five slaves between them. A list of names of sundry persons to whom Governor Scott granted town lots in the town of St George's in the island of Grenada, CO 101/1, f. 245: These 1763 records list three women as owning lots in the town of St George's: Mary Joseph Colett, Madame Larnage and Madame Delesnables.

68. Miscellaneous Accounts Current for Grenada Estates, 1838–1867, Acc. 775/954/4. Lady Cooper of Portland Place, London, gained £5,600.10.09 from Dukenfield Hall Estate (Jamaica) and £228.13.01 for her eighth of a share of Grand Bras Estates Grenada. Although the figures are for May 1837, outside of the period of slavery, they give an idea of the wealth these women gained from plantation production.

69. William Green, *British Slave Emancipation: The Sugar Colonies and the Great Experiment, 1830–1865* (Oxford: Clarendon Press, 1976), 122.

70. Stipendiary Magistrate (SM) C.L. Fraser, Report for the Parish of St Patrick, Belvedere Cottage, 30 November 1837, CO 101/87.

71. Report for St George District for October 1837, SM John Ross, CO 101/84, vol. 2.

72. SM Sinclair Reports for Carriacou, November 1837, CO 101/87; Minutes of the Honourable House of Assembly, Extract from report of proceedings taken by directions of the Lt. Governor. Clarke's Court Estate, 15 September 1837, CO 104/14; Minutes of the Honourable House of Assembly. To the Honourable the speaker and members of the House of Assembly of the island of Grenada and its Dependencies, 18 November 1837, CO 104/14.

73. Papers Relative to the Abolition of Slavery in the British Colonies Number 2, Return of the Number and Nature of the Punishments inflicted on the apprenticed labourers in the colony of Grenada by Special or Stipendiary Magistrates from 1 August 1834 to 31 July 1835 specifying the offences from which they were inflicted separation males from females, CO 101/79.

74. John Ross to Lt. Governor McGregor, St George, 23 August 1837, CO 101/83.

75. Judicial notes of evidence taken in the trial of John Brown an ex officio: Information for an infraction of the Abolition Act by confining Hannah an apprenticed labourer in the stocks, CO 101/85, ff. 304, 310.

76. CO 101/85 (1837), f. 245–48, 251–53.

77. Letter to Colonel C.J. Doyle, Lt Governor, from SM C.L. Fraser, 1 July 1837, CO 101/83 (January to September 1837), vol. 1, f. 249–65.

78. John Ross to Chief Justice Sanderson, 20 November 1837, CO 101/88, ff. 206–19.

79. Minutes of the Honourable House of Assembly, Complaint of Gilchrist against five apprenticed labourers with the different proceedings in that case, Clarke's Court Estate, 15 March 1837, CO 104/14, 3.

80. Papers Relative to the Abolition of Slavery in the British Colonies, CO 101/79, 396. The sums presented were in the currency of the country. Eight shillings sterling was about equal to one pound in current currency.

CHAPTER 3

1. R.T. Smith, "Race, Class and Gender in the Transition to Freedom", in *The Meaning of Freedom: Economics Politics and Culture after Slavery*, ed. Frank McGlynn and Seymour Drescher (Pittsburgh: University of Pittsburgh Press, 1992), 278;

Bridget Brereton, "Family Strategies, Gender and the Shift to Wage Labour in the British Caribbean", in *The Colonial Caribbean in Transition: Essays on Post Emancipation Social and Cultural History*, ed. Bridget Brereton and Kelvin Yelvington (Kingston: University of the West Indies Press,1999), 82.

2.   Grenada Stipendiary Magistrates' Reports for 1841, CO 101/92, f. 18.

3.   Minutes of evidence taken before the Select Committee in the West Indian Colonies, 26 May 1842, 199; George Brizan, *Grenada: Island of Conflict* (London: Macmillan Education, 1998), 135.

4.   Minutes, 26 May 1842, 199.

5.   Brizan, *Grenada*, 145.

6.   SM C. Fraser, District of St John and St Mark, 31 December 1845, Stipendiary Magistrates' Reports 1845–1849, CO 106/13.

7.   Brizan, *Grenada*, 163 and 167; St Joseph's Convent Centenary Magazine, 1876–1976, 5; Blue Books 1880, Return of the number of schools etc., CO 106/74.

8.   Brizan, *Grenada*, 170–71.

9.   David F. Clyde, *Health in Grenada: A Social and Historical Account* (London: Vade-Mecum Press, 1985), 84.

10.   Edward Cox, "Indian Migration to Grenada and St Vincent, 1857–1885" (paper presented at the International Conference on Asian Diasporas to the Americas, University of the West Indies, St Augustine, Trinidad, August 2000); Edward Cox, "Indentured African Labourers to Grenada and St Vincent, 1838–1863" (paper presented at the conference of the Association of Caribbean Historians, Cayenne, April 2000); Brizan, *Grenada*, 194.

11.   "Report on the Condition of Indian Immigrants and the Working of the New Immigration Law in Grenada", D.W. Warner, Inspector of Immigrants, 1880. C 2602: Accounts and Papers 10, 1880: Colonies and British Possessions Barbados, Canada, Fiji, Hong Kong, Jamaica, West Indies, Cyprus, Cambridge University Library, Cambridge.

12.   W.G. Sewell, *The Ordeal of Free Labour in the British West Indies* (London: Frank Cass, 1968), 89.

13.   Beverley Steele, "East Indian Indenture and the work of the Presbyterian Church among the Indians in Grenada", *Caribbean Quarterly* 22 (1976): 30.

14.   George Brizan, "Creole and Immigrant: Aspects of Nineteenth-Century Grenadian Society" (typescript, St George's Public Library, St George's, Grenada, 1981), 9.

15.   "Report on the Condition of Indian Immigrants and the Working of the New Immigration Law in Grenada", D.W. Warner, Inspector of Immigrants, 1880.

C 2602: Accounts and Papers 10, 1880: Colonies and British Possessions Barbados, Canada, Fiji, Hong Kong, Jamaica, West Indies, Cyprus, Cambridge University Library, Cambridge.

16. Supplements to the Grenada Government Gazette: List of Voters for the Parish of St Patrick, no. 16, 13 April 1887; List of Voters for the Parish of St Andrew, no. 18, 27 April 1887; List of Voters for the Parish of St David, no. 24, 1 June 1887; List of Voters for the Parish of St Mark, no. 17, 20 April 1887.

CHAPTER 4

1. Merle Collins, "Sometimes You Have to Drink Vinegar and Pretend You Think Is Honey: Race, Gender and Man/Woman Talk", in *Caribbean Portraits: Essays on Gender Ideologies and Identities*, ed. Christine Barrow (Kingston: Ian Randle, 1998), 381.

2. Ibid., 382.

3. Frederica Lewis (labourer on the Plaisance Estate in St John's from the late 1940s to the late 1990s), interview with author, 15 April 1999.

4. Patrick Antoine, "Report on River Antoine Estate" (unpublished paper, Public Library, St George's, Grenada, 1984), 23.

5. Lewis, interview.

6. M.G. Smith, *Dark Puritan* (Kingston: Department of Extra Mural Studies, University of the West Indies, 1963), 11.

7. Ibid., 12.

8. Thelma Francis (domestic worker for twenty-one years at Presentation Boys College St George's), interview with author, 5 February 1999.

9. Edward Kent (landowner in Carriacou), interview with author, 26 August 2006; Ruskine Patterson (landowner in Carriacou), interview with author, 26 August 2006.

10. Report of General Abstracts of Census of 1921, Grenada, 32.

11. Clyde, *Health in Grenada*, 210.

12. Ibid., 238.

13. Albertina Alexander (domestic worker from the village of Morne Jaloux, St George), interview with author, 9 February 1999.

14. Marriage records of the Presbyterian and Anglican Churches, St George's Grenada, 1903–1919; Judith Mendes (Carriacou resident), interview with author, 1 August 2000.

15.   Veronica Williams, interview with author, 10 February 1999.

16.   M.G. Smith, *Kinship and Community in Carriacou* (New Haven: Yale University Press, 1962), 198–99.

17.   M.G. Smith, *Stratification in Grenada* (Berkley and Los Angeles: University of California Press, 1965), 187–88.

18.   Williams, interview.

19.   Francis, interview.

20.   Sheila Mapp (resident of Carriacou and mother of eight), interview with author, 2 August 2000; Judith Mendes, interview.

21.   Theophilus Albert Marryshow, "The Case of Women", *West Indian*, 13 February 1920, 3–4.

22.   Lady Gloria Williams (teacher in the 1950s; wife of the former governor general, Sir Daniel Williams), interview with author, 1 March 1999.

23.   Enid Charles (employee at a furniture and appliance store, St George's), interview with author, 3 May 1999. The Blue Books for 1900 (CO 106/94) give an example of the kind of curriculum from which girls at the St Joseph's Convent were taught. This consisted of English grammar, composition and paraphrasing, reading, orthography, penmanship, geography, history (English, natural and biblical), arithmetic, algebra, botany, astronomy, domestic economy, French (reading, grammar, exercises and translation), drawing and painting, music (vocal and instrumental), calisthenics, needlework (plain and ornamental).

24.   Education Reports: Primary and Secondary Schools, Girls and Boys attendance including St Joseph's Convent and Girls High School, Blue Books 1900, CO 106/94.

25.   Joyce Cole, *Official Ideology and Education of Women in the English Speaking Caribbean, 1835–1945: With Special Reference to Barbados*, vol. 5, Women in the Caribbean Project (Cave Hill, Barbados: Institute of Social and Economic Research, 1982), 12–14.

26.   Mollie McIntyre (daughter of an estate owner; former president of the Soroptomists Club), interview with author, 9 March 1999.

27.   Alice McIntyre (former employee of the Grenada Cooperative Bank), interview with author, 22 March 1999.

28.   Nellie Payne and Jean Buffong. *Jump Up and Kiss Me* (London: Women's Press, 1996), 36.

29.   Nesha Haniff, *Blaze of Fire: Significant Contributions of Caribbean Women* (Toronto: Black Women and Women of Colour Press, 1988), 198.

30.   Ibid., 200.

31. Mae Nurse (former teacher from the village of St Paul's), interview with author, 23 March 1999.

32. Blanche Sylvester (former teacher from the village of Fontenoy), interview with author, 24 April 1999.

33. Ibid.

34. Charles, interview.

35. Osbourne Ivor O'Brien (former employee of the Grenada Cooperative Bank, the Grenada Nutmeg Association and former manager of the Grenada Telephone Company), interview with author, 31 August 2000.

36. Along with Millicent Douglas and Inez Munro, Marguarite Bryan was also a social worker in 1946. See "Social Welfare", *West Indian*, 15 January 1946, 2; "Marcus Garvey's Visit to Grenada", *West Indian*, 12 September 1937, 3; "Miss Inez Munro presented with M.B.E. Insignia by Administrator", *West Indian*, 29 May 1939, 3; "The Grenada Globe Cinema Ltd", *West Indian*, 15 July 1937, 4.

37. Brizan, *Grenada*, 287–289.

38. Angela Smith, "Industrial Relations in Grenada", in *Labour Relations in the Caribbean Region: Record of Proceedings of, and documents submitted to a Caribbean Regional Seminar on Labour Relations, Port of Spain, March 1973*, Labour Management Relations Series, no. 43 (Geneva: International Labour Office, 1973), 104.

39. Grenada Report of the Labour Department for 1950.

40. Brizan, *Grenada*, 350–51.

41. Edward Cox, " 'Race Men': The Pan-African Aspect of the Political Struggles of William Galway Donovan and T. Albert Marryshow, 1884–1926" (paper presented at the Henry Sylvester Williams Pan-African Conference, University of the West Indies, St Augustine, Trinidad, January 2001)

42. W.L. Heape, "Notice: Women Jurors", *West Indian*, 2 November 1937; C.H. Lucas, "Female Jurors", 26 November 1937.

43. "St Patrick's District Board First to Name Lady Elected Member", *West Indian*, 12 September 1939, 4–5.

44. George Gmelch, *Double Passage: The Lives of Caribbean Migrants Abroad and Back Home* (Ann Arbor: University of Michigan Press, 1993), 41.

45. Brizan, *Grenada*, 249–250.

46. Juliana Aird, interview with author, 1 April 1999.

47. Collins, "Sometimes You Have to Drink Vinegar", 380.

48. Claire-Anna Gill (housewife from the village of Birch Grove, St Andrew), interview with author, 20 October 2009.

CHAPTER 5

1. Report of the Labour Department for 1951, Council Paper no. 4, 1954.
2. The ruling class included the governor, the imperial representatives, the members of the plantocracy and merchants. Most of Grenada's white population during the heyday of sugar cultivation had left the island in the latter part of the nineteenth century. By 1960, whites comprised less than 1 per cent of the population. Thus, except for the governor and some of his officials, the ruling class can be defined as light or pale brown in colour.
3. Brizan, *Grenada*, 277.
4. Grenada Disturbances February–March 1951 (compiled by Government of Grenada, Public Library, St George's, Grenada); Brizan, *Grenada*, 277; Report of the Labour Department for 1951; Council Reports, Report for the Years 1948–1949. (London: Her Majesty's Stationery Office [HMSO]), 9; George Brizan, "The Development of the Labour Movement in Grenada 1940–1960: A Preliminary Analysis" (typescript, University of the West Indies Library, St George's, Grenada, 1975), 27, 37.
5. Interview with Murie Francois, quoted from David Michael Franklyn, "The Role of Women in the Struggle for Social and Political Change in Grenada 1979–1983" (MA thesis, University of the West Indies, Cave Hill, 1989), 43.
6. A.W. Singham, *The Hero and the Crowd in a Colonial Polity* (London: Yale University Press, 1968), 170–71.
7. River Antoine Estate Records, 27 September 1954, 16 October 1954 and 5 January 1955; Colonial Office Report on Grenada for the Years 1955–1956.
8. Rita Knight (estate worker from 1955 on the Douglaston Estate, St John), interview with author, 22 January 1999.
9. Knight, interview.
10. Remittances continue to be a very important source of finance today, not only for Grenadian families but also for families throughout the Caribbean.
11. Douglaston Estate Records, 8–21 September 1967 and 12–25 January 1968.
12. Delta Duprey (estate worker from 1955 on the Douglaston Estate, St John), interview with author, 22 January 1999.
13. Duprey, interview.
14. Knight, interview.
15. Catherine Duprey (daughter of Delta Duprey and previous domestic worker at the Douglaston Estate), interview with author, 22 January 1999.
16. Carl Franklyn (present owner of Panorama Estate), personal interview, 1 Octo-

ber 2006; Nora Holas (owner of inherited property and a shop owner), interview with author, 8 November 2006.

17. Phyllis Pitt (landowner in Richmond, St Andrew), interview with author, 14 October 2006; Sister Gabrielle Mason (daughter of Celestine Mason), interview with author, 10 November 2006.

18. Glenda Mason-Francis (former principal of the Anglican high school), interview with author, 27 april 1999.

19. Gloria Payne-Banfield (former cabinet secretary), interview with author, 22 March 1999.

20. Mason-Francis, interview.

21. Monica Joseph (retired judge), interview with author, 17 March 1999.

22. "Gertrude Protain Lobby for Scholarships for Girls Defeated in Legislative Council", *Citizen's Weekly*, 3 October 1960, 1.

23. Colonial Report (Grenada), Report for the Year 1954 (London: HMSO, 1957), 3.

24. Nadia Benjamin (parliamentary secretary in the Ministry of Education and Social Affairs), interview with author, 24 March 1999.

25. Report, 1968–1969, Grenada Inter-Church Council for Social Welfare, 3, 5, 7.

26. Report of the Commission of Enquiry on the Colony Hospital, 1959, 7, 9.

27. Maude Hutchinson, interview with author, 29 January 1999.

28. Wapel Nedd, interview with author, 29 January 1999.

29. Eric Gairy, "Prime Minister Tells United Nations General Assembly of God and Women" (address, United Nations General Assembly, twenty-third meeting, Tuesday, 17 September 1974).

30. Statement by Marie-Josephine McIntyre, Grenada's permanent representative to the United Nations and Leader of Grenada's Delegation to International Women's Year Conference, 27 June 1975, 1–3.

31. Pamela Steele (former permanent secretary of the Ministry of Communications and Works, the Ministry of Health and the Ministry of Agriculture), interview with author, 26 April 1999.

32. "The Story of Our Advancement", *Farmers Weekly*, 3 July 1971, 4.

33. Report on the Status of Women in Grenada, National Commission on the Status of Women (St George's: Government Printers, 1976), 40–44.

34. Benjamin and Nedd, interview.

35. Marie-Josephine McIntyre (former Grenadian ambassador to the UN), interview with author, 30 January 1999.

36. "Nurses' Demonstration", *Torchlight*, 8 November 1970, 1.

37. "Nurses' Resignation", *Torchlight*, 15 November 1970, 1.

38.   "Apologies to Whom and for What?", *Torchlight*, 29 November 1970, 1.

39.   "Gairy Withholds Nurses' Certificates", *New Jewel*, 3 May 1974, 1.

40.   Veronica Coard (mother of six girls), interview with author, 24 February 1999.

41.   People's Revolutionary Government, *In the Spirit of Butler: Trade Unionism in Free Grenada* (St George's: Fedon, 1982), 53.

42.   Eric Gairy, "Black Power in Grenada", radio broadcast by premier of Grenada, the Honourable E.M. Gairy (St George's: Government Printery, 1970), 3.

43.   Alimenta Bishop (mother of Maurice Bishop, the former prime minister of Grenada), interview with author, 15 June 1996.

44.   "Jewel's Office Invaded Mrs Thomas Arrested", *New Jewel*, 28 September 1973, 1; "The Secret Police Attack Teacher", *New Jewel*, 5 July 1974, 1.

45.   Mary Jane (pseudonym), interview with author, 22 February 1999.

46.   "Women of Grenada", *New Jewel*, 17 May 1974, 7.

47.   Rosemary Porter, "Women and the State: Women's Movements in Grenada and their Role in the Grenada Revolution 1979–1983" (PhD thesis, Temple University, 1986), 222.

48.   Phyllis Coard (president of the NJM/NWO), interview with author, 16 and 25 February 1999.

49.   Miranda Davis, *Third World, Second Sex: Women's Struggles and National Liberation* (London: Zed Books, 1983), 158–59.

50.   Claudette Pitt (executive member of the NWO), interview with author, 27 February 1999.

51.   EPICA Task Force, *Grenada: The Peaceful Revolution* (Washington, DC: EPICA, 1982), 55.

CHAPTER 6

1.   St George's Progressive Women's Association (PWA), Constitution of the St George's PWA, 1977, Public Library, St George's, Grenada.

2.   Dessima Williams, "Grenadian Women Under the New Jewel Movement", *Trans Africa Forum* 4, no. 3 (1987): 55.

3.   Maurice Bishop, "Women Step Forward", in *Maurice Bishop Speaks: The Grenada Revolution, 1979–1983*, ed. Michael Taber and Bruce Marcus (New York: Pathfinder Press, 1983), 37.

4.   Williams, "Grenadian Women", 56.

5.   Rosemary Porter, "Women and the State: Women's Movements in Grenada and

their Role in the Grenada Revolution 1979–1983" (PhD thesis, Temple University, 1986), 333.

6. Phyllis Coard, Memo to NJM Bureau (Public Library, St George's, Grenada, May 1979).

7. Pitt, interview.

8. Phyllis Coard's Notes in Isabel Jamaron's Report on NJM/NWO (Public Library, St George's, Grenada, May 1981).

9. Phyllis Coard, interview.

10. "The Part the NWO Must Play in the Development of Women in Grenada from 1983–1989" (Public Library, St George's, Grenada), 5. This document was published by the National Women's Organisation in 1983. It included the achievements of the organization up to that point and a projection up to 1989.

11. "The Part the NWO Must Play", 6.

12. Tessa Stroude (executive member of the NWO and the Women's Desk), interview with author, 2 February 1999.

13. Phyllis Coard, interview.

14. Stroude, interview.

15. Ibid.

16. Draft Resolution on the Work Programme of the National Women's Organisation for 1981 (Public Library, St George's, Grenada), 1–2.

17. National Women's Organisation (pamphlet, Public Library, St George's, Grenada, November 1981)

18. Davis, *Third World, Second Sex*, 160.

19. "Requin Co-op Gets off the Ground", *Free West Indian*, 6 December 1980, 2.

20. "The Part the NWO Must Play", 6.

21. "Preprimary Schools Open in St Andrew", *Free West Indian*, 6 June 1981, 10; "Successful Year of NWO, *Free West Indian*, 21 November 1981, 5.

22. Dessima Williams, "Women Must Define their Priorities: Grenada, 1979–1983", in *Women in the Rebel Tradition: The English Speaking Caribbean*, ed. WIRE (New York: Women's International Resource Exchange, 1987), 24.

23. Rita Joseph, "The Significance of the Grenada Revolution to Women in Grenada", *Bulletin of Eastern Caribbean Affairs* 7, no. 1 (1981): 17.

24. Report by the national coordinator of the Centre for Popular Education, Valerie Cornwall (Public Library, St George's, Grenada), 5; "The CPE Special", *Free West Indian*, 28 February 1981, 8.

25. Valerie Gordon, interview with author (former coordinator of the Centre for Popular Education), 24 February 1999; Jacqueline Creft, "The Building of Mass

Education in Free Grenada", *Grenada Is Not Alone: Speeches by the PRG at First International Conference in Solidarity with Grenada* (St George's: Fedon, 1982), 52.

26. "CSDP Looks Forward to a Brighter Year", *Free West Indian*, 25 July 1980, 7.

27. Phyllis Coard, interview; "Fisherwomen Join True Blue School", *Free West Indian*, 31 January 1981, 6.

28. "50 Pioneers at First Camp", *Free West Indian*, 25 April 1981, 8

29. The Maternity Leave Law entitled women who had worked for more than eighteen months for the same employer to three months' maternity leave; for two of these three months they were to be fully paid. It also guaranteed women the right to re-employment with the same employer after three months. Women must work for at least 40 per cent of the work week or fortnight to qualify for the three-month maternity leave. The woman must notify her employers at least three weeks before she decides to take her leave and she must notify the employer that she intends to come back to work. Daily paid workers were entitled to one fifth of their annual pay (that was about two and a half months' pay). Information from *Free West Indian*, 11 October 1980, 1.

30. Restaurant owner Evelyn Thompson fired her twenty-five-year-old waitress, Jessica Williams, because she was pregnant. Miss Williams had been employed since May 1979 and worked from 7:00 a.m to 5:00 p.m. for six days a week for $100. Miss Thompson admitted that she had dismissed Miss Williams due to her pregnancy and gave this response to Judge Lyle St Paul. She stated, "I never got maternity leave in the days when I had my children." In "Boss Fined for Firing Pregnant Worker", *Free West Indian*, 2 May 1981, 3.

31. Peggy Nesfield (worked in Ministry of Education and Foreign Affairs,1979 to1983), interview with author, 5 February 1999.

32. Michael Aberdeen, *Grenada Under the PRG* (Port of Spain, Trinidad: People's Popular Movement, 1983), 61.

33. Aberdeen, *Grenada Under the PRG*, 61.

34. Madonna Harford (present president of the Public Workers' Union), 31 October 2006.

35. Jeanette Dubois, (former president of the Grenada Union of Teachers), 31 October 2006.

36. EPICA, *Grenada*, 99; Monica Joseph, interview.

37. Alexander, interview.

38. A bomb was set at Queen's Park at a rally on 19 June 1980. It was probably intended to wipe out the leadership of the PRG, instead three women died – Bernadette Bailey, Laurice Humprey and Laureen Phillip.

39. Colleen Lewis, "Interview with Phyllis Coard: Women's Growing Role in Revolutionary Grenada", *Inter Continental Press* and *Imprecor* 18 (1980): 1193; "34 Women Join Grand Roy Militia", *Free West Indian*, 5 July 1980, 3.

40. Merle Hodge, "Leading Role in Production and Defense: Women in the Grenada Revolution", *Inter Continental Press* and *Imprecor* 18 (1980): 943.

41. Chris Searle, *Grenada: The Struggle against Destabilisation* (London: Writers and Readers Publishing Cooperative, 1983), 109–10.

42. "We Stand Ready to Defend Our Revolution", *New Jewel*, 27 March 1983, 5.

43. Ibid., 5.

44. Claire Steeples (pseudonym), interview with author, 10 February 1999.

45. Ibid.

46. Rita Joseph, interview with author, 9 February 1999.

47. Phyllis Coard, interview.

48. Merle Hodge and Chris Searle, *"Is Freedom We Making": The New Democracy in Grenada"* (Grenada: Government Information Service, 1981), 48–49.

49. Hodge and Searle, *Is Freedom We Making*, 77.

50. Chris Searle, *Carriacou and Petite Martinique in the Mainstream of the Revolution* (St George's: Fedon, 1982), 108.

51. "The Part the NWO Must Play", 8–9.

52. Rosemary Porter, "Women and the State: Women's Movements in Grenada and their Role in the Grenada Revolution 1979–1983" (PhD diss., Temple University, 1986), 349. The Airport Development Committee was set up in St George's in November–December 1979. Other committees were formed in other parishes. Although the Airport Development Committee was organized by women, men were free to join.

53. Phyllis Coard, interview.

54. Beverley Steele (former resident tutor of the UWI Centre, Grenada), interview with author, 19 February 1999.

55. Peggy Antrobus, "Lessons from the Grenada Revolution", *Caricom Perspective* No. 222 (November–December 1983). Women and Development Unit, Extra Mural Department, UWI, Barbados, 1984, 3.

56. Mary Jane, interview.

57. Ibid.

58. Ibid.

59. Lucy Lace (pseudonym), interview with author, 24 February 1999.

60. Mary Theresa (pseudonym), interview with author, 9 March 1999.

61. Mary Annie (pseudonym), interview with author, 26 March 1999.

62. Mary Jane, interview.

63. Bernard Coard, interview with author, 17 August 2000.

64. Ibid.

65. Problems Affecting Women Party Members. Letter Given to the Political Bureau NJM from Chairperson Women's Committee, NJM, 11 May 1982, Document 79–1. Grenada Documents an Overview and Selection (Washington, DC: Department of State and Department of Defense, September 1984).

66. Minutes of Political Bureau Meeting, Wednesday, 22 September 1982, document 81–2. Grenada Documents.

67. Central Committee Report on First Plenary Session, 13–19 July 1983, Document 110-18. Grenada Documents.

68. Byron Campbell (NTS chairman from 1979 to 1983), interview, 30 June 2000.

69. Sheila Rowbotham, *Women in Movement: Feminism and Social Action* (London: Routledge, 1992), 141.

70. Stroude, interview.

71. Ibid.

72. Pitt, interview.

73. Extraordinary Meeting of the Central Committee of the NJM, 14–16 September 1983, Document 112–21. Grenada Documents.

74. Phyllis Coard, interview.

75. Extraordinary General Meeting of the Full Members of NJM, Sunday, 25 September 1983, Document 113–37. Grenada Documents.

76. Mary Jane, interview.

77. Phyllis Coard, interview.

78. Pitt, interview.

79. Ibid.

80. Faye Thompson, interview with author, 24 August 2000.

81. Thompson, interview.

82. Nancy Lou (pseudonym), interview with author, 12 March 1999.

83. Lady Esmai Scoon, interview with author, 17 March 1999.

84. Mary Louise (pseudonym), interview with author, 9 February 1999.

85. Steeples, interview.

86. Ibid.

87. Ibid.

88. "Maurice Bishop Murder Trial", *Grenada Newsletter*, 17 May 1986, 2.

89. Ibid.

90. All the detainees were released between June 2007 and September 2009. The

last seven, including the former deputy prime minister Bernard Coard, were released on Saturday, 5 September 2009.

CONCLUSION

1. Higman, *Slave Populations*, 381.
2. Brereton, "Family Strategies", 100.
3. Woodville Marshall, "The Social and Economic Development of the Windward Islands" (PhD thesis, University of Cambridge, 1963), 148.
4. There were four women in the senate between 1976 and 1981. Three served on the Barbados House of Assembly between 1976 and 1983. There were two ministers between 1976 and 1981. Kenneth O'Brien and Neville Duncan, *Women and Politics in Barbados, 1948–1981* (Cave Hill, Barbados: Institute of Social and Economic Research, 1983), 50–52.
5. Between 1979 and 1983, there were two women in high echelons of power in Dominica, the prime minister and a minister of government. See Lennox Honychurch, *The Dominica Story: A History of the Island* (Roseau: The Dominica Institute, 1984). Between 1979 and 1983 Monserrat had one female minister of government. See Verene Shepherd, ed., *Women in Caribbean History: The British Colonised Territories* (Kingston: Ian Randle, 1999), 183–84.
6. Sheila Rowbotham, *Hidden From History: Rediscovering Women in History from the 17th Century to the Present* (New York: Vintage Books, 1974), xxiv.
7. Catherine A. MacKinnon, "Feminism, Marxism, Method and the State: An Agenda for Theory", *Signs* 7 (1982): 523.
8. Hannah Mitchel, *The Hard Way Up* (London: Faber, 1968), 88.
9. Rowbotham, *Women in Movement*, 204.
10. Minutes of Political Bureau Meeting, Wednesday, 22 September 1982, Document 81-2, *Grenada Documents*; General Committee Report on the First Plenary Session, 13–19 July 1982, Document 110-18, *Grenada Documents*.

Bibliography

REPORTS, LETTERS, NEWSPAPERS AND OTHER DOCUMENTS

Public Library, Grenada

Report of the Labour Department for 1951. Council Paper No. 4 of 1954.

Draft Resolution on the Work Programme of the National Women's Organisation for 1981.

Grenada Inter Church Council for Social Welfare 1969.

Grenada Government Gazette: List of Voters for the Parish of St Patrick, 13 April 1887, Number 16; List of Voters for the Parish of St Mark, 20 April 1887, Number 17; List of Voters for the Parish of St Andrew, 27 April 1887, Number 18; List of Voter for the Parish of St David, 1 June 1887, Number 24.

Gairy, Eric. "Prime Minister Tells United Nations General Assembly of God and Women". Address to the United Nations General Assembly, 23rd Meeting, New York, Tuesday, 17 September 1974.

Gairy, Eric. Radio Broadcast by Premier of Grenada, Honourable E.M. Gairy, on "Black Power in Grenada", 3 and 4 May 1970. St George's, Grenada: Government Printery, 1970.

Report on Grenada for the Years 1955–1956, Colonial Office (CO). London: Her Majesty's Stationery Office.

Report of the Commission of Enquiry on the Colony Hospital, 1959.

Report on the Status of Women in Grenada 1976. National Commission on the Status of Women. St George's: Government Printers, 1976

"The Part the NWO Must Play in the Development of Women in Grenada from 1983–1989". National Women's Organisation, St George's, Grenada, 1983.

Statement by Marie-Josephine McIntyre, Grenada's Permanent Representative to the United Nations and Leader of Grenada's Delegation to International Women's Year Conference, 27 June 1975.

University of the West Indies, Open Campus, Grenada

Constitution of the St George's Progressive Women's Association, 1977.
Parliamentary Select Committee on the West India Colonies, 1842.

University of the West Indies, St Augustine Campus

"Grenada Documents: An Overview and Selection". Released by the Department of
State and the Department of Defense. Washington, DC, 1984.

Cambridge University Library, Cambridge

"Report on the Condition of Indian Immigrants and the Working of the New Immi-
gration Law in Grenada". D.W. Warner, Inspector of Immigrants, 1880. C 2602:
Accounts and Papers 10, 1880: Colonies and British Possessions Barbados, Canada,
Fiji, Hong Kong, Jamaica, West Indies, Cyprus.

Public Record Office, Kew Gardens, London

Series CO 101: Original correspondence between Governors of Grenada and Secretary
of State:
CO 101/1–CO 101/43
CO 101/58–CO 101/64
CO 101/ 78–CO 101/109
Series CO 102: Original correspondences between the colonies and England
(despatches between Secretary of State and Governors)
CO 102/21–22

Series CO 104: Sessional Papers
CO 104/1, 8, 13, 14

Series CO 105: Government Gazettes
CO 105/1–3 (1834–1848)

Series CO 106: Shipping Returns
CO 106/1–CO 106/5 (1764–1809)

Stipendiary Magistrates' Reports
CO 106/13–14 (1845–1853)

Blue Books
CO106/15–124 (1821–1930)

Series CO, T 71: Grenada Slave Registration Volumes

T71/264, 266 (1817)

T 71/326,327 (1833)

Chancery Masters Exhibits. C 110/103–107. Boccage, Boulogne, Pearl, Plaisance, Dunfermline and Madey's Plantations, Grenada: Accounts and Inventories, 1796–1823.

London Metropolitan Archives, London

Cooper Franks Ms. Acc. 775: Accounts of Grand Bras Plantations, Grenada, 1764–1840.

Herefordshire Record Office, Hereford

Moccas Mss. Lataste Plantation, Grenada: Accounts and Correspondences, 1785– 1835.

River Antoine Estate

River Antoine Estate Records. Pay Lists: For the third week ending 18 September 1948,
27 September 1954, 16 October 1954, 5 January 1955; for the two weeks ending 30
August 1975.

Douglaston Estate

Douglaston Estate Records. Pay Lists: For the period 8 to 21 September 1967, 12 to 25
January 1968, 5 to 18 November 1976.

Westerhall Estate

Westerhall Estate Records. Pay List for the period 11 to 24 May 1973.

NEWSPAPERS

Grenada Free Press and Public Gazette (St George's), 1829, 1834.

Farmers Weekly (Port of Spain), 1971.

West Indian (St George's), 1937, 1939, 1946, 1951, 1974.

St George's Chronicle and Grenada Gazette (London) 1815, 1821, 1823, 1834, 1835.

New Jewel (St George's), 1973–1976, 1983.

Free West Indian (St George's), 1980–1981.

ORAL SOURCES

Adams, Canice. Interview with author. La Florissante Gardens, Dabadie, Trinidad,
24 January 2001.

Aird, Juliana. Interview with author. Lucas Street, St George's, Grenada, 1 April 1999.

Alexander, Albertina. Interview with author. Morne Jaloux, St George, Grenada, 9 February 1999.

Allen, Nita. Interview with author. Aboud Circular, St James, Trinidad, 21 June 1999.

Annie, Mary*. Interview with author. St George's, Grenada, 26 March 1999.

Benjamin, Nadia. Interview with author. Victoria Street, Grenville, St Andrew, Grenada, 24 March 1999.

Bishop, Alimenta. Interview with author. St Paul's, St George, Grenada, 15 June 1996.

Campbell, Byron. Interview with author. Church Street, St George's Grenada, 30 June 2000.

Charles, Enid. Interview with author. Archibald Avenue, St George's, Grenada, 3 May 1999.

Coard, Bernard. Interview with author. Her Majesty's Prison, Richmond Hill, St George's, Grenada, 17 August 2000.

Coard, Phyllis. Interview with author. Her Majesty's Prison, Richmond Hill, St George's, Grenada, 16 and 25 February 1999.

Coard, Veronica. Interview with author. Green Street, St George's, Grenada, 24 February 1999.

Dubois, Jeanette. Interview with author. Tanteen, St George's Grenada, 31 October 2006.

Duprey, Delta. Interview with author. Douglaston Estate, Florida, St John, Grenada, 22 January 1999.

Duprey, Catherine. Interview with author. Douglaston Estate, Florida, St John, Grenada, 22 January 1999.

Francis, Thelma. Interview with author. Bocas, St Paul's, St George, Grenada, 5 February 1999.

Franklyn, Carl. Interview with author. Panorama Estate, St Patrick, Grenada, 1 October 2006.

Gordon, Valerie (formerly known as Cornwall). Interview with author. H.A. Blaize Street, St George's, Grenada, 24 February 1999.

Harford, Madonna. Interview with author. Marine Villa, St George's, Grenada. 31 October 2006.

Holas, Nora. Interview with author. St Patrick, 8 November 2006.

Hutchinson, Maude. Interview with author. Mount Rose, St Patrick, Grenada, 29 January 1999.

Jane, Mary*. Interview with author. St Andrew, Grenada, 22 February 1999.

Joseph, Monica. Interview with author. Lance aux Epines, St George, Grenada, 17 March 1999.

Kent Edward. Interview with author. Craigston Carriacou, 26 August 2006.

Knight, Rita. Interview with author. Douglaston Estate, St John, Grenada, 22 January 1999.

Lace, Lucy*. Interview with author. St George's, Grenada, 24 February 1999.

Lewis, Frederica. Interview with author. Plaisance Estate, Florida, St John, Grenada, 15 April 1999.

Louise, Mary*. Interview with author. St George's, Grenada, 9 February 1999.

Lou, Nancy*. Interview with author. St George's Grenada, 12 March 1999.

Mapp, Sheila. Interview with author. Main Street, Hillsborough, Carriacou, 2 August 2000.

Mason, Gabrielle (Sister). Interview with author. St George's Grenada (via telephone) 10 November 2006.

Mason-Francis, Glenda. Interview with author. Anglican High School, Tanteen, St George's, Grenada, 27 April 1999.

McIntyre, Alice. Interview with author. Upper Lucas Street, St George's, Grenada, 22 March 1999.

McIntyre, Mollie. Interview with author. St Paul's, St George, Grenada, 9 March 1999.

McIntyre, Marie-Josephine. Interview with author. Lance aux Epines, St George, Grenada, 30 January 1999.

Mendes, Judith. Interview with author. Main Street, Hillsborough, Carriacou, 1 August 2000.

Nedd, Wapel. Interview with author. Pearls St Andrew, Grenada, 29 January 1999.

Nesfield, Peggy. Interview with author. Bain Alley, St George's, Grenada, 5 February 1999.

Nurse, Mae. Interview with author. St Paul's, St George, Grenada, 23 March 1999.

O'Brien, Ivor Osbourne. Interview with author. Morne Jaloux, St George, Grenada, 31 August 2000.

Patterson, Ruskine. Interview with author. Hillsborough, Carriacou, 26 August 2006.

Payne-Banfield, Gloria. Interview with author. University of the West Indies Centre, Marryshow House, H. A. Blaize Street, St George's, Grenada, 22 March 1999.

Pitt, Claudette. Interview with author. Bathway, St Patrick, Grenada, 27 February 1999.

Pitt, Phyllis. Interview with author. Richmond, St Andrew, Grenada, 10 November 2006.

Phillip, Thelma. Interview with author. Springs, St George, Grenada, 5 February 1999.

Protain, Gertude. Interview with author. Observatory Road, St George's, Grenada, 15 March 1999.

Scoon, Esmai. (Lady) Interview with author. Madigras, St Paul's, St George, Grenada, 17 March 1999.

St Bernard, Gloria. Interview with author. Cathedral House, Church Street, St George's, Grenada, 27 April 1999.

Steele, Pamela. Interview with author. Woolwich Road, St George's Grenada, 26 April 1999.

Steeples, Claire*. Interview with author. St George's Grenada, 10 February 1999.

Stroude, Tessa. Interview with author. Tanteen, St George's, Grenada, 2 February 1999.

Sylvester, Blanche. Interview with author. Fontenoy, St George, Grenada, 24 April 1999.

Theresa, Mary*. Interview with author. St George's, Grenada, 9 March 1999.

Thompson, Faye. Interview with author. Woodlands, St George, 24 August 2000.

Williams, Gloria (Lady) Interview with author. Governor General's Residence Upper Lucas Street St George's, Grenada, 1 March 1999.

*Pseudonyms used at the interviewees' request

BOOKS, ARTICLES, DISSERTATIONS, AND PUBLISHED AND UNPUBLISHED PAPERS

Aberdeen, Michael. *Grenada Under the PRG*. Port of Spain, Trinidad: People's Popular Movement, 1983.

Ambursley, Fitzroy and James Dunkerley. *Grenada: Whose Freedom?* London: Latin American Research Bureau and Action, 1984.

Antoine, Patrick. Report on River Antoine Estate. Unpublished paper, Public Library, St George's, Grenada, 1984.

Antrobus, Peggy. "Lessons from the Grenada Revolution", *Caricom Perspective*, no. 222 (November–December 1983). Women and Development Unit, Extra Mural Department, University of the West Indies, Barbados.

Aymer, Paula. *Uprooted Women: Migrant Domestics in the Caribbean*. Westport: Praeger, 1997.

Barrow, Christine, ed. *Caribbean Portraits: Essays on Gender Ideologies and Identities*. Kingston: Ian Randle, 1998.

Beckles, Hilary. *Afro-Caribbean Women and Resistance to Slavery in Barbados*. London: Karnak House, 1988.

———. *Centering Women: Gender Relations in Caribbean Slave Society*. Kingston: Ian Randle, 1999.

————. *Natural Rebels: A Social History of Enslaved Black Women in Barbados*. London: Zed Books, 1989.

Binder, Wolfgang, ed. *Slavery in the Americas*. Wurzburg: Konighausen and Newmann, 1993.

Bishop, Maurice. "Women Step Forward". In *Maurice Bishop Speaks: The Grenada Revolution, 1979–1983*, edited by Michael Taber and Bruce Marcus, 32–41. New York: Pathfinder, 1983.

Bremer, Thomas, and Ulrich Fleischmann, eds. *Alternative Cultures in the Caribbean*. Frankfurt: Vervuert Verlag, 1993.

Brereton, Bridget. "Caribbean Women in the Post-Emancipation Century, 1838–1938: Agenda for Research". Paper presented at the UNESCO conference Slavery and the Shaping of Caribbean Society, University of the West Indies, St Augustine, Trinidad, 8–10 December 1988.

————. "Family Strategies, Gender and the Shift to Wage Labour in the British Caribbean". In *The Colonial Caribbean in Transition: Essays on Post Emancipation Social and Cultural History*, edited by Bridget Brereton and Kelvin Yelvington, 77–107. Kingston: University of the West Indies Press, 1999.

Brereton, Bridget, and Kevin Yelvington, eds. *The Colonial Caribbean in Transition: Essays on Post Emancipation Social and Cultural History*. Kingston: The Press, University of the West Indies Press, 1999.

Brierley, John. "Small Farming in Grenada West Indies. An Investigation of its Nature and Structure". PhD thesis, Department of Geography, University of Manitoba, Winnepeg, 1974.

Brinkley Frances, Kay. *This Is Grenada*. Port of Spain: Caribbean Printers, 1967.

Brizan, George. *Brave Young Grenadians: Loyal British Subjects*. Port of Spain: Paria Publishing Company, 2002.

————. Creole and Immigrant in Aspects of Nineteenth Century Grenadian Society. Typescript, University of the West Indies Library, St George's Grenada, 1981.

————. "The Development of the Labour Movement in Grenada 1940–1960: A Preliminary Analysis". Typescript, University of the West Indies Library, St George's, Grenada, 1975.

————. *Grenada: Island of Conflict*. London: Macmillan Education, 1998.

————. "The Grenadian Peasantry and Social Revolution, 1930–1951". Working Paper no. 21. Kingston: Institute of Social and Economic Research, 1979.

Brodber Erna. *Perspectives of Caribbean Women*. Vol. 4, Women in the Caribbean Project. Cave Hill, Barbados: Institute of Social and Economic Research, 1982.

Browne, G. *Labour Conditions in the West Indies*. London: Her Majesty's Stationery Office, 1939.

Buffong, Jean, and Nellie Payne. *Jump Up and Kiss Me*. London: Women's Press, 1996.

Bush, Barbara. "Defiance or Submission? The Role of Women in Slave Resistance in the British Caribbean". *Immigrants and Minorities* 1 (1982): 17–38.

———. *Slave Women in Caribbean Society, 1650–1838*. Kingston: Heinemann, 1990.

Charlton, Sue Ellen. *Women in Third World Development*. London: Westview Press, 1984.

Clarke, Edith. *My Mother Who Fathered Me*. London: Allen and Unwin, 1966.

Clarke, Steve. *Grenada Workers and Farmers: Government with a Revolutionary Proletarian Leadership*. New York: Pathfinder, 1980.

Clyde, David F. *Health in Grenada: A Social and Historical Account*. London: Vade-Mecum, 1985.

Cole, Joyce. *Official Ideology and the Education of Women in the English Speaking Caribbean, 1835–1945: With Special Reference to Barbados*. Vol. 5, Women in the Caribbean Project. Cave Hill, Barbados: Institute of Social and Economic Research, 1982.

Coleridge, Henry. *Six Months in the West Indies*. London: John Murray, 1825.

Collins, Merle. *Because the Dawn Breaks*. London: Karia, 1985.

Collins, Merle. "Sometimes You Have to Drink Vinegar and Pretend You Think Is Honey: Race, Gender and Man/Woman Talk". In *Caribbean Portraits: Essays on Gender Ideologies and Identities*, edited by Christine Barrow, 378–90. Kingston: Ian Randle, 1998.

Collins Hill, Patricia, and Margaret Anderson. *Race, Class and Gender*. California: Wadsworth, 1992.

Cox, Edward. "Fedon Rebellion, 1795–1796: Causes and Consequences". *Journal of Negro History* 67 (1982): 7–19.

———. *Free Coloreds in the Slave Societies of St Kitts and Grenada, 1763–1833*. Knoxville: University of Tennessee Press, 1984.

———. "Indentured African Labourers to Grenada and St Vincent, 1836–1863". Paper presented at the Association of Caribbean Historians Conference, Cayenne, April 2000.

———. "Indian Migration to Grenada and St Vincent, 1857–1885". Paper presented at the International Conference on Asian Diasporas in the Americas. University of the West Indies, St Augustine, Trinidad, August 2000.

———. " 'Race Men': The Pan-African Aspect of the Political Struggles of William Galway Donovan and T. Albert Marryshow, 1884–1926". Paper presented at the Henry Sylvester Williams Pan-African Conference, the University of the West Indies, St Augustine, Trinidad, January 2001.

Craton, Michael. "Changing Patterns of Slave Families in the British West Indies". *Journal of Interdisciplinary History* 10 (1979): 1–35.

———. "The Passion to Exist: Slave Rebellions in the British West Indies, 1650–1832". *Journal of Caribbean History* 13 (1980): 1–20.

———. *Testing the Chains: Resistance to Slavery in the British West Indies*. Ithaca: Cornell University Press, 1982.

Creft, Jacqueline. "The Building of Mass Education in Free Grenada". In *Grenada Is Not Alone: Speeches by the PRG at First International Conference in Solidarity with Grenada*, 49–60. St George's: Fedon, 1982.

Curtin, Philip. *The Atlantic Slave Trade: A Census*. Madison: University of Wisconsin Press, 1969.

David, Christine. *Folklore in Carriacou*. St Michael: Coles Printery, 1985.

Davis, Miranda. *Third World, Second Sex: Women's Struggles and National Liberation*. London: Zed Books, 1983.

Devas, Raymund. *Conception Island, or the Troubled Story of the Catholic Church in Grenada*. London: Sands and Co., 1932.

———. *A History of the Island of Grenada 1498–1796*. St George's, Grenada: Carenage Press, 1974.

Drescher, Seymour, and Frank McGlynn, eds. *The Meaning of Freedom: Economy, Politics, and Culture after Slavery*. Pittsburgh: Pittsburgh University Press, 1992.

Ellis, Pat. *Women of the Caribbean*. London: Zed Books, 1986.

Emmanuel, Patrick. *Crown Colony Politics in Grenada, 1917–1951*. Cave Hill, Barbados: Institute of Social and Economic Research, 1978.

Emmanuel, Patrick, Farley Brathwaite and Eudine Barriteau. *Political Change and Public Opinion in Grenada, 1979–1984*. Cave Hill, Barbados: Institute of Social and Economic Research, 1988.

Engels, Frederick. *The Origin of the Family Private Property and the State*. London: Lawrence and Wishart, 1972.

Engerman, Stanley, and Eugene Genovese, eds. *Race and Slavery in the Western Hemisphere: Quantitative Studies*. Princeton: Princeton University Press, 1975.

Ecumenical Program for Inter-American Communication and Action (EPICA) Task Force. *Grenada: The Peaceful Revolution*. Washington, DC: EPICA, 1982.

Fletcher, L.P. "The Decline of Friendly Societies in Grenada: Some Economic Aspects". *Caribbean Studies* 12 (1972): 99–111.

Fox-Genovese, Elizabeth. "Placing Women's History in History". *New Left Review* (1982): 5–29.

———. "Strategies and Forms of Resistance: Focus on Slave Women in the United States". In *In Resistance: Studies in African Caribbean and Afro-American History*, edited by Gary Okihino, 146–165. Amherst: University of Massachusetts Press, 1986.

Franklyn, David Michael. "The Role of Women in the Struggle for Social and Political Change in Grenada, 1979–1983". Caribbean Studies thesis, Department of History, University of the West Indies, Cave Hill, 1989.

Garraway, D.G. *A Short Account of the Insurrection of 1795–1796*. St George's, Grenada: Chas. Wells and Son, 1877.

Gasper, David Barry, and Darlene Clark Hine, eds. *More than Chattel: Black Women and Slavery in the Americas*. Indianapolis: Indiana University Press, 1996.

Gittens, Knight. *The Grenada Handbook and Directory, 1946*. Bridgetown: Advocate Company, 1946.

Gmelch, George. *Double Passage: The Lives of Caribbean Migrants Abroad and Back Home*. Ann Arbor: University of Michigan Press, 1993

Goveia, Elsa. *The West Indian Slave Laws of the Eighteenth Century*. Barbados: Caribbean University Press, 1970.

Green, William. *British Slave Emancipation: The Sugar Colonies and the Great Experiment, 1830–1865*. Oxford: Oxford University Press, 1976.

Grenada Government. *Centre for Popular Education – Adult Education*. Books 1, 2, 3 and 4. Havana: Pueblo y Educacion, Ministry of Culture, 1982.

Haniff, Nesha. *Blaze of Fire: Significant Contributions of Caribbean Women*. Toronto: Black Women and Women of Colour Press, 1988.

Harewood, Jack. "Employment in Grenada in 1960". *Social and Economic Studies* 15 (1966): 203–38.

Hart, Keith, ed. *Women and the Sexual Division of Labour in the Caribbean*. Kingston: The Press, University of the West Indies, 1996.

Hay, John. *A Narrative of the Insurrection of Grenada*. London: J. Ridgeway, 1823.

Higman, Barry. *Slave Populations of the British Caribbean, 1807–1834*. Baltimore: Johns Hopkins University Press, 1984.

Hill, Donald. "The Impact of Migration in the Metropolitan and Folk Society of Carriacou and Grenada". *Anthropological Papers of the American Museum of Natural History* 54, part 2 (1977): 238–367.

Hodge, Merle. "Leading Role in Production and Defense: Women in the Grenada Revolution". *Intercontinental Press* and *Imprecor* 18 (1980): 943–44.

Honychurch, Lennox. *The Dominica Story: A History of the Island*. Roseau: The Dominica Institute, 1984.

Hodge, Merle, and Chris Searle. *"Is Freedom We Making": The New Democracy in Grenada*. Grenada: Government Information Service, 1981.

Hooks, Bell. *Ain't I a Woman: Black Women and Feminism*. London: Pluto Press, 1982.

Jacobs, Richard W. *The Grenada Revolution at Work*. Pleasantville: University of the West Indies, St Augustine, 1979.

Jacobs, Richard and Ian Jacobs. *Grenada: Route to Revolution*. Havana: Casa de las Americas, 1980.

Joseph, Rita. "The Significance of the Grenada Revolution to Women in Grenada". *Bulletin of Eastern Caribbean Affairs* 7, no. 1 (1981): 16–19.

Kiple, Kenneth. *The Caribbean Slave: A Biological History*. New York: Cambridge University Press, 1984.

Kiple, Kenneth, and Virginia Kiple. *Another Dimension to the Black Diaspora: Diet, Disease and Racism*. Cambridge: Cambridge University Press, 1981.

———. "Deficiency Diseases in the Caribbean". *Journal of Interdisciplinary History* 11 (1980): 197–215.

Klein, Herbert. *African Slavery in Latin America and the Caribbean*. Oxford: Oxford University Press, 1986.

———. "African Women in the Atlantic Slave Trade". In *Women and Slavery in Africa*, edited by C. Robertson and M. Klein, 29–38. Madison: University of Wisconsin Press, 1983.

———. *The Middle Passage: Comparative Studies in the Atlantic Slave Trade*. Princeton: Princeton University Press, 1978.

Klein, Herbert, and Stanley Engerman. "Fertility Differentials Between Slaves in the United States and the British West Indies". *William and Mary Quarterly* 35 (1978): 357–74.

Klein, Martin, and Claire Robertson, eds. *Women and Slavery in Africa*. Madison: University of Wisconsin Press, 1983.

Kleysen, Brenda. *Women Small Farmers in the Caribbean*. San Jose, Costa Rica: Inter-American Institute for Cooperation on Agriculture and Inter-American Development Bank, 1996.

Koplan, Jeffrey. "Slave Mortality in Nineteenth-Century Grenada". *Social Science History* 7 (1983): 311–19.

Kossek, Brigitte. "Racist and Patriarchal Aspects of Plantation Slavery in Grenada: White Ladies, Black Women Slaves and Rebels". *Studien Zur Neuen Welt* 4 (1993): 277–303.

Lambert, Sheila, ed. *House of Commons Sessional Papers of the Eighteenth Century.* Delaware: Scholarly Resources, 1975.

Lewis, Arthur. *The Evolution of the Peasantry in the British West Indies.* London: n.p., 1936.

Lewis, Colleen. "Interview with Phyllis Coard: Women's Growing Role in Revolutionary Grenada". *Intercontinental Press* and *Imprecor* 18 (1980): 1192–93.

Lewis, David. *Reform and Revolution in Grenada 1950 to 1981.* Havana: Casa de las Americas, 1984.

Lewis, Gordon. *Grenada: The Jewel Despoiled.* Baltimore: Johns Hopkins University Press, 1987.

Lopez-Springfield, Consuelo. *Daughters of Caliban: Caribbean Women in the Twentieth Century.* Indianapolis: Indiana University Press, 1997.

Lucey, Sheila. *Frances Moloney: Co-founder of the Missionary Sisters of St Columban.* Dublin: Dominican Publications, 1999.

MacKinnon, Catherine A. "Feminism, Marxism Method and the State: An Agenda for Theory". *Signs* 7 (1982): 515–44.

Mandle, Jay. *Big Revolution, Small Country: The Rise and Fall of the Grenada Revolution.* Lanham, Maryland: North–South Publishing, 1985.

Marshall, Bernard. "Society and Economy in the British Windward Islands 1763–1823". PhD thesis, University of the West Indies, Mona, 1972.

Marshall, Woodville. "The Ex-slaves as Wage Labourers on the Sugar Estates in the British Windward Islands, 1836–1846". Paper presented at the Eleventh Conference of Caribbean Historians, Curaçao, 1979.

———. "Metayage in the Sugar Industry of the British Windward Islands, 1836–1865". *Jamaica Historical Review* 1 (1965): 28–55.

———. "Notes on Peasant Development in the West Indies since 1838". *Social and Economic Studies* 17, (1968): 252–63.

———. "The Post Slavery Labour Problem Revisited". Elsa Goveia Memorial Lecture, Department of History, the University of the West Indies, Mona, 1991.

———. "Provision Ground and Plantation Labour in Four Windward Islands'. Competition for Resources during Slavery". In *Cultivation and Culture: Labour and the Shaping of Slave Life in the Americas*, edited by Philip Morgan and Ira Berlin. London: University of Virginia Press 1993.

———. "The Social and Economic Development of the Windward Islands". PhD thesis, University of Cambridge, 1963.

———. "Social and Economic Problems in the Windward Islands, 1838–1865: The Caribbean in Transition". Papers in Social Political and Economic Development, Second Caribbean Scholars Conference, Mona Jamaica, 14–19 April 1964.

————. "The Termination of Apprenticeship in Barbados and the Windward Islands: An Essay on Colonial Administration and Politics". *Journal of Caribbean History* 2 (1971): 1–45.

Martin, Tony, ed. *In Nobody's Backyard: The Grenada Revolution in Its Own Words, the Revolution at Home.* 2 vols. Dover: The Majority Press, 1983–85.

Massiah, Joycelin. *Indicators of Women in Development.* Women, Work and Development. Cave Hill, Barbados: Institute of Social and Economic Research, 1984.

————, ed. *Women and the Family.* Vol. 2, Women in the Caribbean Project. Cave Hill, Barbados: Institute of Social and Economic Research, 1982.

————. *Women as Heads of Households in the Caribbean: Family Structure and Feminine Status.* Women in a World Perspective. Paris: UNESCO, 1983.

Mathurin, Lucille. *The Rebel Women in the British West Indies during Slavery.* Kingston: African Caribbean Publications, 1975.

Mathurin-Mair, Lucille. "Women Field Labourers in Jamaica During Slavery". In *Slavery Freedom and Gender: The Dynamics of Caribbean Society*, edited by Brian Moore, B.W. Higman, Carl Campbell, Patrick Bryan, 183–96. Kingston: University of the West Indies Press, 2001.

McBarnette, Colville. Allegations of Human Rights Violations in Grenada. Unpublished paper, Public Library, St George's, Grenada, 1977.

McDaniel, Lorna. *The Big Drum Ritual of Carriacou: Praise Songs in Rememory of Flight.* Gainesville: University Press of Florida, 1998.

————. "The Philips: A Free Mulatto Family of Grenada". *Journal of Caribbean History* 24, no. 2 (1990): 179–94.

Meeks, Brian. "Social Formation and People's Revolution: A Grenadian Study". PhD thesis, University of the West Indies, Mona, 1988.

Miller, Errol. *Men at Risk.* Kingston: Jamaica Publishing House, 1991.

Mitchel, Hannah. *The Hard Way Up.* London: Faber, 1968.

Mohammed, Patricia. "Writing Gender into History: The Negotiation of Gender Relations Among Indian Men and Women in Post Indenture Trinidadian Society 1917–1947". In *Engendering History: Caribbean Women in Historical Perspective*, edited by Verene Shepherd, Bridget Brereton and Barbara. Bailey, 20–47. London: James Currey, 1995.

Mohammed, Patricia, and Catherine Shepherd, eds. *Gender in Caribbean Development.* Women and Development Studies Project. St Augustine, Trinidad and Tobago: University of the West Indies, 1988.

Moitt, Bernard. "Women, Work and Resistance in the French Caribbean During Slavery, 1700–1848". Paper presented at the symposium Engendering History Current Directions in the Study of Women and Gender in Caribbean History, 10–12 November 1993.

Momsen, Janet, ed. *Women and Change in the Caribbean*. London: Indiana University Press, 1993.

Mondesire, Alicia, and Leith Dunn. "Towards Equality in Development: A Report on the Status of Women". Sixteenth Commonwealth Caribbean Countries and Caribbean Community, Caribbean Secretariat, Georgetown, Guyana, 1995.

Morgan, Philip, and Ira Berlin, eds. *Cultivation and Culture: Labour and the Shaping of Slave Life in the Americas*. Charlotteville: University of Virginia Press, 1993.

Morrisey, Marietta. *Slave Women in the New World: Gender Stratification in the Caribbean*. Lawrence: University of Kansas Press, 1989.

O'Brien, Kenneth, and Neville Duncan. *Women and Politics in Barbados, 1948–1981*. Cave Hill, Barbados: Institute of Social and Economic Research, 1983.

Okihiro, Gary, ed. *In Resistance: Studies in African Caribbean and Afro-American History*. Amherst: University of Massachusetts Press, 1986.

Passee, Thomas Edmund. *An Epic on the Miserable State of Grenada, British West Indies*. Grenada: n.p., 1883.

Patterson, Orlando. *The Sociology of Slavery*. London: MacGibbon and Kee, 1967.

Perrot, Michelle, ed. *Writing Women's History*. Oxford: Blackwell, 1984.

People's Revolutionary Government. *In the Spirit of Butler: Trade Unionism in Free Grenada*. St George's: Fedon, 1982.

Porter, Rosemary Anne. "Women and the State: Women's Movements in Grenada and Their Role in the Grenada Revolution, 1979–1983". PhD thesis, Temple University, 1986.

Reddock, Rhoda. *Women, Labour and Politics in Trinidad and Tobago*. London: Zed Books, 1994.

Reddock, Rhoda, and Shobita Jain, eds. *Women Plantation Workers' International Experiences*. Oxford: Berg, 1998.

Richardson, Bonham. *Economy and Environment in the Caribbean: Barbados and the Windwards in the late 1800s*. Kingston: The Press, University of the West Indies, 1997.

Richardson, David, ed. *Abolition and its Aftermath*. London: Frank Cass, 1985.

Rowbotham, Sheila. *Hidden from History: Rediscovering Women in History from the Seventeenth Century to the Present*. New York: Vintage Books, 1974.

———. *Women in Movement: Feminism and Social Action*. London: Routledge, 1992.

Rubin, Vera, and Arthur Tuben, eds. *Comparative Perspectives on Slavery in the New World: Plantation Societies*. New York: New York Academy of Sciences, 1977.

Schoenhals, Kai, and Richard Melanson. *Revolution and Intervention in Grenada: The New Jewel Movement, the United States, and the Caribbean*. London: Westview Press, 1985.

Schuler, Monica. "Day to Day Resistance to Slavery in the Caribbean during the 18th Century". *African Studies Association of the West Indies* 6 (1973): 57–75.

Searle, Chris. *Carriacou and Petite Martinique in the Mainstream of the Revolution*. St George's: Fedon, 1982.

———. *Grenada: The Struggle against Destabilisation*. London: Writers and Readers Publishing Cooperative, 1983.

Senior, Olive. *Working Miracles: Women's Lives in the English Speaking Caribbean*. London: James Currey, 1991.

Sewell, W.G. *The Ordeal of Free Labour in the British West Indies*. London: Frank Cass, 1968.

Shepherd, C. *Peasant Agriculture in the Leeward and Windward Islands*. St Augustine, Trinidad: Imperial College of Tropical Agriculture, 1945.

Shepherd, Verene. *Women in Caribbean History: The British Colonised Territories*. Kingston: Ian Randle, 1999.

Shepherd, Verene, Bridget Brereton and Barbara Bailey, eds. *Engendering History: Caribbean Women in Historical Perspective*. London: James Currey, 1995.

Sheridan, Richard. *Doctors and Slaves: A Medical and Demographic History of Slavery in the British West Indies, 1680–1834*. Cambridge: Cambridge University Press, 1985.

Singham, A.W. *The Hero and the Crowd in a Colonial Polity*. New Haven: Yale University Press, 1968.

Smith, Angela. "Industrial Relations in Grenada". In *Labour Relations in the Caribbean Region: Record of Proceedings of, and Documents Submitted to a Caribbean Regional Seminar on Labour Relations, Port of Spain, March 1973*, Labour Management Relations Series, no. 43. Geneva: International Labour Office, 1973.

Smith, George. *The Laws of Grenada from the Year 1763 to the Year 1805*. London: n.p., 1808.

Smith, M.G. *Dark Puritan*. Kingston: Department of Extra Mural Studies, University of the West Indies, 1963.

———. *Kinship and Community in Carriacou*. New Haven: Yale University Press, 1962.

———. *Stratification in Grenada*. Berkeley and Los Angeles: University of California Press, 1965.

———. *West Indian Family Structure*. Seattle: University of Washington Press, 1962.

Smith, R.T. "Race, Class and Gender in the Transition to Freedom". In *The Meaning of Freedom: Economics Politics and Culture after Slavery*, edited by Frank McGlynn and Seymour Drescher, 257–87. Pittsburgh: University of Pittsburgh Press, 1992.

St Bernard, Andrea. "National Report for the Fourth Conference on Women". Department of Women's Affairs, St George's, Grenada, April 1993.

Steele, Beverley. "East Indian Indenture and the Work of the Presbyterian Church among the Indians in Grenada". *Caribbean Quarterly* 22 (1976): 28–39.

Sunshine, Cathy, and Philip Wheaton. *Death of a Revolution: An Analysis of the Grenada Tragedy and the United States Invasion.* Washington, DC: EPICA, 1984.

Taber, Michael, and Bruce Marcus, eds. *Maurice Bishop Speaks: The Grenada Revolution 1979–1983.* New York: Pathfinder, 1984.

Walvin, James, and David Eltis. *The Abolition of the Atlantic Slave Trade: Origins and Effects in Europe Africa and the Americas.* Madison: University of Wisconsin Press, 1981.

Williams, Dessima. "Grenadian Women Under the New Jewel Movement", *Trans Africa Forum* 4, no. 2 (1987): 53–67.

———. "Women Must Define their Priorities: Grenada, 1979–1983". In *Women in the Rebel Tradition: The English Speaking Caribbean*, 23–28. New York: Women's International Resource Exchange, 1987.

Williams, Eric. *From Columbus to Castro: The History of the Caribbean, 1492–1969.* London: Andre Deutsch, 1970.

WIRE (Women's International Resource Exchange). *Women in the Rebel Tradition: The English Speaking Caribbean.* New York: WIRE, 1987.

Index

adultery, society's response to, 66–67
African cultural practices, 31–32, 146
agricultural cooperative, 119–20
agricultural labourers. *See* estate
 workers
Aird, Juliana, 7, 76–77
Alexander, Albertina, 64, 126
Alexis, Annette, 124
Allen, Nita, 7
Alleyne, Candia, 125
Andrew, Judy, 56
Andrews, Pauline, 152
Anglican High School, 51, 87
apprenticeship, 4, 12, 16, 42–47
Archer, M.E., 61
Art Club, 93
Augusta-Charles, Louise, 61

Bain, Fitzroy, 137
Bain, Norris, 143
Bain-Horsford, Yolande, 153
Bascus, Leah, 78
Bee Wee Ballet, 93
Belfon, Jane, 125
Bell, Rose, 73
Belmar, Gemma, 141, 143
Belmar, Sister, 104
Belmar, Sylvia, 143

Benjamin, Nadia, 8, 89, 96, 100–101
Bernadine, Franka, 153
Bernard, Joan, 104
big drum dancing, 31, 146
birth rates
 of female slaves, 2, 160n21, 160n22
 of immigrant population, 5
 infant mortality, 5, 16, 29–30, 62, 148
 post-emancipation, 52
Bishop, Alimenta, 106
Bishop, Maurice, 14–15
 death of, 138, 139–41
 democratic centralism, view of, 137
 empowerment of women, 113, 123,
  129, 144
 on establishment of NWO, 108
 and the Forum, 102
 joint leadership proposal, 136–39
 Movement for the Advancement of
  Community Effort, 102–3
 People's Congress (NJM), 105–6
Bishop, Rupert, 106
Black Power Movement (US), 109–10
Blaize, Gascoigne, 81
Blaize, H.A., 14
Bonaparte, Dorris, 107
Bourne, Lew, 125
Bowen, Joy, 104

Braveboy, Dorcas, 125
Britain
    amelioration policies, 12, 23–24, 36,
        145, 146
    colonial rule of Grenada, 11, 13
    Moyne Commission, 68
    Wood Commission (1921), 13
Bronlow, Lord, 107
Burke, June, 104
Buxo, Pamela, 125
Byelands Bakery Cooperative, 119
Bynoe, Dame Hilda, 68, 94, 101

Calliste, Mary, 83
Campbell, Byron, 135
Canadian Save the Children Fund, 8, 89
Cape, Angela, 126
Caribbean Regional Seminar on
    Women, 98
Caribbean Women's Association, 101
Castro, Fidel, 102, 115
Centre for Popular Education, 120–21,
    125, 129
charitable organizations, 89–92
    as foundation for political careers, 8,
        96–97
Charles, Claris, 153
Charles, Enid, 69, 73, 100
Charles, Mavis, 104
Charles, Shirley, 73
Chateau, Magdalene, 104
Cherubim, Porgie, 140
children
    apprenticeship of, 16, 47
    child dispersion, 7, 78
    childraising responsibilities, 65–67
    disease and illness, 62, 65
    as estate workers, 48, 49, 50
    illegitimate, 66–67, 131
    malnutriton, 26–28, 89

milk distribution programmes, 88–90,
    118, 130
School Children's Immunization Law,
    124
Church of England, Sunday school, 32,
    50
Coard, Bernard, 108, 133, 138
Coard, Phyllis
    on benefits of the revolution to
        women, 129
    on criticism of NWO, 131
    and death of Bishop, 138, 139, 143
    on joint leadership proposal, 137
    on NWO ideology, 122
    on objective of NJM/NWO, 117–18
    as president of NWO, 113–14, 115
    in PRG government, 125
    on shortcomings of PRG, 133–34
    women's movements, 108–9
Coard, Veronica, 104
Coleridge, Henry, 39
Collins, Merle, 57, 126
Colonial Development and Welfare
    Fund Scholarships, 68
Colony Hospital
    conditions at (1849), 51–52
    conditions at (1959), 90
Commercial and Industrial Workers
    Union, 104–5
Commission of Enquiry (Duffus
    Commission), 101
Community School Day Programme
    (CSDP), 118, 121–22, 125, 132
Creft, Jacqueline, 125, 140–41
    on the "new education", 121

David, Christine, 126
David, Marcella, 125
David-Antoine, Ann, 153
day-care centres, 99, 130, 134

day nurseries, 92, 120
De Gale, Lady, 107
disease and illness
  1854 cholera pandemic, 52, 148
  feeding programmes, 89–90, 118, 130
  housing conditions, effect on health,
    62
  malnutrition, 26–28, 89
  of slave children, 29–30
District Boards, women in, 75–76, 93
Divi Divi Dance Group, 92
domestic workers
  duties, 70–71
  migration, 7, 77–78, 79, 147–48
Donovan, William Galway, 13
Douglas, Millicent, 73–74,
dressmakers and seamstresses, 41, 46
Dubois, Jeanette, 105, 124–25
Duncan, Grace, 152
Duncan, Magdeline, 153
Duprey, Catherine, 86
Duprey, Cindy, 86
Duprey, Delta, 85, 86

Edgar, Catherine, 83
education
  Caribbean comparisons, 69
  Centre for Popular Education, 120–21,
    125, 129
  class distinctions, 69–70
  Community School Day Programme
    (CSDP), 121–22, 125, 132
  curriculum, gender bias of, 51, 68–70,
    87–88, 166n23
  European gender ideology, influence
    on, 5–6, 148
  fees, 50, 56, 68, 69, 83–84
  in historical analysis, 15
  Marryshow Award, 154
  mass literacy campaign, 120–21

  as means of advancement, 5–6, 79,
    87–88
  National Commission on the Status
    of Women recommendations, 99
  the "new education", 121
  NISTEP (National In-Service Teacher
    Education Programme), 121–22, 125,
    132
  opportunities for women, 50, 67–70
  scholarships, 9, 88, 99, 149
  schoolbooks and uniforms pro-
    gramme, 120
  secondary education, 9, 56, 68, 87, 130,
    154
  Sunday school, 50
  truancy, 129
emancipation, and ex-slave family strategy, 4, 6, 16, 48–49
employment, of women, 79
  agricultural work, 48, 49, 70, 83–87
  civil service, 71–72, 87
  discrimination against, 6, 111, 144
  domestic workers, 70–71
  marriage, and job security, 72–73, 102
  maternity leave. See maternity leave;
    Maternity Leave Law
  National Commission on the Status
    of Women, 99
  street vending, 70
  teaching, 41, 46, 68, 72
empowerment, defined, 8–9
Engels, Frederick, 135
estate workers
  gendered occupational strategy, 4,
    147–48
  general strike (1951), effect on, 80–87
  generational cycle of, 86
  living conditions, 83–87
  minimum daily wage, 74, 80, 82
  population records, 16

estate workers (*continued*)
  post-emancipation exodus, 48–50, 56,
    147, 148
  wage disparity, 5, 58
  working conditions, 5, 58–61
European gender ideology
  in Caribbean context, 6
  "drudge" status of African women,
    20
  influence on education curriculum, 5–
    6, 51, 148
  sexuality of white females, 41–42
  and slave society, 2–3

family forms
  in Caribbean ideology, 6–7
  child dispersion, 7, 78
  ex-slave family strategy, 4, 6, 16, 48–49
  female heads of households, 6–7
Fanon, Frantz, 102
Federación de Mujeres (Cuba), 115
Federation of the West Indies, 14
Fédon Rebellion, 11–12, 34–35
Felix, Lorraine, 122, 129
femininity, cultural definition of, 15
Fletcher, Mavis, 96
Fletcher, Sharon, 125
Foresters' Social Workers League, 89,
    90, 91
the Forum, 102
Francis, Thelma, 60–61, 67
Francois, Augustina, 56
Francois, Marcelane, 56
Francois, Murie, 82, 138
free coloured/free black class
  discrimination against, 37
  Fédon Rebellion, support of, 35
  internal market system, affect on, 38
  manumission of female slaves, 3
  occupations of, 18, 38, 46

population, ratio to slaves, 39, 40
  as property owners, 37–38, 162n65,
    162n67, 162n68
  social and family life, 38–39

Gairy, Cynthia, 96–97, 98, 107
Gairy, Eric Matthew, 99
  Caribbean Regional Seminar on
    Women, 98
  Commercial and Industrial Workers
    Union, 104–5
  crimes against the people, 105–6
  demonstrations against, 14, 103–8
  early political successes, 81–82, 110
  female opposition to, 8, 100–102, 103–
    8, 149
  female presence in administration, 8,
    93–98, 149
  female support for, 82–83, 97–98
  general strike (1951), 14, 80–81, 82, 148
  Green Beasts, 105, 106
  and Grenada Women's League, 92
  intimidation tactics, 103–7
  Mongoose Gang, 101, 105, 106, 107
  National Commission on the Status
    of Women, 98–99
  sexual demands, 8
  squandermania, 102, 110
  as "Uncle Gairy", 81
  unwillingness to share power, 100–101
  use of rhetoric, 81
  violence and victimization, use of, 110
  women's rights, promotion of, 94–95
Garvey, Marcus, 74
gender boundaries
  division of labour, 15
  educational opportunities for women,
    67–70
  relationships and parenthood, 65–67
  and societal status, 57–58

gendered occupational strategy, of
ex-slaves, 4, 147–48
gender system, in historical analysis, 15
General Workers' Union, 82
Gilbert, Pat, 104
Gill, Claire-Anna, 78
Glean, Florence, 86
Glean, Muriel, 73
GNP (Grenada National Party), 8, 14,
100
Gordon, Valerie, 121, 125
GPP (Grenada People's Party), 14, 80
Grammar School, 51
Green Beasts, 105, 106
Grenada
colonial agricultural economy, 11, 13,
Crown Colony government, 13
in Federation of the West Indies, 14
Fédon Rebellion, 11–12
general history of, 10–15
general strike (1951), 14
independence of, 14
National Insurance Scheme, 152
patriarchal attitude of society, 122–24
socialist revolution, 111, 114–44
Treaty of Paris, 11
Treaty of Versailles, 11
universal adult suffrage, 14, 81, 110
US invasion, 15, 141–43
Grenada Agricultural Association
general strike (1951), 14, 74, 80–81, 82,
148
Grenada Board of Tourism, 94
Grenada Boys Secondary School, 51, 87
Grenada Civil Service Association, 124
Grenada Cooperative Nutmeg Associa-
tion, 75
Grenada Election Act (1792), 37
Grenada Manual and Mental Workers
Union, 14, 80–81, 124

Grenada National Organization of
Women, 154
Grenada National Party (GNP), 8, 14,
100
Grenada People's Party. See GPP
(Grenada People's Party)
Grenada Representative Association, 13
Grenada Trade Union, 74
Grenada Union of Teachers, 105, 124–25
Grenada United Labour Party. See
GULP (Grenada United Labour
Party)
Grenada Women's League, 8, 90, 92,
104, 123
Grenada Workers' Union, 74
Guardian Act, 22–26, 145
GULP (Grenada United Labour Party),
14, 80, 153. See also Gairy, Eric
Matthew
New Jewel criticism, 107–8
women in public office, 93–98

Hall, Sister Rose, 90
Happy Hill School, 67
Harris, Gloria, 104
health care. See also disease and illness
estate provision for, 30, 51, 63–64
estate records of, 16
of free children during apprenticeship, 42–43
hospital conditions, 51–52, 90
housing conditions, effect on health,
62
medical fees, 63
National Commission on the Status
of Women recommendations, 99
pregnancy support services, 64–65
Report of the Commission of
Enquiry on the Colony Hospital
(1959), 90

health care (*continued*)
sick leave, 80–81
traditional medicine, 63
UNICEF milk-feeding programme,
88–89
higglers, 27, 46
historiography, and women's history, 15
Hodge, Merle, 140–41
Holas, Nora, 86
Holder, Sister, 104
Home Career Programme, 154
Home Industries' Association, 89, 90, 91
Homemakers Association, 8, 89, 92
Hood, Brenda, 153
Horsford, Bridget, 126
Hosten, Jennifer, 95
Hosten, Mary, 73
house repair material, 120
Hutchinson, Maude, 92
Hypolite, Patricia, 120

illness. *See* disease and illness
indentureship
East Indian population (1866–1896), 55
female immigration during, 4–5
health care, 53
of Indian women, 53–55
male to female ratio, 53
racial composition of immigrants, 12–
13,
infant mortality
1928–37, 62
estate records of, 16
of estate women labourers, 5, 148
as gynaecological resistance, 32
malnutrition and disease, 29–30
Inter Church Council, 88, 89–90
International Women's Conference
(1975), 95
International Women's Year (1975), 98

Jamaica
Morant Bay Rebellion, 13, 158n5
women's movements, 108–9
James, Yvonne, 125
Jamoron, Isabel (Cuba), 115
Japal, J., 124
JEWEL (Joint Endeavour for Welfare
Education and Liberation), 103
Jno-Baptiste, Jean, 56
John, Marva, 104
Joint Endeavour for Welfare Education
and Liberation (JEWEL), 103
Joseph, Helena, 127
Joseph, Monica, 87, 88, 126
Joseph, Rita, 109, 115, 118, 129
judicial system,
women as jurors, 75–76
women in legal profession, 153
J.W. Fletcher Memorial, 67

Keens-Douglas, Sister Ann, 87
Kent, Betty, 78
Kerr, Rita, 78
King, Martin Luther, 102
kinship behaviour, 15
Knight, Rita, 83–85
Knight-Phillip, Thelma, writings of, 93

labourer, defined, 65
Lady Cinty, 126
Lambert, Edlyn, 137
land ownership, 37–38, 61, 86–87
Legislative Council
women admitted to, 93–94
women excluded from, 75
Lenin, on women in mass movements,
108
Lewis, Frederica, 59–60
Lewis, Loraine, 138
Lioness Club, 8, 89, 90, 91, 123

Louison, George, 137

Maitland, Fred, female slave resistance, 4
Malcolm X, 102
Manley, Michael, 108
manumission
during apprenticeship, 45
Caribbean rates of, 146
as part of amelioration, 36
and self purchase, 46
Mapp, Catherine, 130
Mark, Cecelia, 56
marriage
among free coloureds, 38–39
job discrimination and, 6, 72–73, 102
NWO view of, 131
relationships and parenthood, 65–67
rules of, 65–67
Marryshow, Theophilus Albert, 100
on educational opportunities for women, 67–68
Grenada Representative Association and, 13
Marshall, Debbie, 64
Marxism, and empowerment of women, 135, 150
masculinity, cultural definition of, 15
Mason, Celestine, 86–87
Mason-Francis, Glenda, 87
Maternity and Child Welfare League, 64–65
maternity leave
and employment, 72–73
and estate women labourers, 5
in Jamaica, 109
National Commission on the Status of Women recommendations, 99, 102
under PRG, 123, 129

Maternity Leave Law, 9, 73, 134, 149, 172n29, 172n30
amendment, 152
Matthew, Yvonne, 104
May, Aletta, 128
McClean, Herbert, 100
McIntyre, Alice, 114
McIntyre, Alice, 70
McIntyre, Marie-Josephine, 95, 100–101
McIntyre, Mollie, 70, 91
midwifery
bush midwives, 64
Maternity and Child Welfare League, 64–65
Midwives Ordinance (1926), 65
National Commission on the Status of Women recommendations, 99
migration
child dispersion, 7, 78
destinations, choice of, 76, 77
as form of resistance, 147–48
male to female ratio, 76
remittance money, 78, 84
role in Caribbean family form, 6–7
of women as domestic workers, 7, 77–78, 79, 148
milk distribution programmes, 88–90, 118, 130
miscegenation, 5, 39
Mitchell, James (St Vincent), 126
Model School, 51
Modeste-Curwen, Clarice, 153
Mohammed, Patricia, 6
Mongoose Gang, 101, 105, 106–7
Morant Bay Rebellion (Jamaica), 13, 158n5
Morne Rouge Club, 93
Mothers' Union, 90
Movement for the Advancement of Community Effort, 102–3

Movement for the Assemblies of the
    People, 103
Munro, Inez, 73–74
Munro, Margaret, 78

National Commission on the Status of
    Women, 98–99
National Cooperative Development
    Agency, 119–20
National Democratic Congress, 152
National In-Service Teacher Education
    Programme. See NISTEP (National
    In-Service Teacher Education Pro-
    gramme)
National Women's Organisation. See
    NWO (National Women's Organisa-
    tion)
National Youth Organization, 122
Neckles, Margaret, 153
Nedd, Sheila, 73
Nedd, Wapel, 8, 92–93, 96, 100–101
Nesfield, Peggy, 122–24
New Jewel Movement. See NJM (New
    Jewel Movement)
New Jewel newspaper, 107–8
New National Party government, 152,
    153
NISTEP (National In-Service Teacher
    Education Programme), 121–22, 125,
    132
NJM (New Jewel Movement)
    coup against Gairy government, 110
    formation of, 14, 103
    goals of, 103
    NJM/NWO formation, 108–10
    PRG joint leadership proposal, 136–40
    sexual exploitation within, 135
    shortcomings, 150–51
    strike action (1973–74), 105–6
    women's involvement in, 8

NJM/NWO
    as broad-based women's group, 115–18
    formation of, 108–10
    hierarchical structure, 116–17
    membership, 115
Nkrumah, Kwame, 102
Noel, Sister, 104
Noel, Vincent, 140, 141
Nunez, Emmeline, 73
Nurse, Mae, 72
nurses' demonstrations, 103–4
NWO (National Women's Organisa-
    tion)
    activities of, 119–28, 144
    cooperatives, establishment of, 119–20
    criticism of, 130–32
    milk distribution programmes, 119
    NJM/NWO formation, 108–10, 115–18
    non-traditional jobs, promotion of, 122
    stance on feminism, 128

obeah, practice of, 29, 31
oral history, 16–17
Ortega, Daniel, 132
Osbourne, Phyllis, 73

parenthood
    empowerment of women, and male
        chauvinism, 124, 134
    gender boundaries, 65–67
Parochial Boards, 55–56
Paryag, Luna, 73
Paul, Akima, 154
Paul, Norman, 60
pauper, defined, 65
Payne, Nellie, 70–71
Payne-Banfield, Gloria, 87, 93, 96, 125
People's Alliance, 14
People's Revolutionary Army. See PRA
    (People's Revolutionary Army)

People's Revolutionary Government.
  See PRG (People's Revolutionary
  Government)
Peters, Ann, 153
Philip, Honoré
  estates bequeathed to Jeanette Philip,
    3, 37–38
  manumission as reward, 35
Philip, Jeanette
  estates bequeathed by Honoré Philip,
    3, 37–38
Philip, Judith, 38
Pierre, Agatha, 92
Pierre, Emmaline, 153
Pierre, Peggy, 56
Pioneers, 122
Pitt, Claudette, 115, 125, 129, 137, 139
Pitt, Phyllis, 87
plantocracy, and Guardian Act, 22–23,
  24–26, 145
political mobilization of women,
  109–10, 112–28
  women in public office, 93–98, 110–11
Pope, Germaine, 124
PRA (People's Revolutionary Army)
  death of Bishop, 139–41
  disbanded, 153
  military training, 128
  National Liberation Army and, 133
  US invasion of Grenada, 141–43
pregnancy
  and maternity leave, 72–73, 99, 102,
    149, 152, 172n29, 172n30
pregnancy support services
  Inter Church Council educational
    programmes, 88
  Maternity and Child Welfare League,
    64–65
  milk-feeding programmes, 88–89, 118,
    130

National Commission on the Status
  of Women recommendations, 99
pre-primary schools, 120, 134
Presbyterian Women's Guild, 123
PRG (People's Revolutionary Government), 112–44
  activities of, 119–28
  army and militia, women's participa-
    tion, 126, 127–28
  Community School Day Programme
    (CSDP), 121–22, 125, 132
  criticism of, 130
  demonstrations against, 138–39
  empowerment of women, 123, 129,
    149
  equal work for equal pay policy, 5, 9,
    123, 149
  initiatives for women, 123–24
  leadership of, 14–15
  maternity leave, 123, 129, 134, 149, 152,
    172n29, 172n30
  National Liberation Army, 133
  NISTEP (National In-Service Teacher
    Education Programme), 121–22, 125,
    132
  NJM joint leadership proposal, 136–39
  public meetings and accountability,
    119
  School Children's Immunization Law,
    124
  sexual exploitation within, 135
  shortcomings, 9, 133–36, 150–51
  socialist ideology, and empowerment
    of women, 8–9, 114–15
  societal attitude change, and male
    chauvinism, 124
  Trade Union Recognition Law, 124
  women in government, 125–26, 149
  Women's Desk as tool of, 119

Progressive Women's Association
(PWA). *See* PWA (Progressive
Women's Association)
Protain, Gertrude, 88, 94
provision grounds, 26–27, 49–50
Public Workers Union, 124
Purcell, Joan, 152, 153
PWA (Progressive Women's Associa-
tion), 8, 112–14
Pygmalion Glee Club, 92

racism, and slavery, 21
Raeburn, Kaywana, 154
Rapier, Florence, 95, 96,125
Reagan, Ronald, 127
Renwick, Daisy, 73
Richmond Hill Club, 93
road repair projects, 120
Roberts, Glenis, 153
Rodney, Walter, 102
Romain, Patsy, 109, 119
Ross, Joan, 126
Rowbotham, Sheila, on Marxist
ideology, 135, 150
Rowley, Louise, 71–72, 91
Rowley, Pansy, 73, 91–92
Royal Grenada Police Force, 153

Sadler, Lady Haynes, 65
scholarships, 9, 69
  Colonial Development and Welfare
  Fund Scholarships, 68
  unavailability of to Gairy opposition,
  104
School Children's Immunization Law,
124
School for the Deaf, 91, 92
Scoon, Lady Esmai, 102, 141–42
sexual exploitation
  Guardian Act, 22–23, 24–26, 145
  within PRG and NJM, 135

of slave labour, 21–22
sexual vulnerability, of white women
  vs. black women, 3, 41–42
Sisters of St Joseph of Cluny, 51
slavery
  amelioration policies, 12, 23–24, 36,
    145, 146
  apprenticeship system, 4, 12, 16,
    42–47
  birth rates, 22–24, 145, 146, 159n19
  and European gender ideology, 2–3
  European religious standards, 31, 32
  Fédon Rebellion, 11–12, 34–35
  freedom through self purchase, 35
  Guardian Act, 22–23, 24–26, 145
  health care, 30, 51
  infant mortality, 5, 29–30
  length of workday, 20
  malnutrition, and slave diet, 26–28
  manumission, 3, 35, 36, 45, 46, 146
  mortality rates in slave trade, 19
  normalization of sex ratios, 19
  slave infertility, 26, 28
  slave marriages, 31
  slave population, natural decrease, 16,
    24–25, 30, 160n21, 160n22
  slave trade, male to female ratio, 18–
    19
  treatment of by white women, 41
  as "un-freedom", 3
  value of slaves following abolition, 23
slave women
  abortions, as gynaecological resist-
    ance, 23, 29, 32
  in African internal slave trade, 19
  contraceptive measures, 28–29
  as field labourers, 2, 19–20
  Guardian Act, 22–23, 24–26, 145
  malnutrition, and slave diet, 26–28, 145
  manumission, 3, 36, 146

maternal mortality rate, 29
as producers and reproducers, 2, 18, 22–24, 46, 145, 147,
punishment of, 20–21, 43–44, 159n10
resistance, forms of, 4, 32–35, 46, 147
runaways, 32–34
small farmer class, creation of, 12
Smith, M.G., *Dark Puritan*, 60
Snagg, Ferdisha, 154
socialist ideology, and empowerment of women, 8–9, 108, 135, 150
socialist revolution, 112–44
  collapse of, 136–44
  coup against Gairy government, 110–11
  criticism of, 131–32
  freedom of speech during, 132
  joint leadership proposal, 136–39
  NJM/NWO collaboration, 115–18
  PWA (Progressive Women's Association), 112–14
  Women's Desk the, 118–19
  women's support for, 126–28
  women's views on, 129–32
social welfare programmes, 118–20
social work, 73–74
Soroptomists' Club, 8, 89, 90, 91, 123
St Bernard, Gloria, 100
St Bernard, Joan, 107
St Bernard, Maureen, 138
Steele, Pamela, 95, 102
St George Girls High School, 51, 56
St George's Workers' Union, 74
St John's Labour Party/General Workers' Union, 74
St Joseph's Convent, 56, 69
St Paul's Academy of Dramatic Arts, 93
Strachan, Winnifred, 153
strike actions

general strike (1951), 14, 80–81, 82, 148
strike (1973–74), 105–6
Stroude, Chris, 140–41
Stroude, Lucy, 104–5
Stroude, Tessa, 115, 117, 118, 120, 129
  women's rights, and male chauvinism, 135–36
Sylvester, Blanche, 72, 73, 100
Sylvester, Cyril, 93–94
Sylvester, Eva, 93–94

Taylor, Regina, 126
teachers
  Gairy intimidation of, 105, 107
  Grenada Union of Teachers, 124–25
  salaries, 68, 72
  white women as, 41, 46
Telesford, Winifred, 92
Thomas, Ethlina, 106–7
Thompson, Faye, 138, 139–40
trade unions, 74–75. *See also unions by name*
  female membership of, 124–25
  general strike (1951), 14, 80–81, 82
  strike actions, 74–75
  Trade Union Recognition Law, 124
  transformation into political power, 81–82
True Blue Fisheries School, 122

United Nations Educational Scientific and Cultural Organization (UNESCO), 89
United Nations International Children's Emergency Fund (UNICEF), 88–89
US invasion of Grenada, 15, 141–43

Vin Vwei La Grenade Group, 93

voting rights
  Grenada Election Act (1792), 37
  universal adult suffrage, 14, 81, 110
  voting qualifications, 55–56, 75

wage disparity
  after general strike (1951), 82, 149
  in employment of women, 6, 111
  equal work for equal pay policy, 9, 99,
    123
  estate workers, 5, 58, 83–87
  immigrant women, 55, 56
  minimum daily wage, Jamaica, 109
Wells, Lottie, 74
Whiteman, Unison, 137, 141
white population, 168n2
  ratio to blacks and coloureds, 39, 40
  white women, in colonial Grenada,
    39–42, 46, 146–47
Williams, Dessima, 112–13, 120, 125
Williams, Lady Gloria, 68, 78
Williams, Veronica, 65, 66, 67
Wilson, Erma, 104
Woman's Cricket Association, 92–93
women, post-emancipation (1838–99),
  48–56

diet and nutrition, 50
economic difficulties of, 49–50
educational issues, 50–51
exodus from the estates, 48–50
wages, 50
women, post-emancipation (1900–
  1950), 57–79
  gender boundaries, 57–58, 61
  wage disparity, 58
  working conditions, estate labour,
    58–61
women, post-emancipation (1951–79),
  80–111. *See also* PRG (People's Revolutionary Government); socialist revolution
  general strike (1951), effect on estate
    workers, 80–87
Women's Desk, 118–28
women's groups, 7–8, 90–93, 109
Woodroffe, Myra, 78
World War II, 78

X, Malcolm, 102

YWCA (Young Women's Christian
  Association), 7, 8, 74, 89, 90, 91–92,
  154

www.ingramcontent.com/pod-product-compliance
Lightning Source LLC
Chambersburg PA
CBHW030649270326
41929CB00007B/282